A PLUME BOOK

VLAD THE IMPALER

SID JACOBSON WAS THE MANAGING EDITOR AT HARVEY COMICS IN NEW YORK FOR MORE THAN TWENTY-FIVE YEARS, THEN EXECUTIVE EDITOR AT MARVEL COMICS, AND EDITOR IN CHIEF AT HARVEY LOS ANGELES. HE CREATED SEVERAL ICONIC CHARACTERS INCLUDING RICHIE RICH AND WENDY THE GOOD LITTLE WITCH.

ERNIE COLÓN HAS CREATED THE ART FOR MANY COMIC BOOK SERIES AND GRAPHIC NOVELS, INCLUDING *RICHIE RICH, CASPER THE FRIENDLY GHOST, AMETHYST: PRINCESS OF GEMWORLD,* AND THE HISTORICAL FANTASY *ARAK,* AMONG MANY OTHERS.

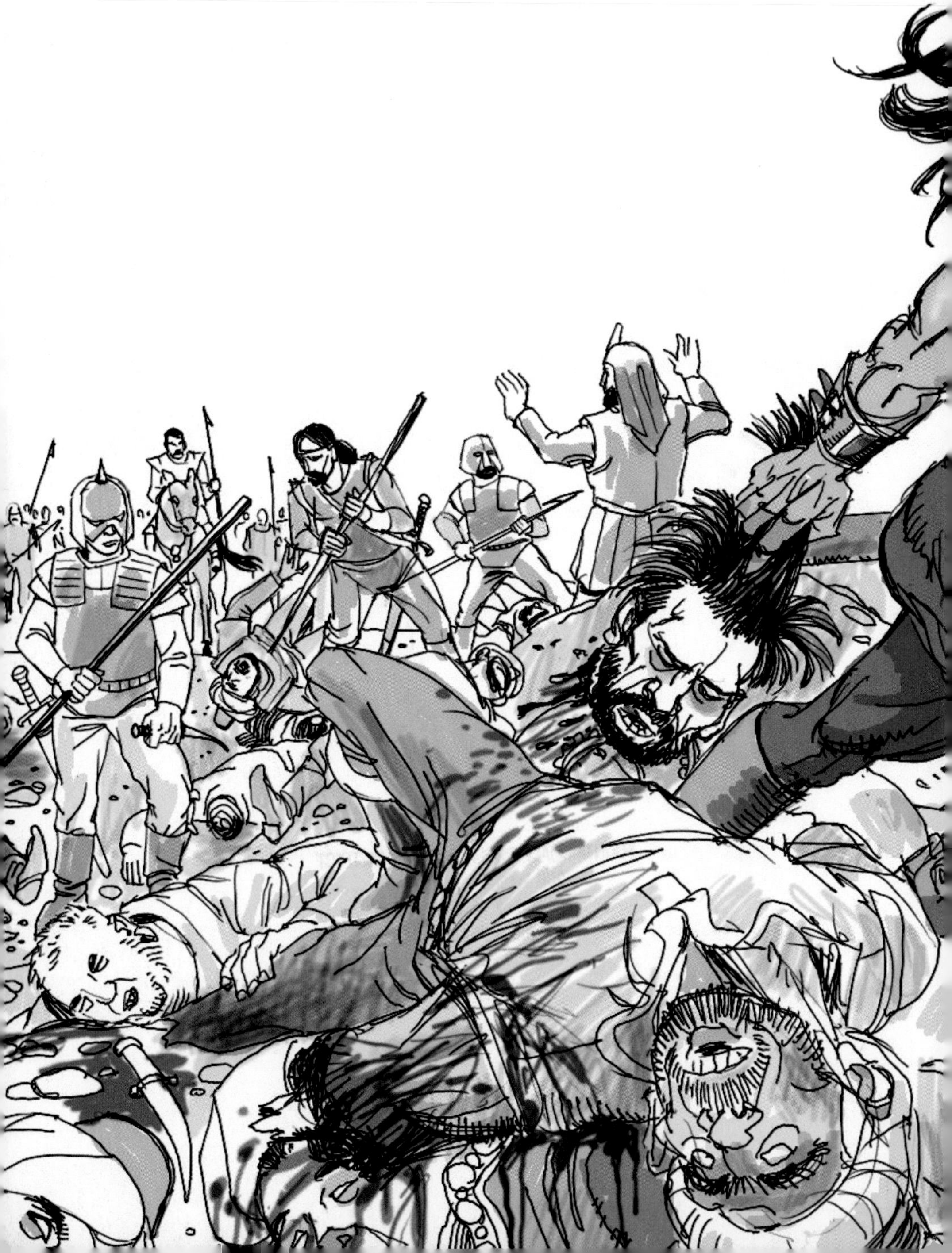

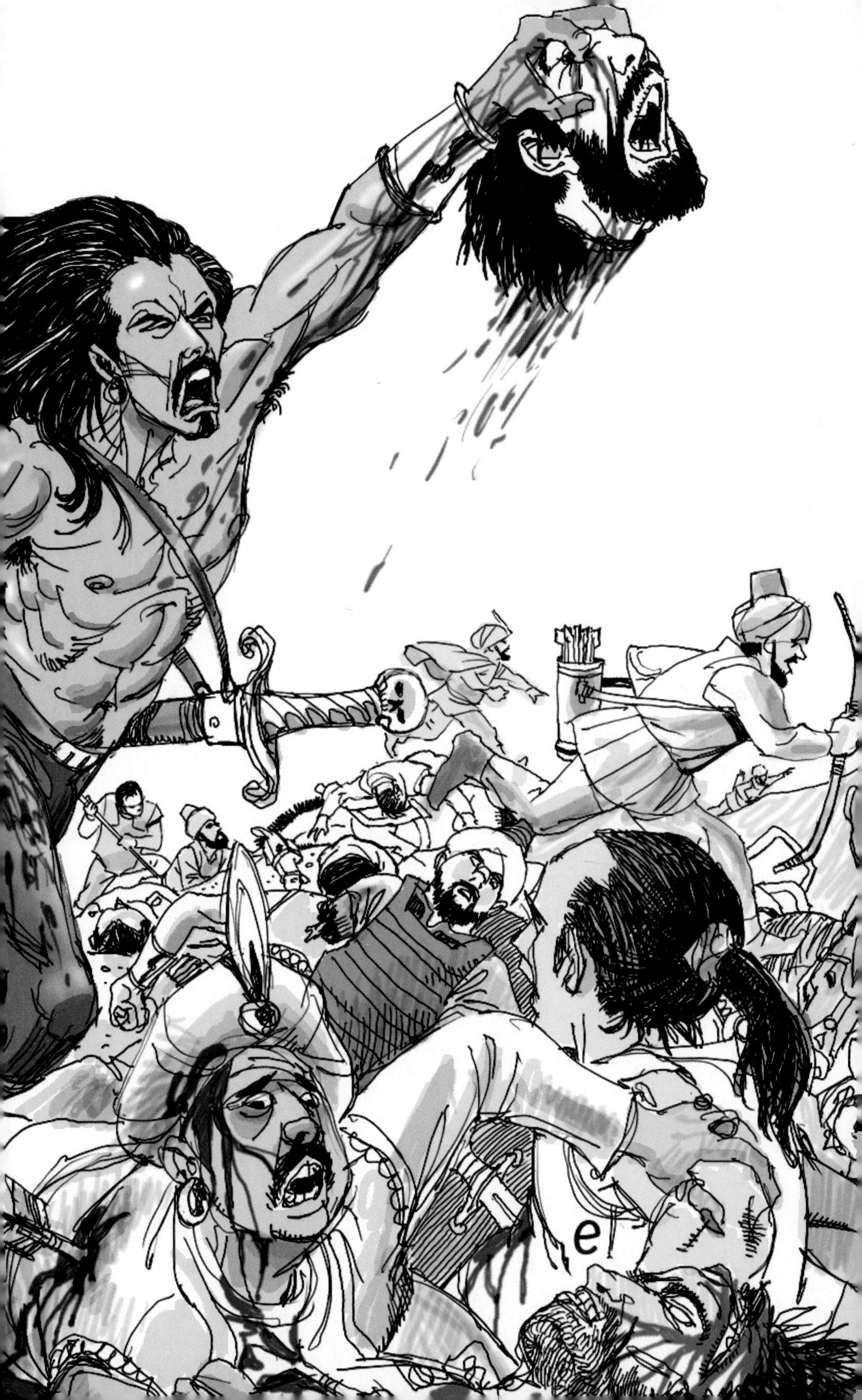

VLAD
THE IMPALER

THE MAN WHO WAS DRACULA

SID JACOBSON AND ERNIE COLÓN

A PLUME BOOK

PLUME
PUBLISHED BY THE PENGUIN GROUP
PENGUIN GROUP (USA) INC., 375 HUDSON STREET, NEW YORK, NEW YORK 10014, U.S.A.
PENGUIN GROUP (CANADA), 90 EGLINTON AVENUE EAST, SUITE 700, TORONTO, ONTARIO, CANADA M4P 2Y3 (A DIVISION OF PEARSON PENGUIN
CANADA INC.)
PENGUIN BOOKS LTD., 80 STRAND, LONDON WC2R 0RL, ENGLAND
PENGUIN IRELAND, 25 ST. STEPHEN'S GREEN, DUBLIN 2, IRELAND (A DIVISION OF PENGUIN BOOKS LTD.)
PENGUIN GROUP (AUSTRALIA), 250 CAMBERWELL ROAD, CAMBERWELL, VICTORIA 3124, AUSTRALIA (A DIVISION OF PEARSON
AUSTRALIA GROUP PTY. LTD.)
PENGUIN BOOKS INDIA PVT. LTD., 11 COMMUNITY CENTRE, PANCHSHEEL PARK, NEW DELHI – 110 017, INDIA
PENGUIN GROUP (NZ), 67 APOLLO DRIVE, ROSEDALE, NORTH SHORE 0632, NEW ZEALAND (A DIVISION OF PEARSON NEW ZEALAND
LTD.)
PENGUIN BOOKS (SOUTH AFRICA) (PTY.) LTD., 24 STURDEE AVENUE, ROSEBANK, JOHANNESBURG 2196, SOUTH AFRICA

PENGUIN BOOKS LTD., REGISTERED OFFICES: 80 STRAND, LONDON WC2R 0RL, ENGLAND

PUBLISHED BY PLUME, A MEMBER OF PENGUIN GROUP (USA) INC. PREVIOUSLY PUBLISHED IN A HUDSON STREET PRESS EDITION.

FIRST PLUME PRINTING, OCTOBER 2010
10 9 8 7 6 5 4 3 2 1

TEXT COPYRIGHT © SID JACOBSON, 2009
ILLUSTRATIONS COPYRIGHT © ERNIE COLÓN, 2009
ALL RIGHTS RESERVED

Ⓟ REGISTERED TRADEMARK—MARCA REGISTRADA

THE LIBRARY OF CONGRESS HAS CATALOGUED THE HUDSON STREET PRESS EDITION AS FOLLOWS:

JACOBSON, SIDNEY.
VLAD THE IMPALER : THE MAN WHO WAS DRACULA / SID JACOBSON AND ERNIE COLÓN.
P. CM.
ISBN 978-1-59463-058-3 (HC.)
ISBN 978-0-452-29657-2 (PBK.)
1. VLAD III, PRINCE OF WALLACHIA, 1430 OR 31-1476 OR 7—COMIC BOOKS, STRIPS, ETC. 2. GRAPHIC NOVELS. I. COLÓN,
ERNIE. II. TITLE.
PN6727.J35V56 2009
741.5973—DC22
2009028610
PRINTED IN THE UNITED STATES OF AMERICA

Unlike the protagonist of the story you are about to read,

we gratefully dedicate this book to our respective wives,

Ruth Ashby Colón and Shure Jacobson,

for their patience and their unqualified love.

ACKNOWLEDGMENTS

WE WOULD LIKE TO THANK AND ACKNOWLEDGE THE THOUGHTFUL AND PRECISE AID WE RECEIVED IN THE LAYOUT ART BY FRANCESCO GUERRINI (ALCADIA SRC), ITALY; THE SYMPATHETIC, INTELLIGENT, AND CONSISTENT POLISHING BY OUR EDITOR, ANNA STERNOFF, WHO TOOK AN "ORPHANED" BOOK AND MADE IT ONE OF HER VERY OWN; AND TO OUR AGENT, LYDIA WILLS, WHO KEEPS LEADING US TO PLACES WE NEVER DREAMED WE'D BE. WE WOULD ALSO LIKE TO THANK LAVINA LEE, MATTHEW BOEZI, AMY HILL, ALISSA AMELL, AND JASON JOHN-SON FOR THEIR SPECIAL HELP AND SKILLS IN BRINGING THIS BOOK TO COMPLETION IN THE FACE OF THE DEMONS OF TIME.

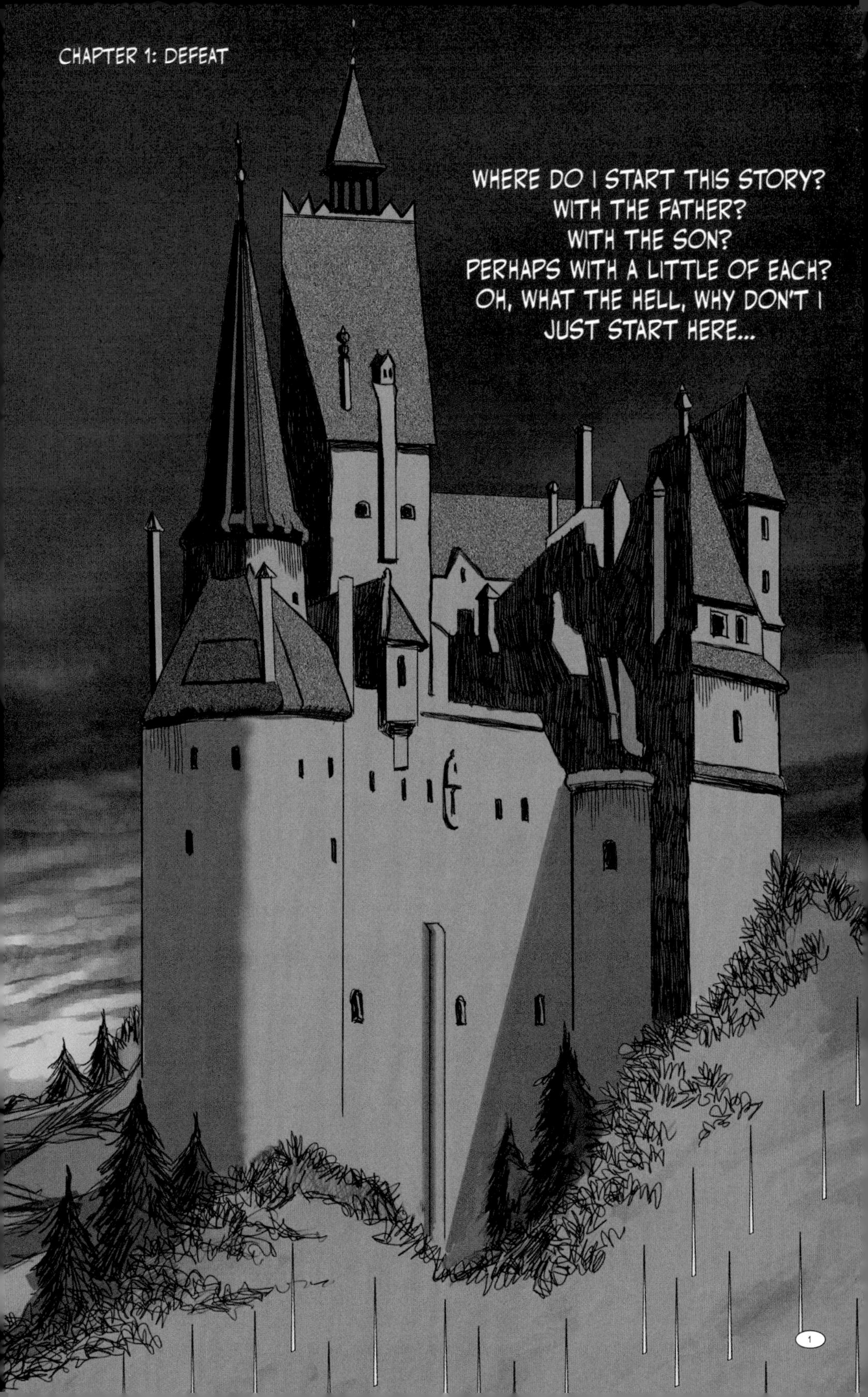
CHAPTER 1: DEFEAT
WHERE DO I START THIS STORY? WITH THE FATHER? WITH THE SON? PERHAPS WITH A LITTLE OF EACH? OH, WHAT THE HELL, WHY DON'T I JUST START HERE...

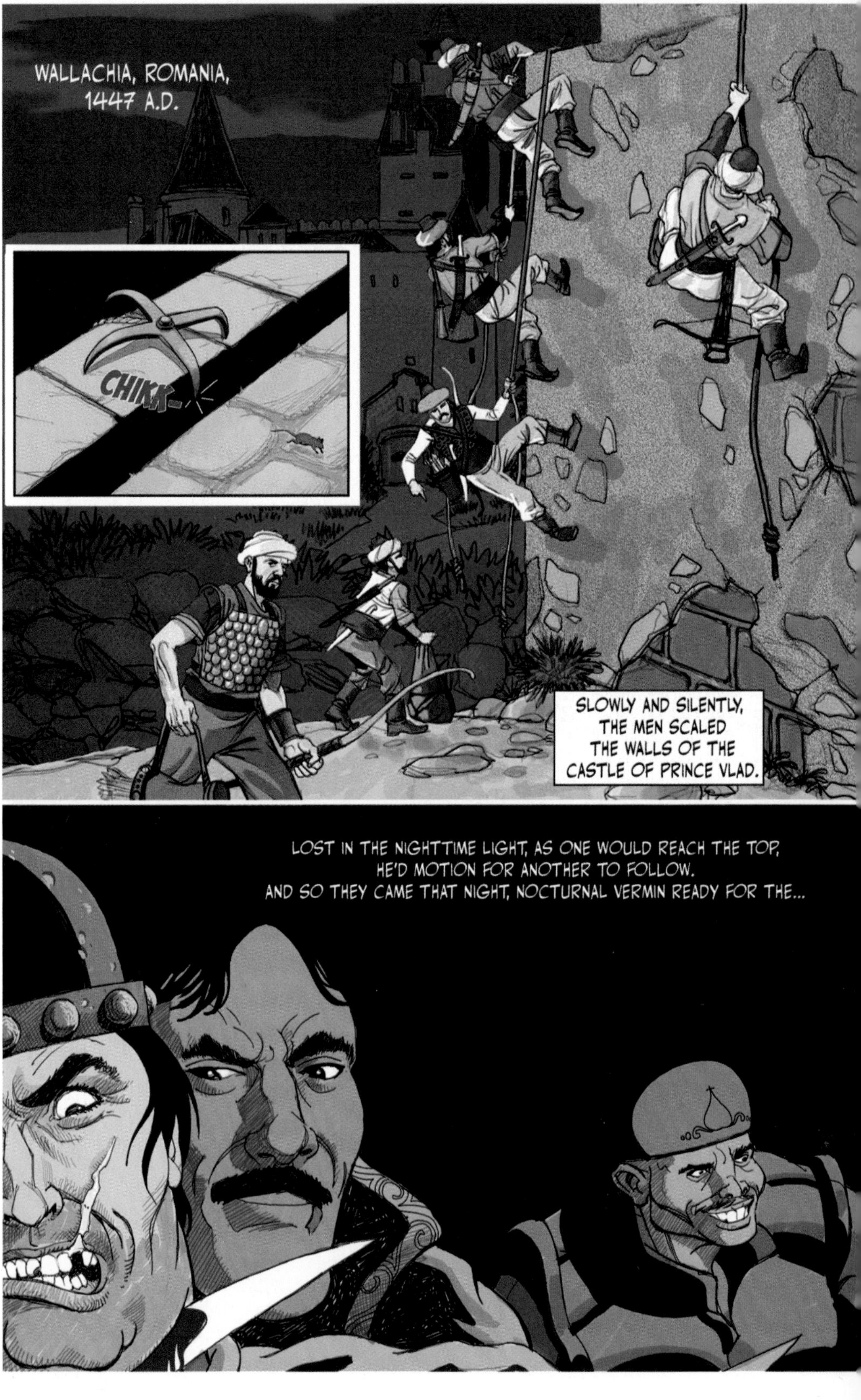
WALLACHIA, ROMANIA, 1447 A.D.
CHIKK-
SLOWLY AND SILENTLY, THE MEN SCALED THE WALLS OF THE CASTLE OF PRINCE VLAD.
LOST IN THE NIGHTTIME LIGHT, AS ONE WOULD REACH THE TOP, HE'D MOTION FOR ANOTHER TO FOLLOW. AND SO THEY CAME THAT NIGHT, NOCTURNAL VERMIN READY FOR THE...

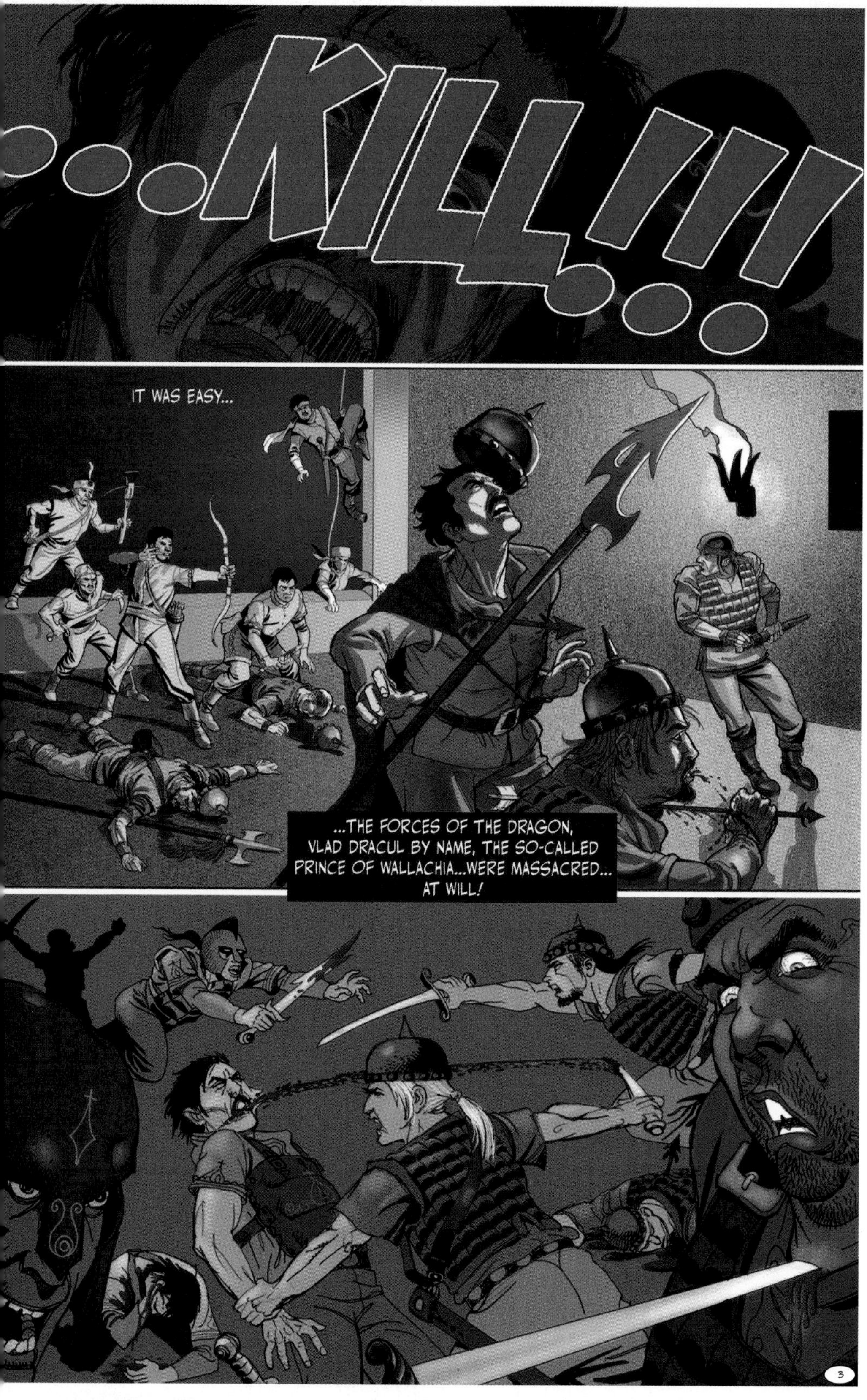
...KILL!!!!...
IT WAS EASY...
...THE FORCES OF THE DRAGON, VLAD DRACUL BY NAME, THE SO-CALLED PRINCE OF WALLACHIA...WERE MASSACRED... AT WILL!

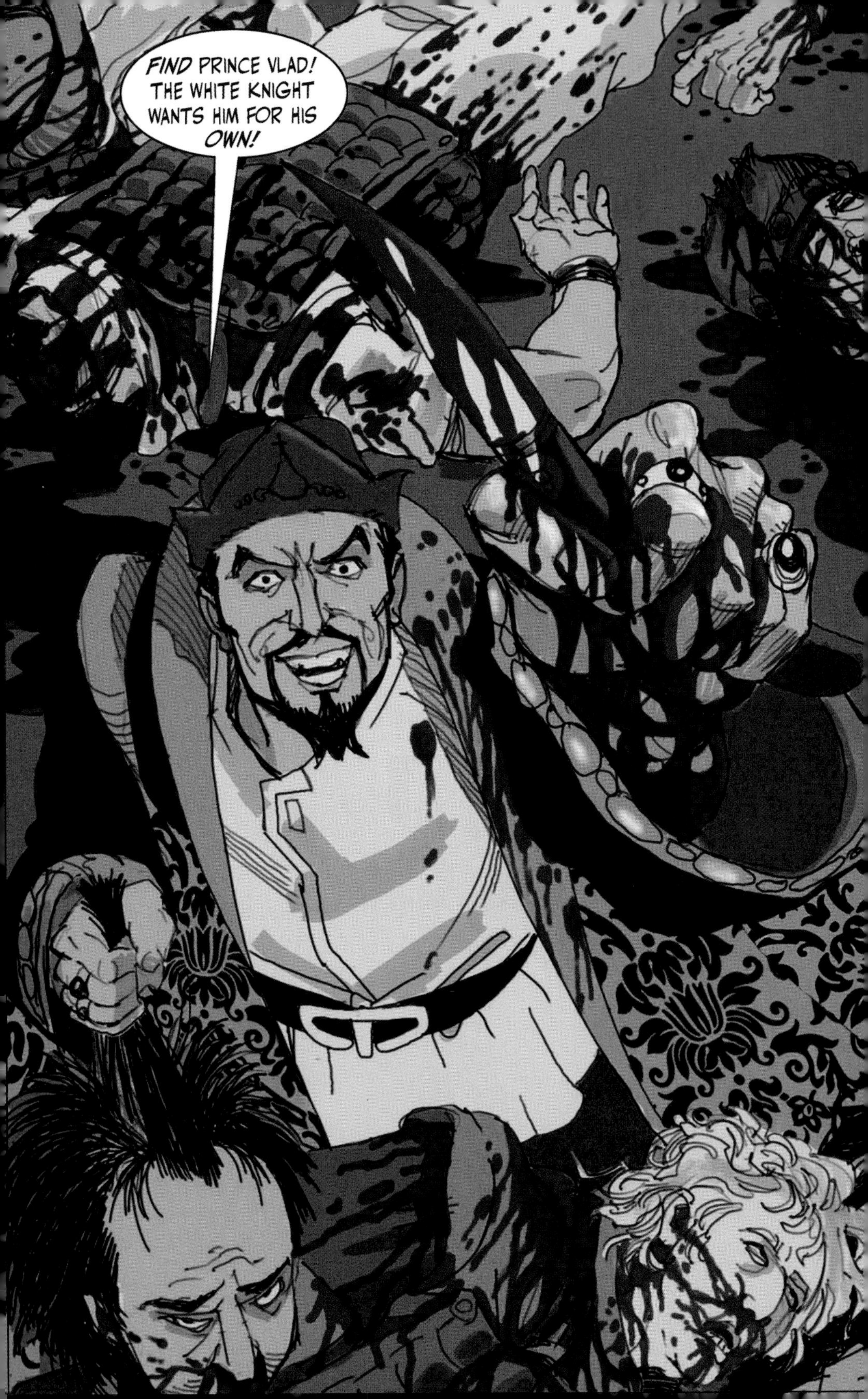
FIND PRINCE VLAD! THE WHITE KNIGHT WANTS HIM FOR HIS OWN!

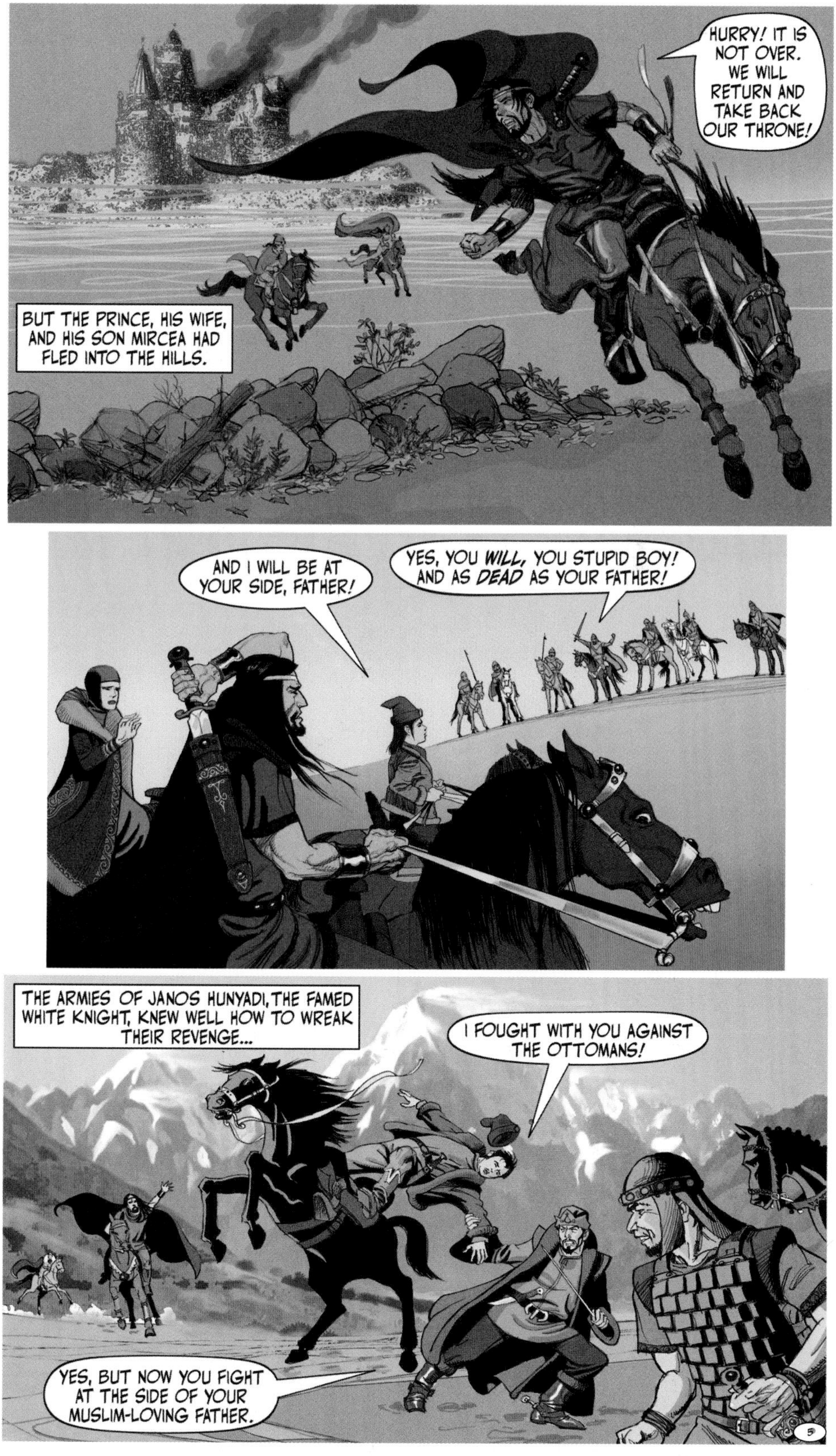
HURRY! IT IS NOT OVER. WE WILL RETURN AND TAKE BACK OUR THRONE!
BUT THE PRINCE, HIS WIFE, AND HIS SON MIRCEA HAD FLED INTO THE HILLS.
AND I WILL BE AT YOUR SIDE, FATHER!
YES, YOU WILL, YOU STUPID BOY! AND AS DEAD AS YOUR FATHER!
THE ARMIES OF JANOS HUNYADI, THE FAMED WHITE KNIGHT, KNEW WELL HOW TO WREAK THEIR REVENGE...
I FOUGHT WITH YOU AGAINST THE OTTOMANS!
YES, BUT NOW YOU FIGHT AT THE SIDE OF YOUR MUSLIM-LOVING FATHER.
5

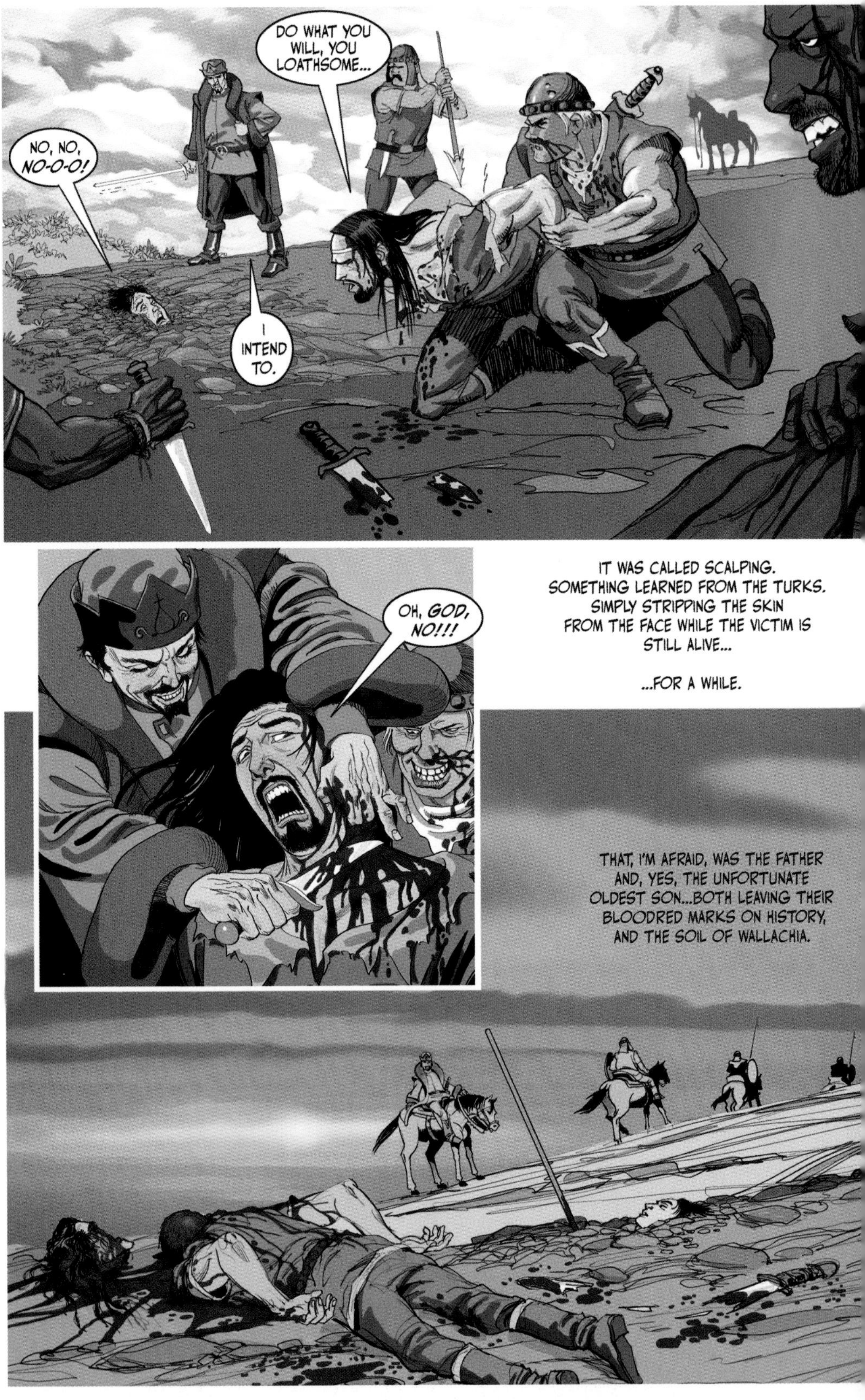
NO, NO, NO-O-O!
DO WHAT YOU WILL, YOU LOATHSOME...
I INTEND TO.
IT WAS CALLED SCALPING. SOMETHING LEARNED FROM THE TURKS. SIMPLY STRIPPING THE SKIN FROM THE FACE WHILE THE VICTIM IS STILL ALIVE...
...FOR A WHILE.
OH, GOD, NO!!!
THAT, I'M AFRAID, WAS THE FATHER AND, YES, THE UNFORTUNATE OLDEST SON...BOTH LEAVING THEIR BLOODRED MARKS ON HISTORY, AND THE SOIL OF WALLACHIA.

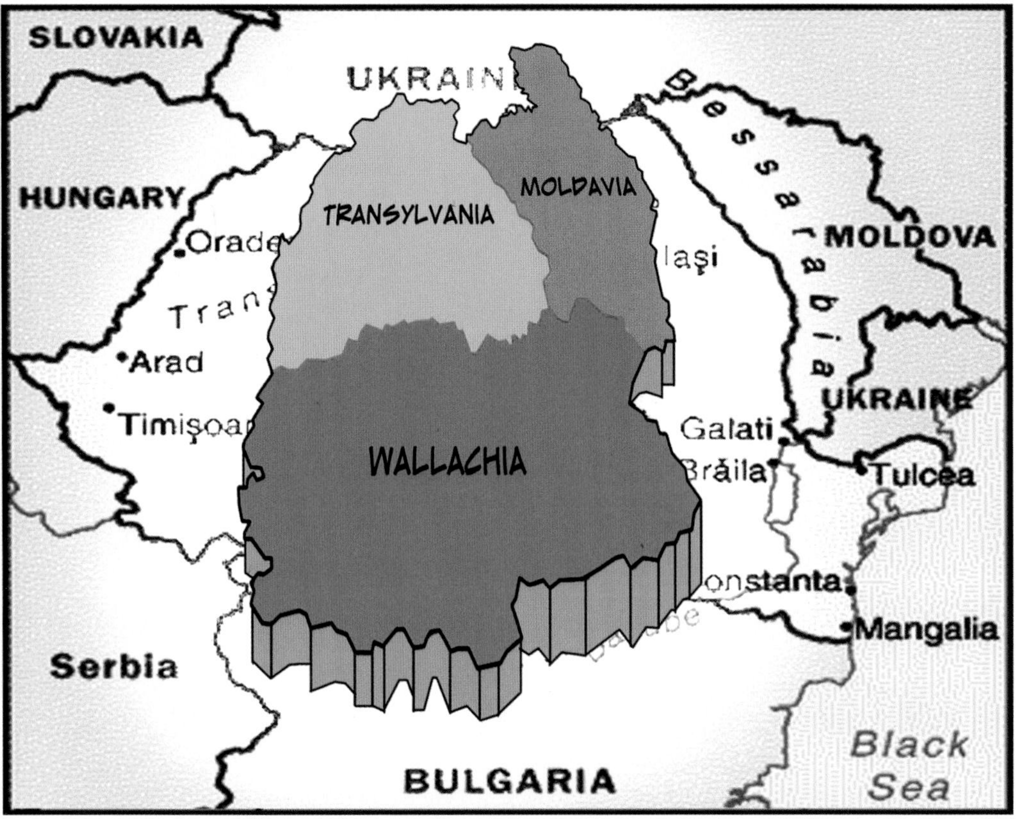
SLOVAKIA
UKRAIN
Bessarabia
HUNGARY
MOLDAVIA
TRANSYLVANIA
MOLDOVA
.Orade
Iaşi
Tran
•Arad
•Timişoar
UKRAINE
Galati
WALLACHIA
Brăila
Tulcea
onstanta
Mangalia
Serbia
Black Sea
BULGARIA

BUT WHAT THE HELL, YOU MAY ASK.
IS THIS WALLACHIA? AND WHAT KIND OF HISTORY AM I TALKING ABOUT? ALONG WITH MOLDAVIA AND TRANSYLVANIA, WALLACHIA WAS AND IS PART OF ROMANIA.

BACK IN THE 1400'S, WALLACHIA WAS A PRINCIPALITY.
THOUGH IT WAS GOVERNED BY ITS OWN PRINCES, THE OTTOMAN EMPIRE EXERCISED POLITICAL CONTROL OVER THE AREA AND TRIBUTES WERE PAID TO THE TURKISH SULTAN.
MOST TROUBLES CAME FROM CHRISTIAN PRINCES WARRING EACH OTHER FOR THE CROWN--JUST LIKE YOU WITNESSED BETWEEN PRINCE VLAD II AND THE WHITE KNIGHT. THE MUSLIMS, IN THEIR OWN WAY, WERE PUSSYCATS.

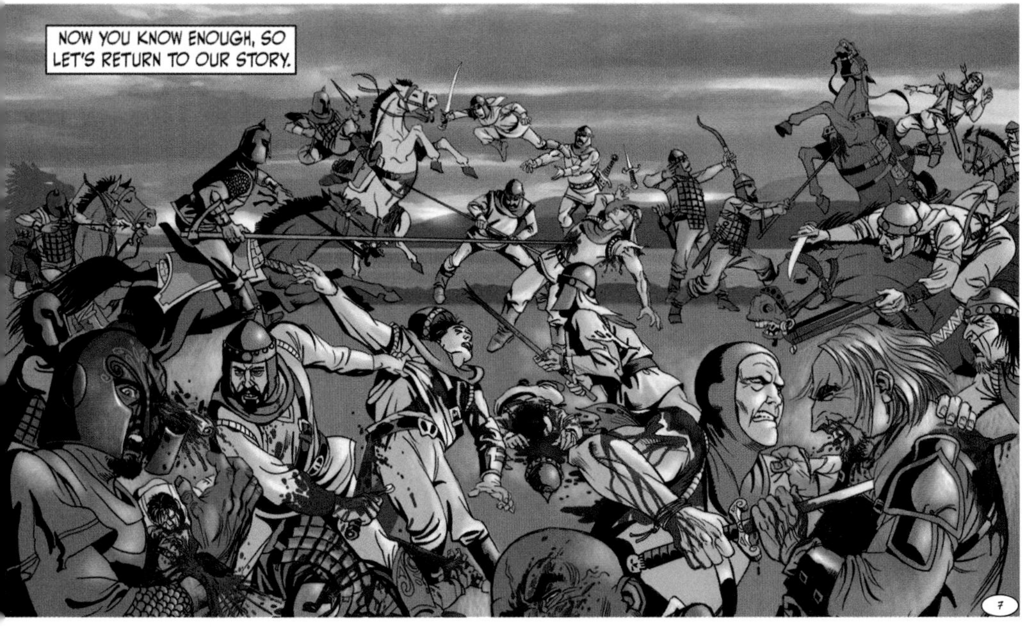
NOW YOU KNOW ENOUGH, SO LET'S RETURN TO OUR STORY.

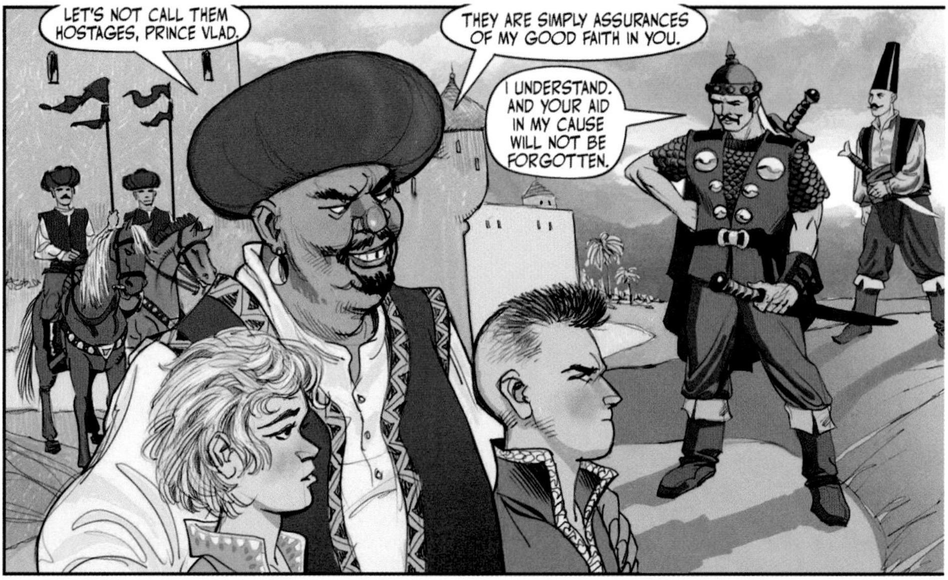
LET'S NOT CALL THEM HOSTAGES, PRINCE VLAD.
THEY ARE SIMPLY ASSURANCES OF MY GOOD FAITH IN YOU.
I UNDERSTAND. AND YOUR AID IN MY CAUSE WILL NOT BE FORGOTTEN.

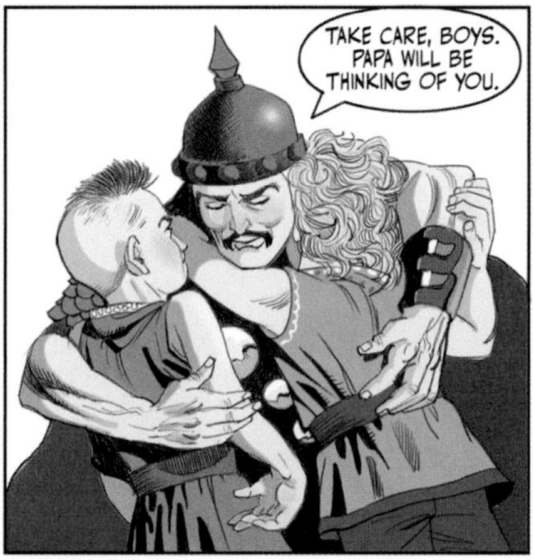
TAKE CARE, BOYS. PAPA WILL BE THINKING OF YOU.

AS YOU MIGHT NOT KNOW, THERE WERE TWO OTHER SONS. SEVERAL YEARS EARLIER THEY WERE LEFT IN THE HANDS OF SULTAN MURAD OF THE OTTOMAN EMPIRE, IN ADRIANOPLE, IN EASTERN EUROPEAN TURKEY.

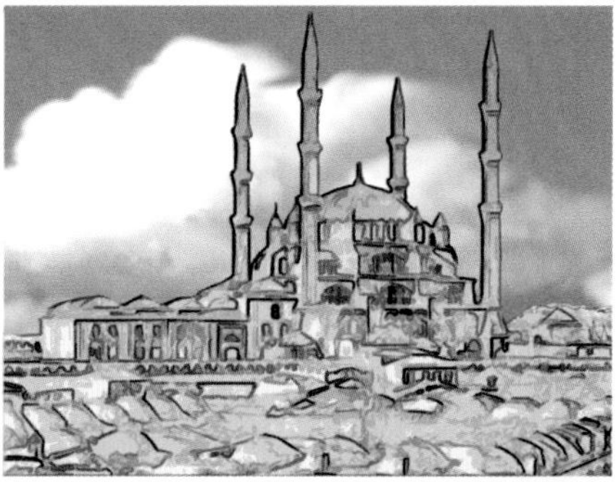

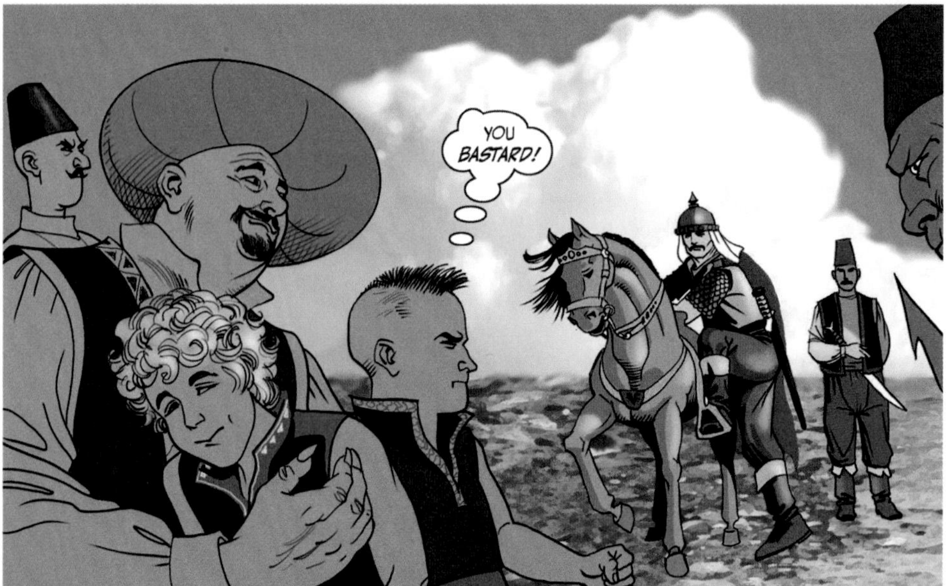
YOU *BASTARD!*

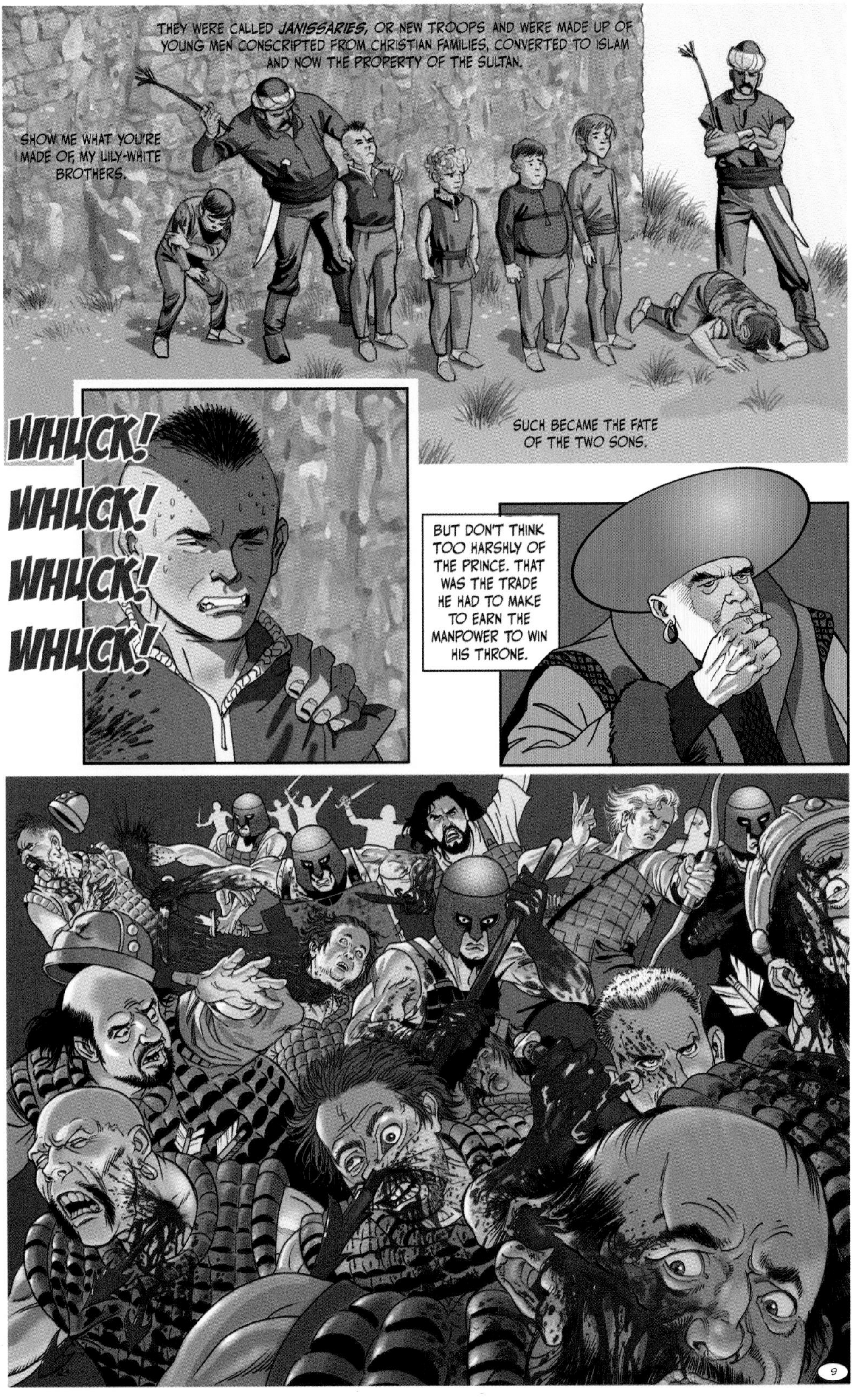
THEY WERE CALLED *JANISSARIES,* OR NEW TROOPS AND WERE MADE UP OF YOUNG MEN CONSCRIPTED FROM CHRISTIAN FAMILIES, CONVERTED TO ISLAM AND NOW THE PROPERTY OF THE SULTAN.
SHOW ME WHAT YOU'RE MADE OF, MY LILY-WHITE BROTHERS.
SUCH BECAME THE FATE OF THE TWO SONS.
WHUCK! WHUCK! WHUCK! WHUCK!
BUT DON'T THINK TOO HARSHLY OF THE PRINCE. THAT WAS THE TRADE HE HAD TO MAKE TO EARN THE MANPOWER TO WIN HIS THRONE.

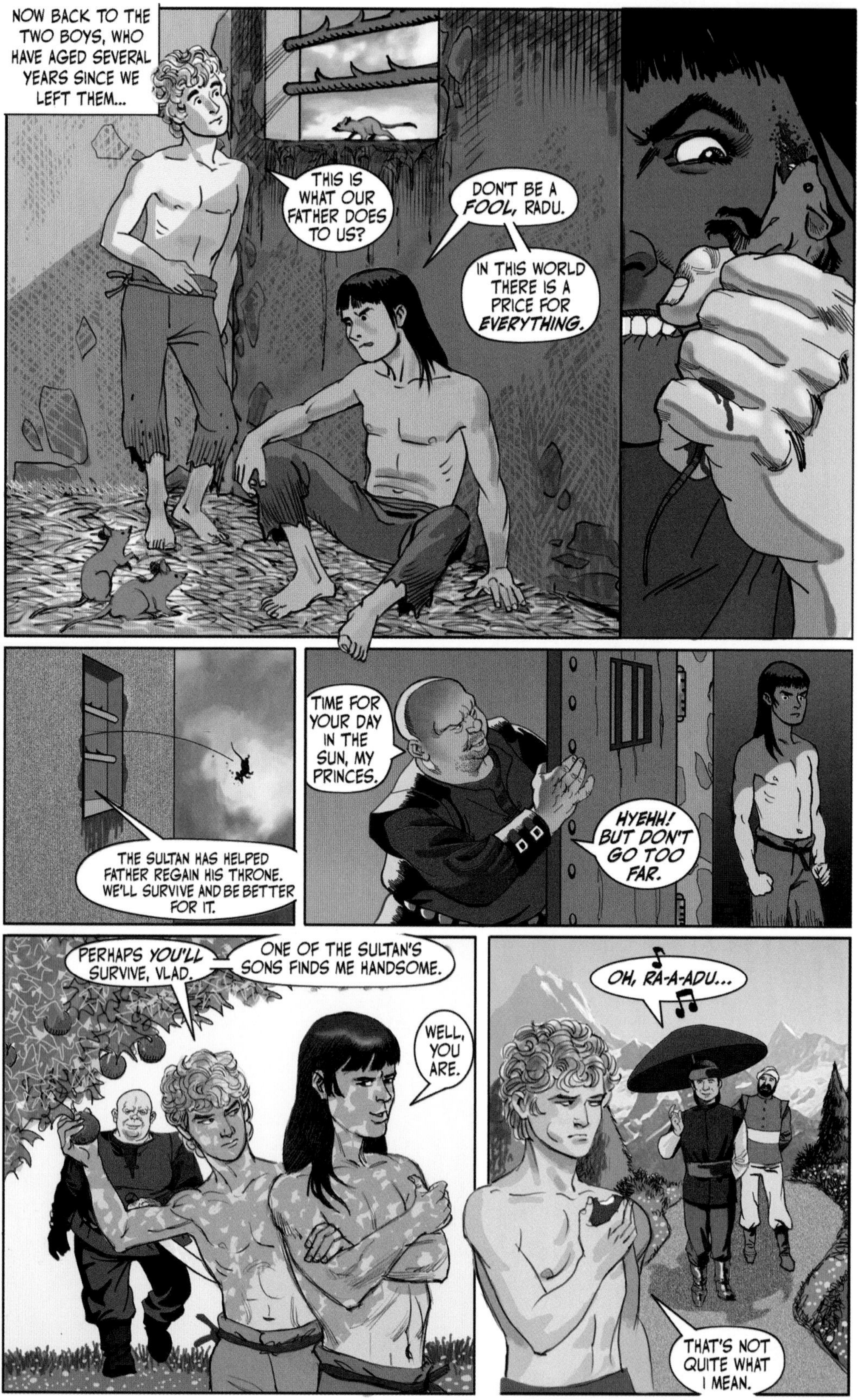
NOW BACK TO THE TWO BOYS, WHO HAVE AGED SEVERAL YEARS SINCE WE LEFT THEM...
THIS IS WHAT OUR FATHER DOES TO US?
DON'T BE A FOOL, RADU.
IN THIS WORLD THERE IS A PRICE FOR EVERYTHING.
THE SULTAN HAS HELPED FATHER REGAIN HIS THRONE. WE'LL SURVIVE AND BE BETTER FOR IT.
TIME FOR YOUR DAY IN THE SUN, MY PRINCES.
HYEHH! BUT DON'T GO TOO FAR.
PERHAPS YOU'LL SURVIVE, VLAD.
ONE OF THE SULTAN'S SONS FINDS ME HANDSOME.
WELL, YOU ARE.
OH, RA-A-ADU...
THAT'S NOT QUITE WHAT I MEAN.

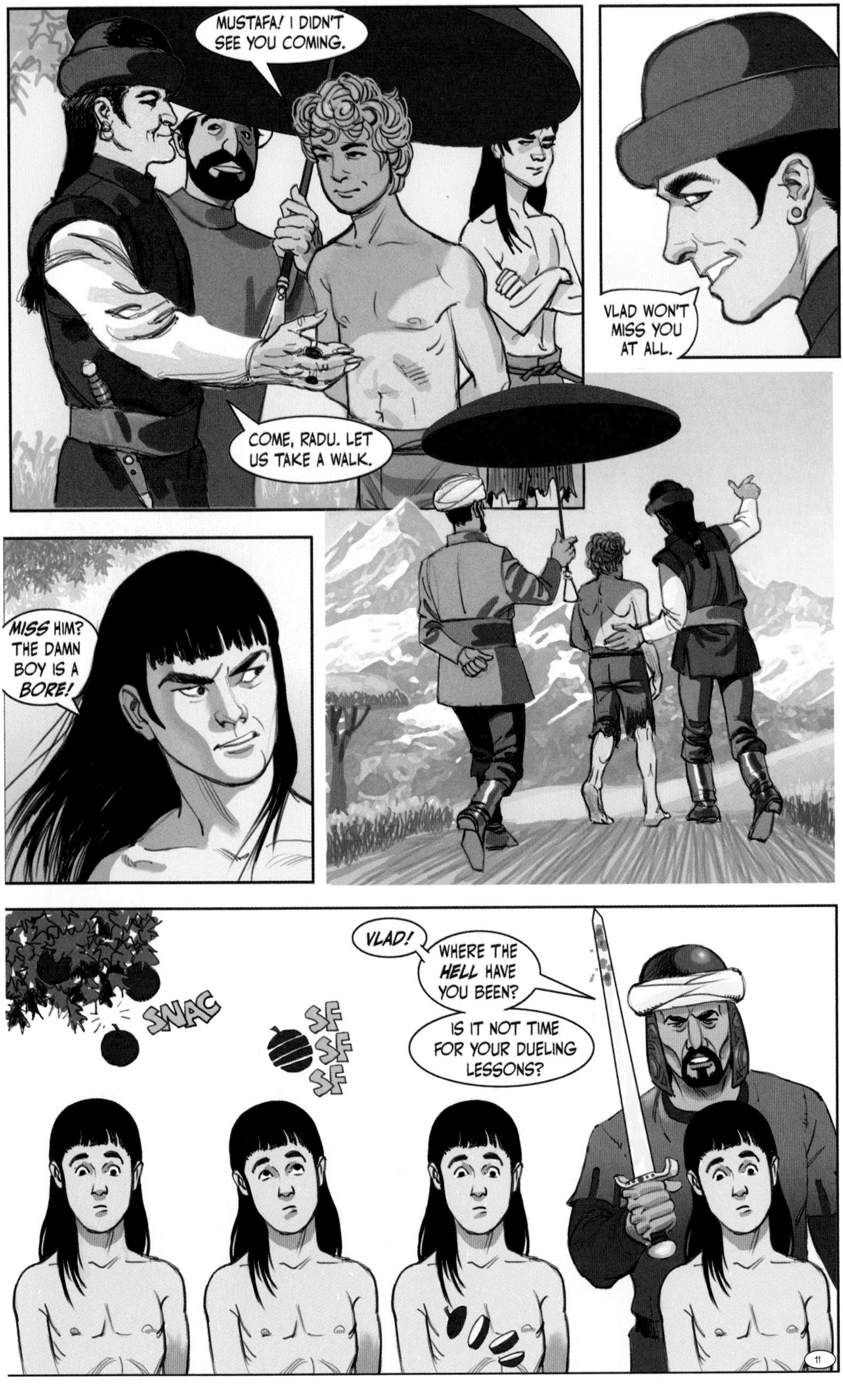
MUSTAFA! I DIDN'T SEE YOU COMING.
VLAD WON'T MISS YOU AT ALL.
COME, RADU. LET US TAKE A WALK.
MISS HIM? THE DAMN BOY IS A BORE!
SNAC
SF SF SF
VLAD!
WHERE THE HELL HAVE YOU BEEN?
IS IT NOT TIME FOR YOUR DUELING LESSONS?

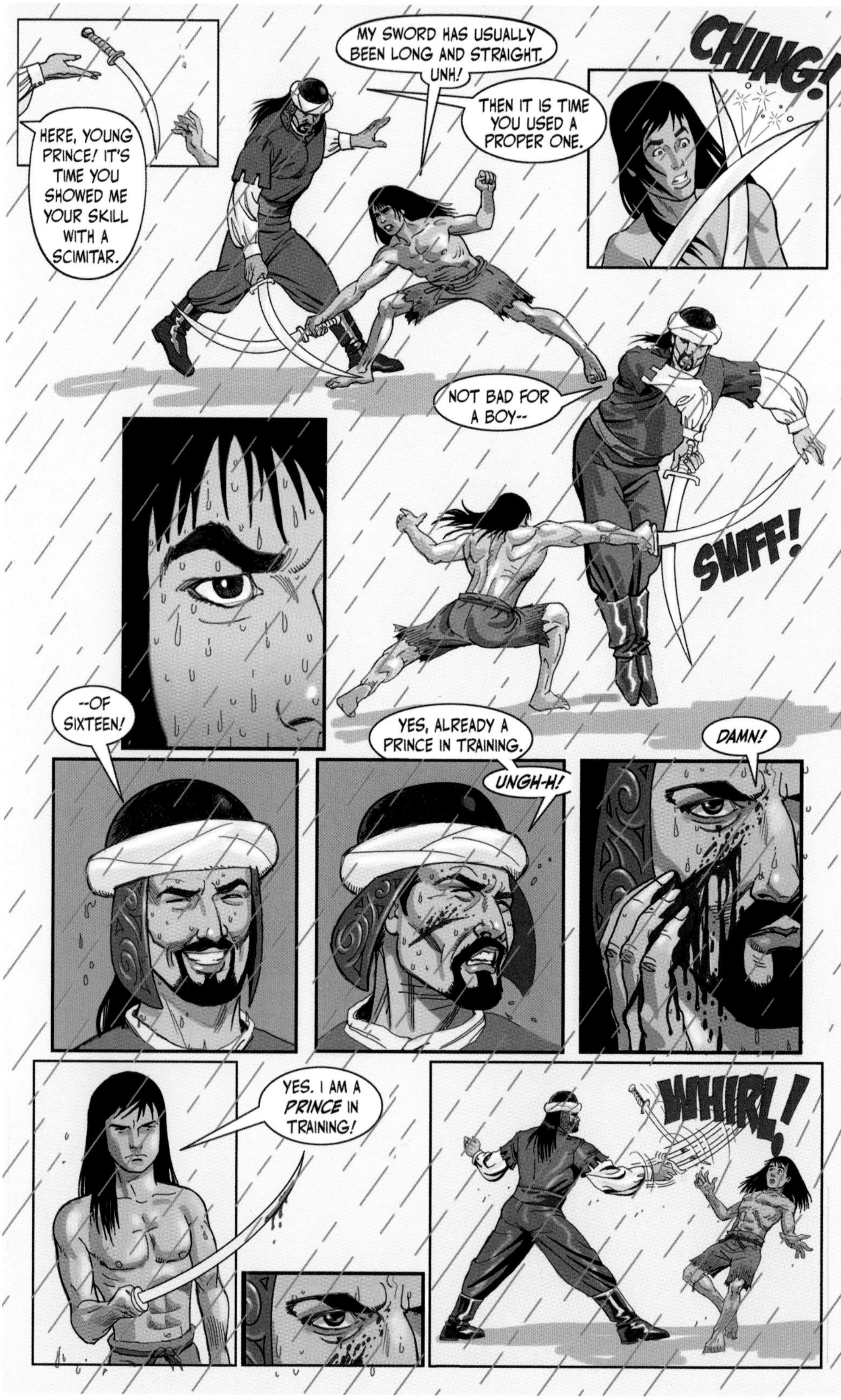
HERE, YOUNG PRINCE! IT'S TIME YOU SHOWED ME YOUR SKILL WITH A SCIMITAR.
MY SWORD HAS USUALLY BEEN LONG AND STRAIGHT.
UNH!
THEN IT IS TIME YOU USED A PROPER ONE.
CHING!
NOT BAD FOR A BOY--
SWFF!
--OF SIXTEEN!
YES, ALREADY A PRINCE IN TRAINING.
UNGH-H!
DAMN!
YES. I AM A PRINCE IN TRAINING!
WHIRL!

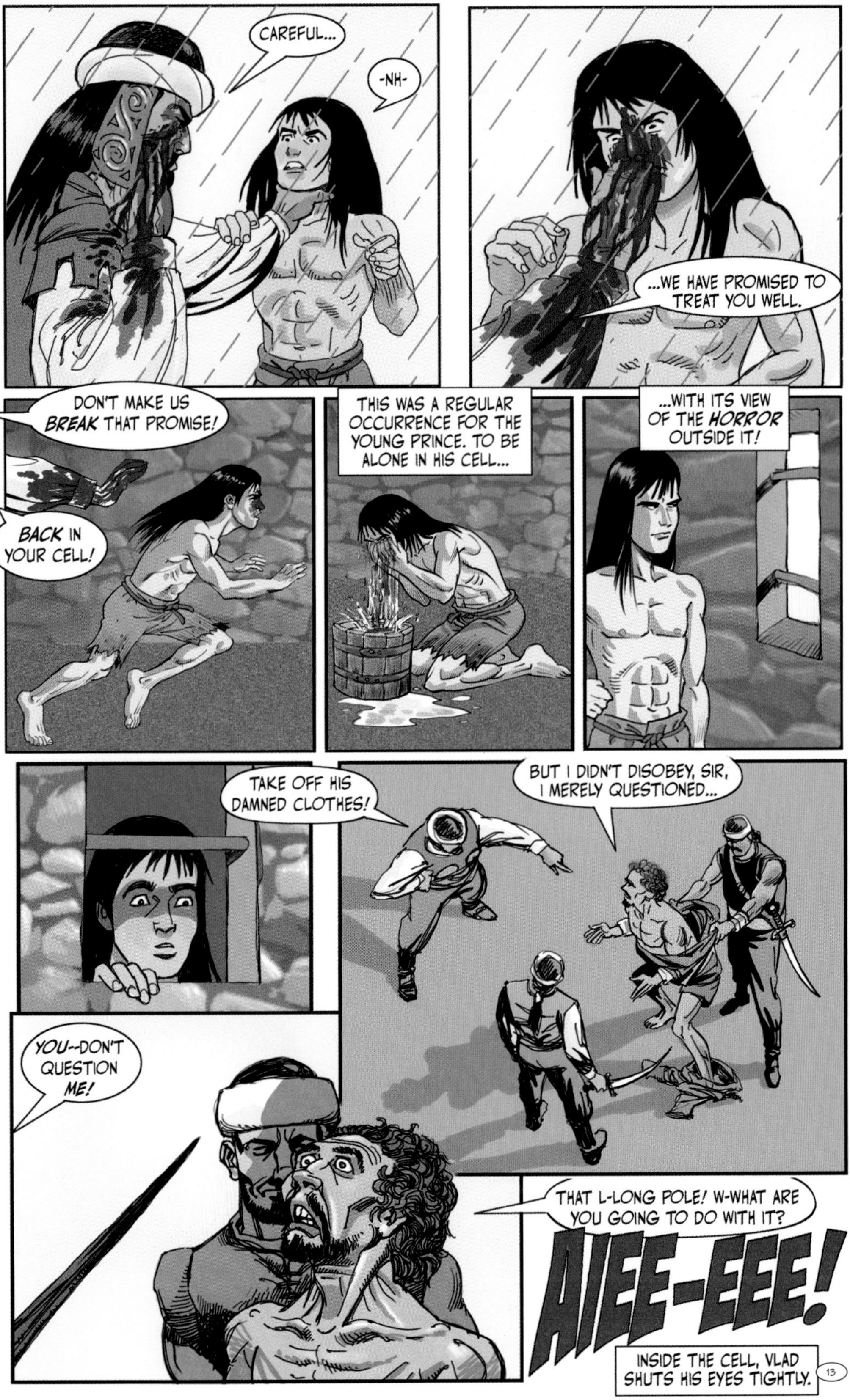
CAREFUL...
-NH-
...WE HAVE PROMISED TO TREAT YOU WELL.
DON'T MAKE US BREAK THAT PROMISE!
BACK IN YOUR CELL!
THIS WAS A REGULAR OCCURRENCE FOR THE YOUNG PRINCE. TO BE ALONE IN HIS CELL...
...WITH ITS VIEW OF THE HORROR OUTSIDE IT!
TAKE OFF HIS DAMNED CLOTHES!
BUT I DIDN'T DISOBEY, SIR, I MERELY QUESTIONED...
YOU--DON'T QUESTION ME!
THAT L-LONG POLE! W-WHAT ARE YOU GOING TO DO WITH IT?
AIEE-EEE!
INSIDE THE CELL, VLAD SHUTS HIS EYES TIGHTLY.

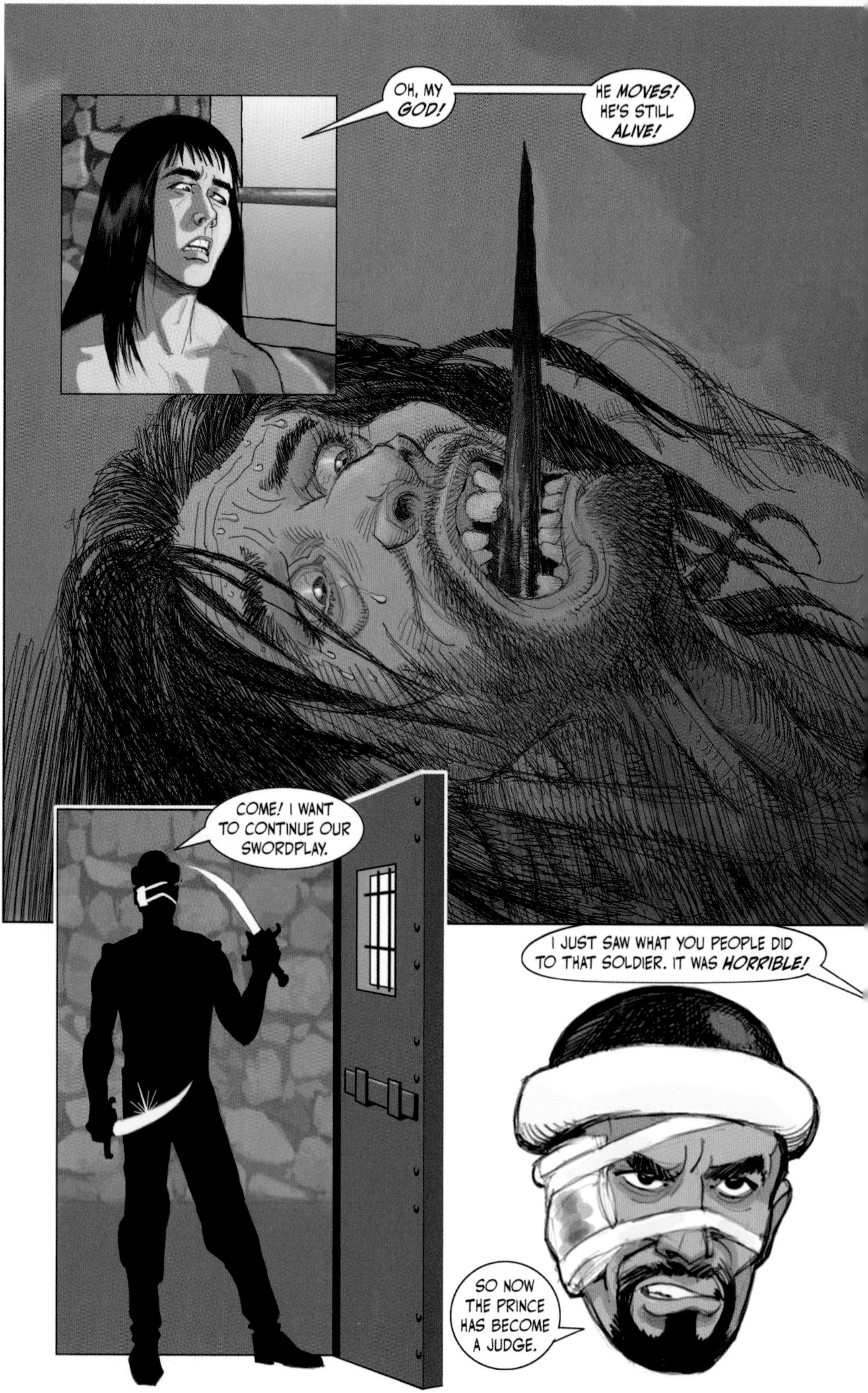
OH, MY GOD!
HE MOVES! HE'S STILL ALIVE!
COME! I WANT TO CONTINUE OUR SWORDPLAY.
I JUST SAW WHAT YOU PEOPLE DID TO THAT SOLDIER. IT WAS HORRIBLE!
SO NOW THE PRINCE HAS BECOME A JUDGE.

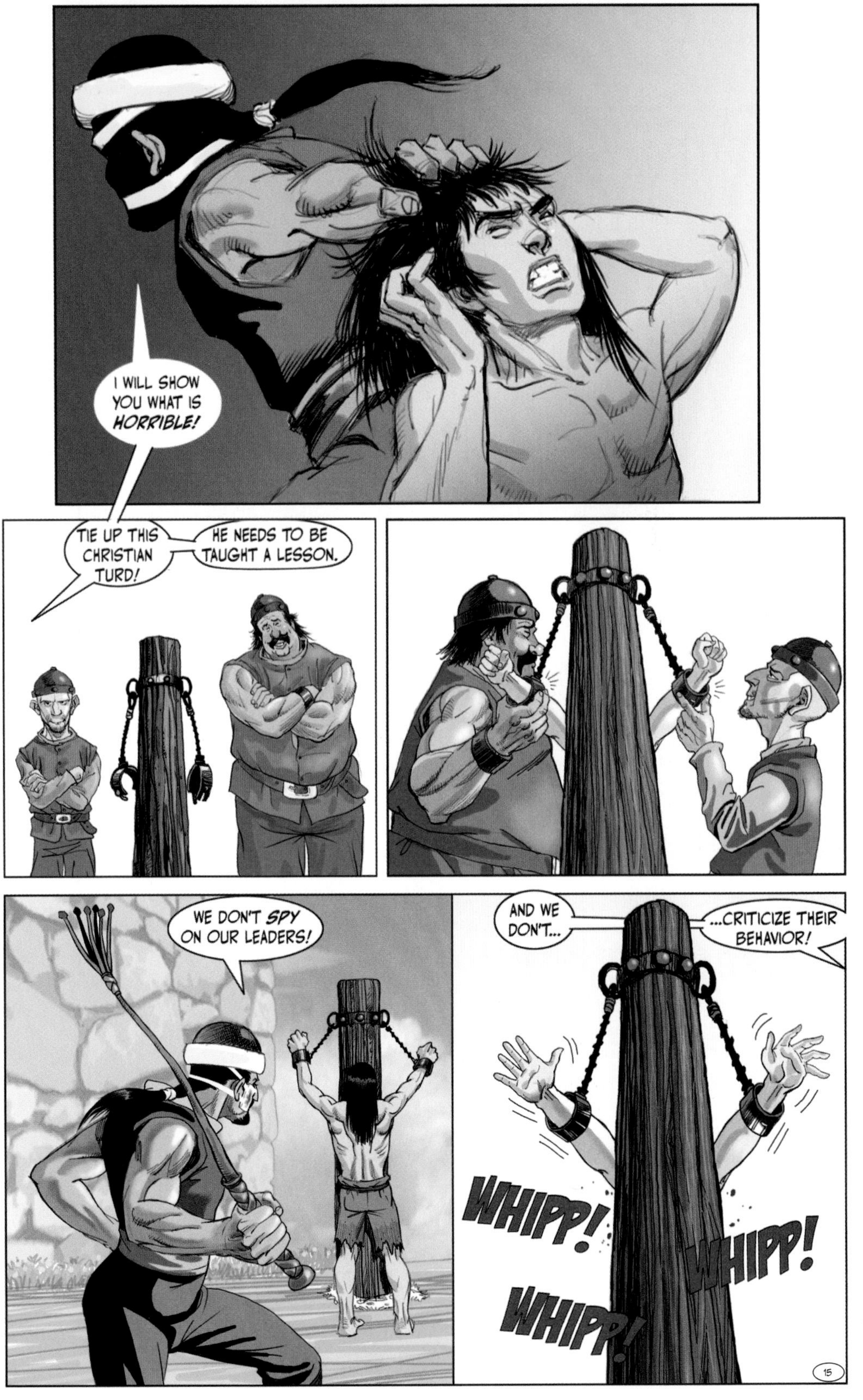
I WILL SHOW YOU WHAT IS HORRIBLE!
TIE UP THIS CHRISTIAN TURD!
HE NEEDS TO BE TAUGHT A LESSON.
WE DON'T SPY ON OUR LEADERS!
AND WE DON'T...
...CRITICIZE THEIR BEHAVIOR!
WHIPP!
WHIPP!
WHIPP!

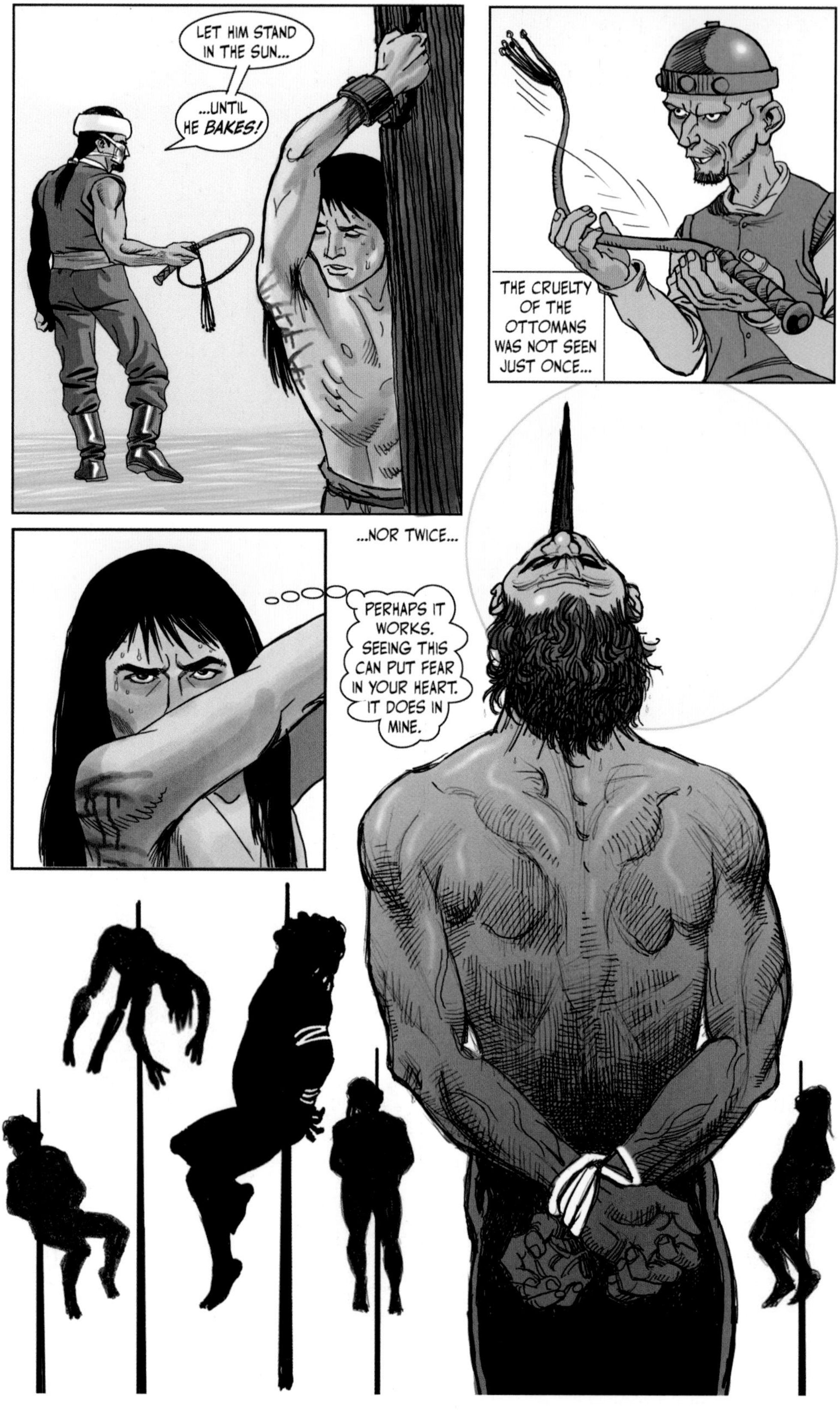
LET HIM STAND IN THE SUN...
...UNTIL HE *BAKES!*
THE CRUELTY OF THE OTTOMANS WAS NOT SEEN JUST ONCE...
...NOR TWICE...
PERHAPS IT WORKS. SEEING THIS CAN PUT FEAR IN YOUR HEART. IT DOES IN MINE.

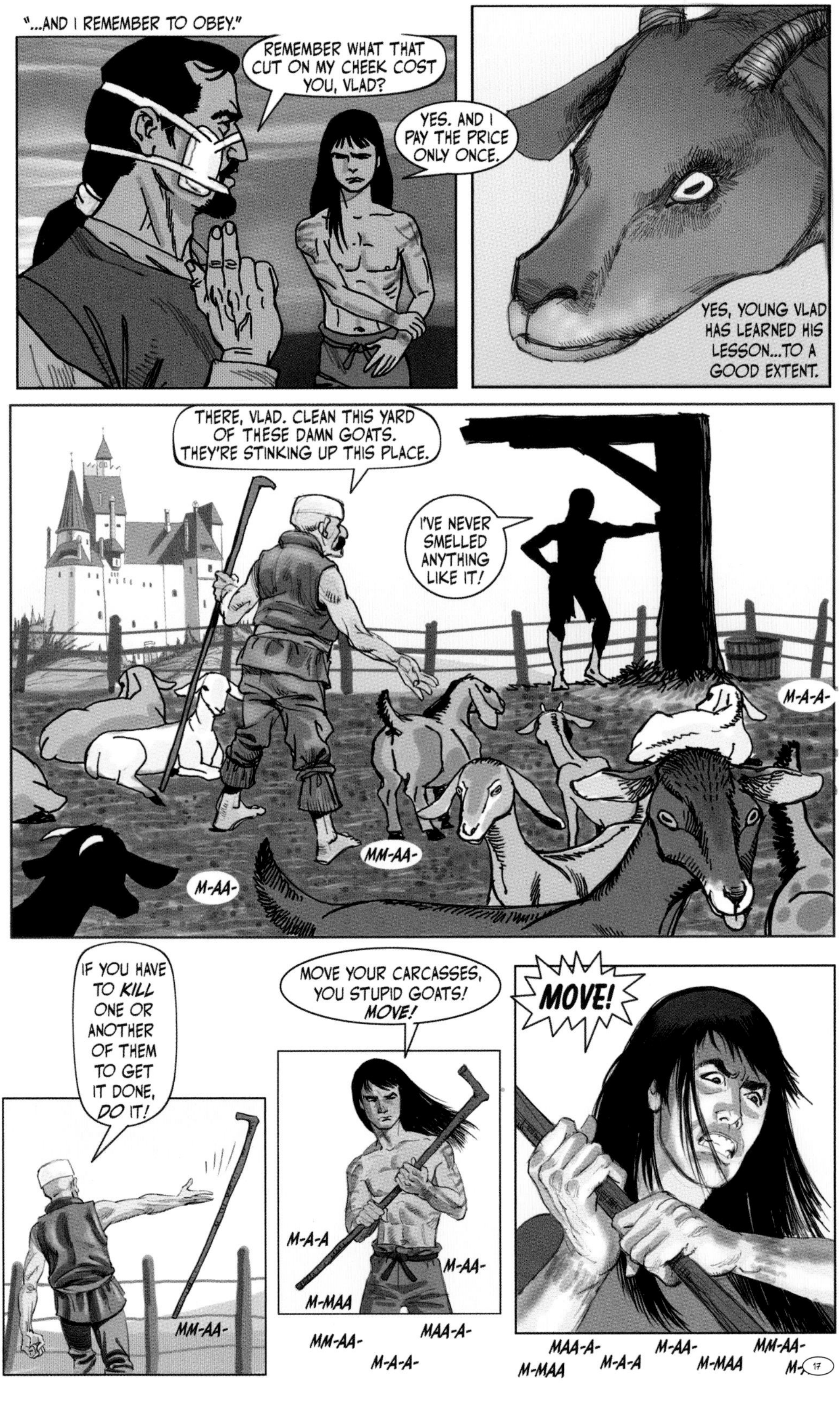
"...AND I REMEMBER TO OBEY."
REMEMBER WHAT THAT CUT ON MY CHEEK COST YOU, VLAD?
YES. AND I PAY THE PRICE ONLY ONCE.
YES, YOUNG VLAD HAS LEARNED HIS LESSON...TO A GOOD EXTENT.
THERE, VLAD. CLEAN THIS YARD OF THESE DAMN GOATS. THEY'RE STINKING UP THIS PLACE.
I'VE NEVER SMELLED ANYTHING LIKE IT!
M-A-A-
MM-AA-
M-AA-
IF YOU HAVE TO KILL ONE OR ANOTHER OF THEM TO GET IT DONE, DO IT!
MM-AA-
MOVE YOUR CARCASSES, YOU STUPID GOATS! MOVE!
M-A-A
M-AA-
M-MAA
MM-AA-
MAA-A-
M-A-A-
MOVE!
MAA-A-
M-MAA
M-A-A
M-AA-
M-MAA
MM-AA-

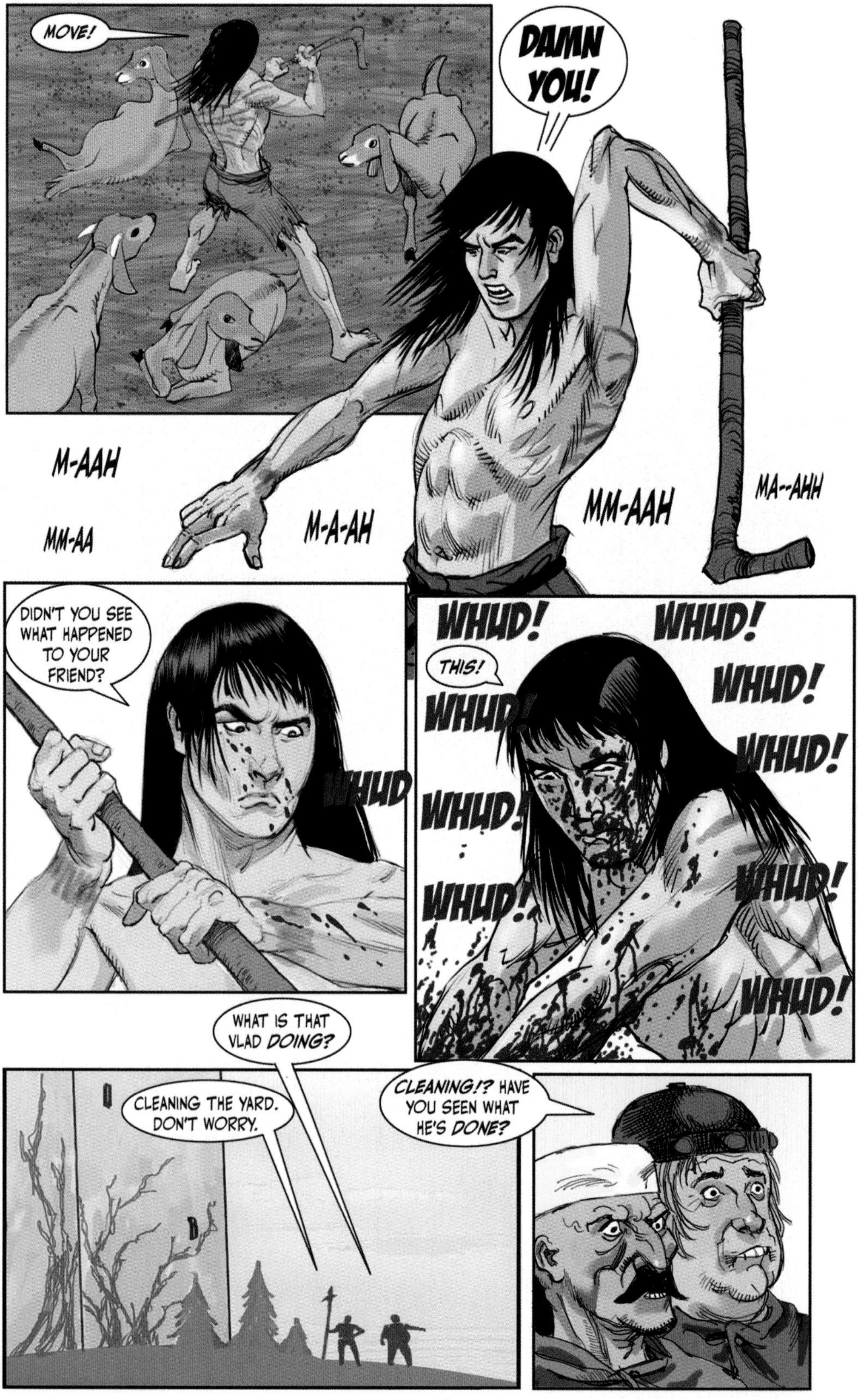
MOVE!
DAMN YOU!
M-AAH
MM-AA
M-A-AH
MM-AAH
MA--AHH
DIDN'T YOU SEE WHAT HAPPENED TO YOUR FRIEND?
WHUD
WHUD!
WHUD!
THIS!
WHUD!
WHUD!
WHUD!
WHUD!
WHUD!
WHUD!
WHUD!
WHAT IS THAT VLAD *DOING?*
CLEANING THE YARD. DON'T WORRY.
CLEANING!? HAVE YOU SEEN WHAT HE'S *DONE?*

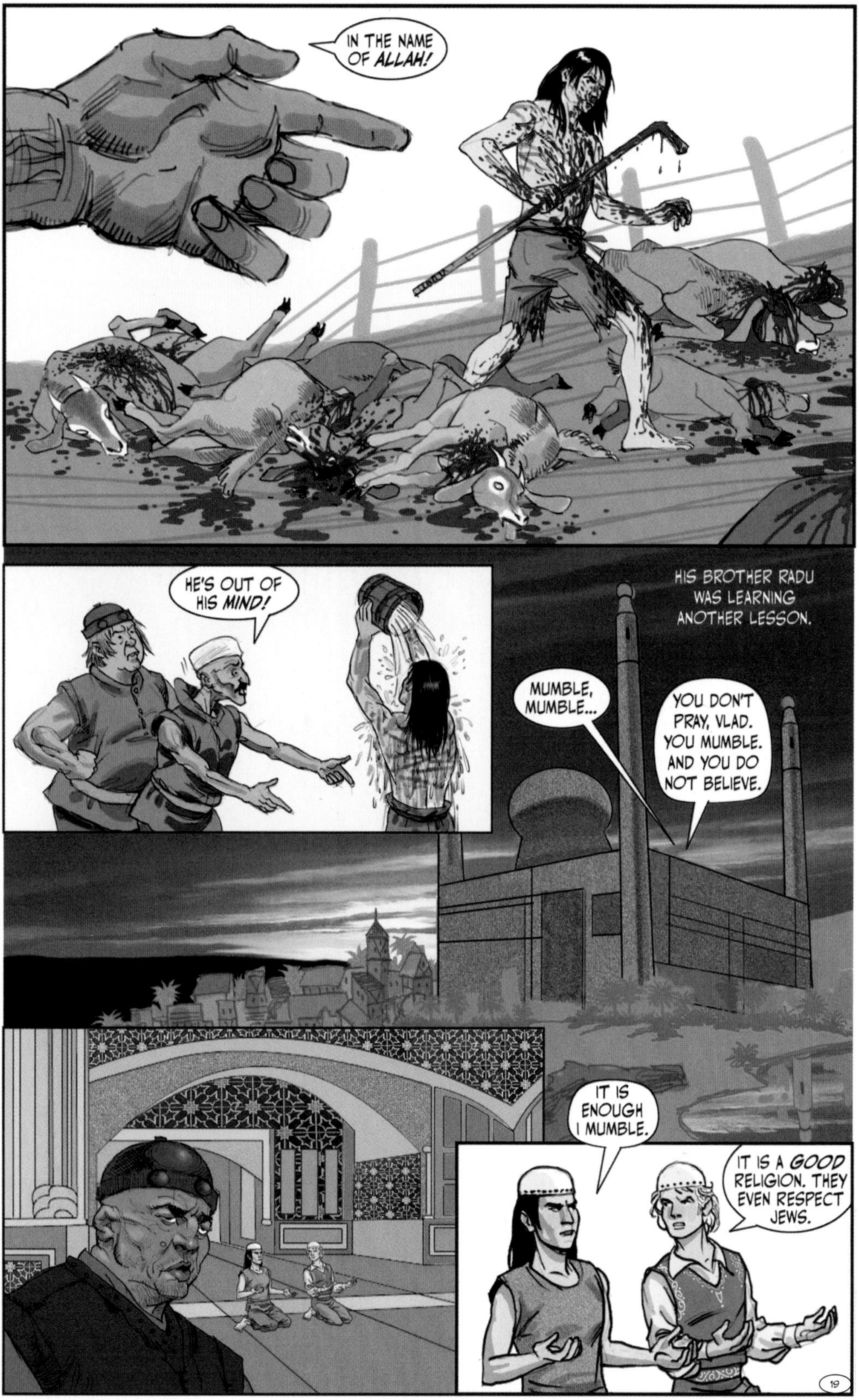
IN THE NAME OF *ALLAH!*
HE'S OUT OF HIS *MIND!*
HIS BROTHER RADU WAS LEARNING ANOTHER LESSON.
MUMBLE, MUMBLE...
YOU DON'T PRAY, VLAD. YOU MUMBLE. AND YOU DO NOT BELIEVE.
IT IS ENOUGH I MUMBLE.
IT IS A *GOOD* RELIGION. THEY EVEN RESPECT JEWS.

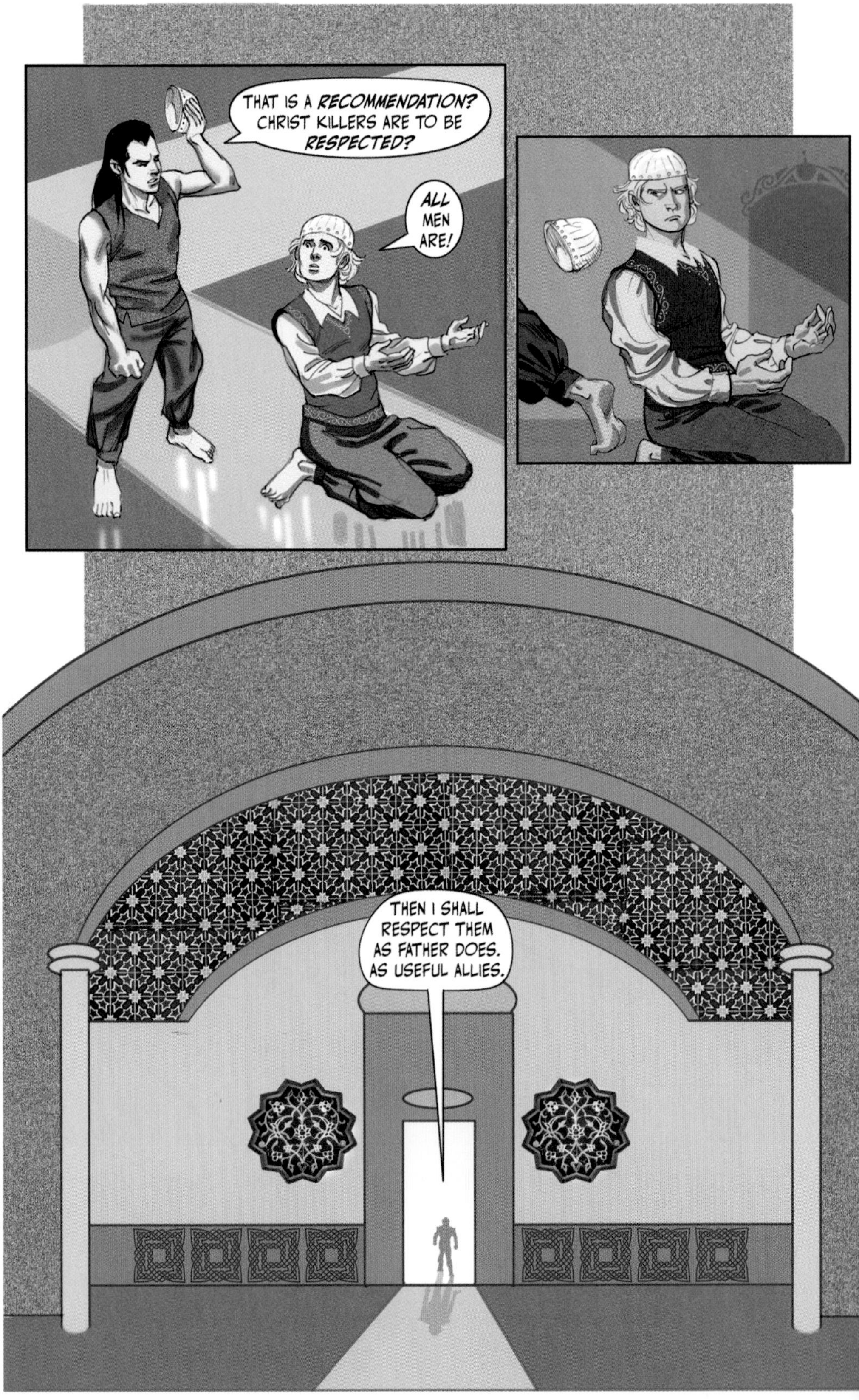
THAT IS A *RECOMMENDATION?* CHRIST KILLERS ARE TO BE *RESPECTED?*
ALL MEN ARE!
THEN I SHALL RESPECT THEM AS FATHER DOES. AS USEFUL ALLIES.

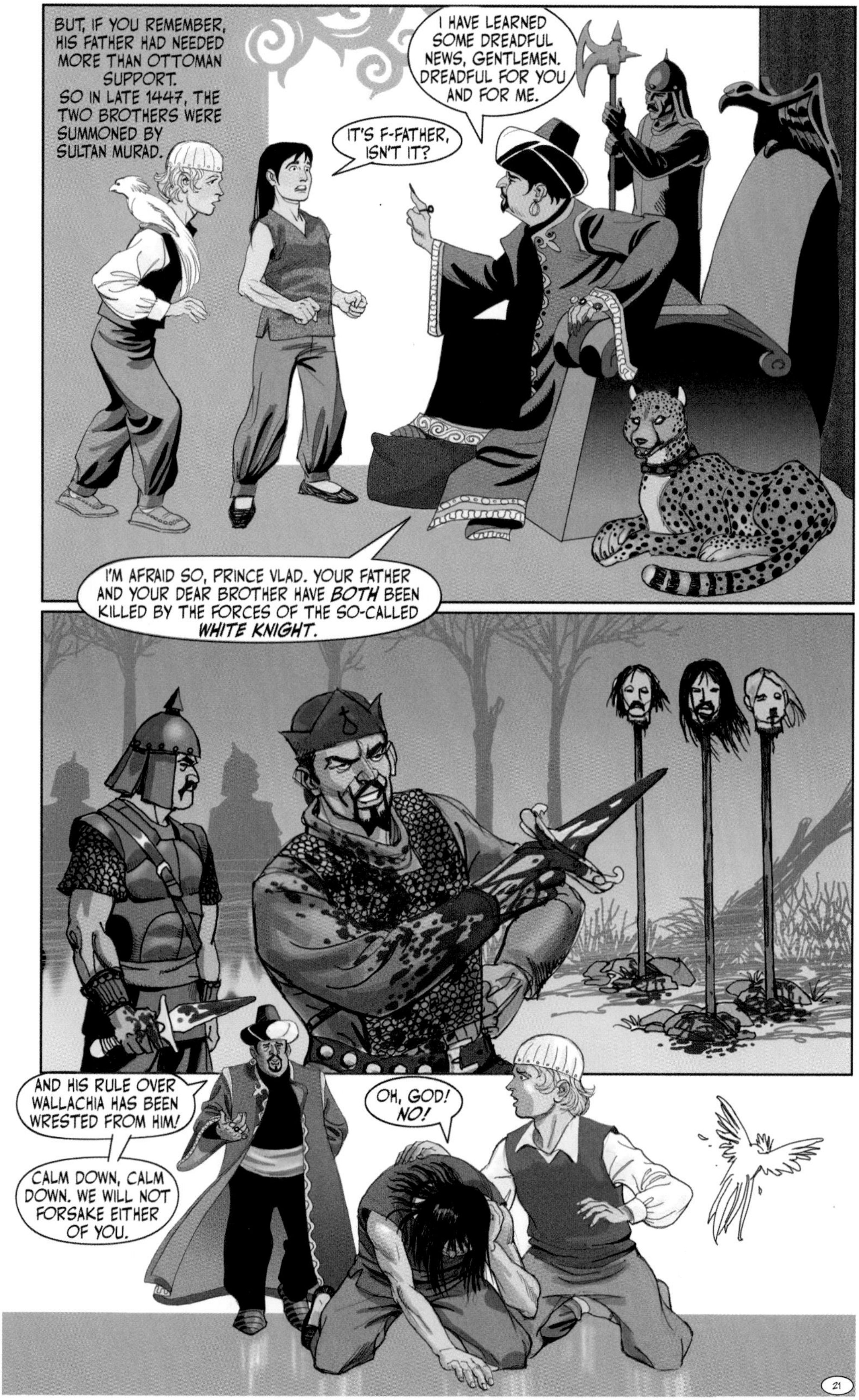

BUT, IF YOU REMEMBER, HIS FATHER HAD NEEDED MORE THAN OTTOMAN SUPPORT.
SO IN LATE 1447, THE TWO BROTHERS WERE SUMMONED BY SULTAN MURAD.
I HAVE LEARNED SOME DREADFUL NEWS, GENTLEMEN. DREADFUL FOR YOU AND FOR ME.
IT'S F-FATHER, ISN'T IT?
I'M AFRAID SO, PRINCE VLAD. YOUR FATHER AND YOUR DEAR BROTHER HAVE *BOTH* BEEN KILLED BY THE FORCES OF THE SO-CALLED *WHITE KNIGHT*.
AND HIS RULE OVER WALLACHIA HAS BEEN WRESTED FROM HIM!
OH, GOD! *NO!*
CALM DOWN, CALM DOWN. WE WILL NOT FORSAKE EITHER OF YOU.

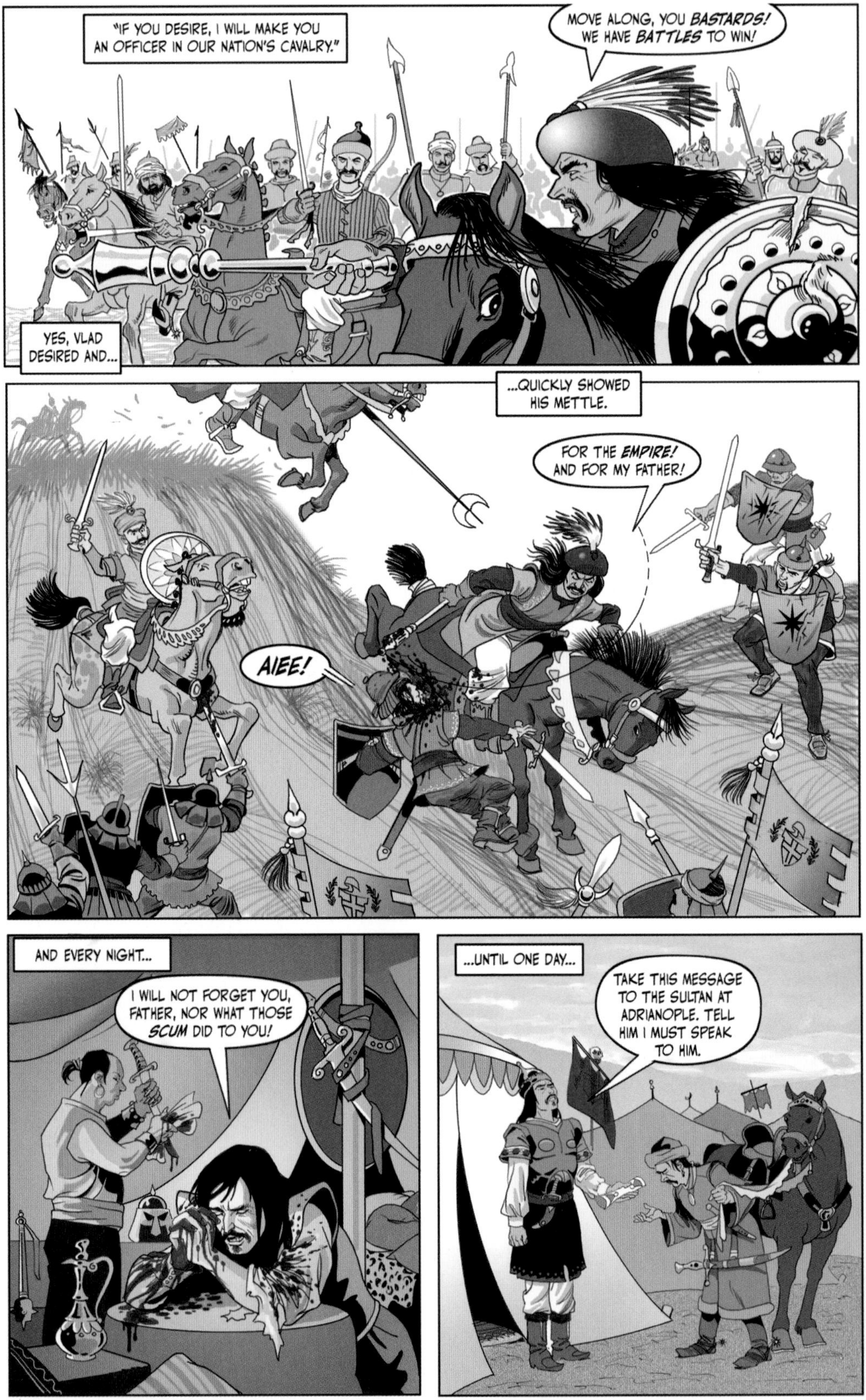
"IF YOU DESIRE, I WILL MAKE YOU AN OFFICER IN OUR NATION'S CAVALRY."
MOVE ALONG, YOU *BASTARDS!* WE HAVE *BATTLES* TO WIN!
YES, VLAD DESIRED AND...
...QUICKLY SHOWED HIS METTLE.
FOR THE *EMPIRE!* AND FOR MY FATHER!
AIEE!
AND EVERY NIGHT...
I WILL NOT FORGET YOU, FATHER, NOR WHAT THOSE *SCUM* DID TO YOU!
...UNTIL ONE DAY...
TAKE THIS MESSAGE TO THE SULTAN AT ADRIANOPLE. TELL HIM I MUST SPEAK TO HIM.

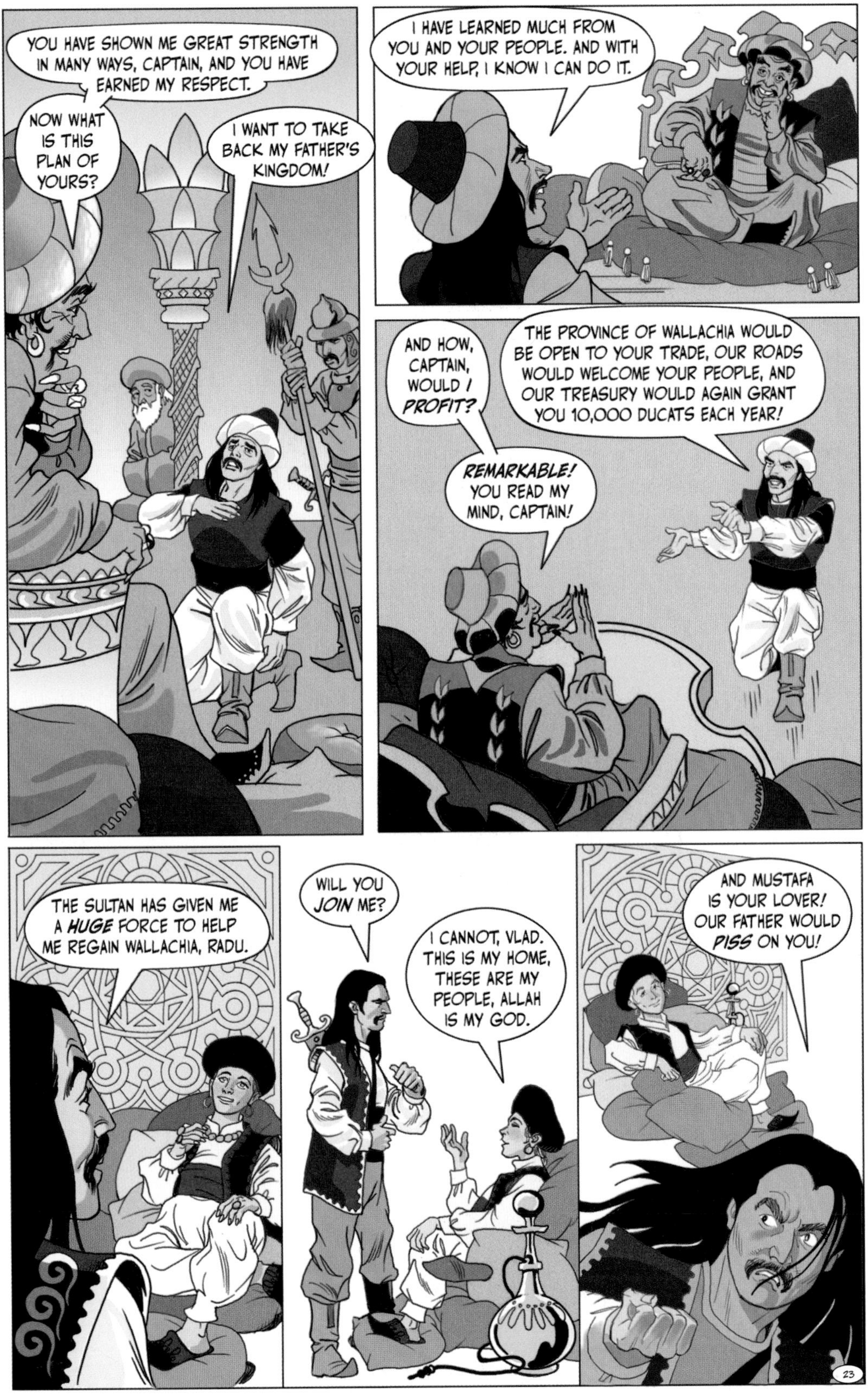
YOU HAVE SHOWN ME GREAT STRENGTH IN MANY WAYS, CAPTAIN, AND YOU HAVE EARNED MY RESPECT.
NOW WHAT IS THIS PLAN OF YOURS?
I WANT TO TAKE BACK MY FATHER'S KINGDOM!
I HAVE LEARNED MUCH FROM YOU AND YOUR PEOPLE. AND WITH YOUR HELP, I KNOW I CAN DO IT.
AND HOW, CAPTAIN, WOULD *I* ***PROFIT?***
THE PROVINCE OF WALLACHIA WOULD BE OPEN TO YOUR TRADE, OUR ROADS WOULD WELCOME YOUR PEOPLE, AND OUR TREASURY WOULD AGAIN GRANT YOU 10,000 DUCATS EACH YEAR!
REMARKABLE! YOU READ MY MIND, CAPTAIN!
THE SULTAN HAS GIVEN ME A ***HUGE*** FORCE TO HELP ME REGAIN WALLACHIA, RADU.
WILL YOU *JOIN* ME?
I CANNOT, VLAD. THIS IS MY HOME, THESE ARE MY PEOPLE, ALLAH IS MY GOD.
AND MUSTAFA IS YOUR LOVER! OUR FATHER WOULD *PISS* ON YOU!

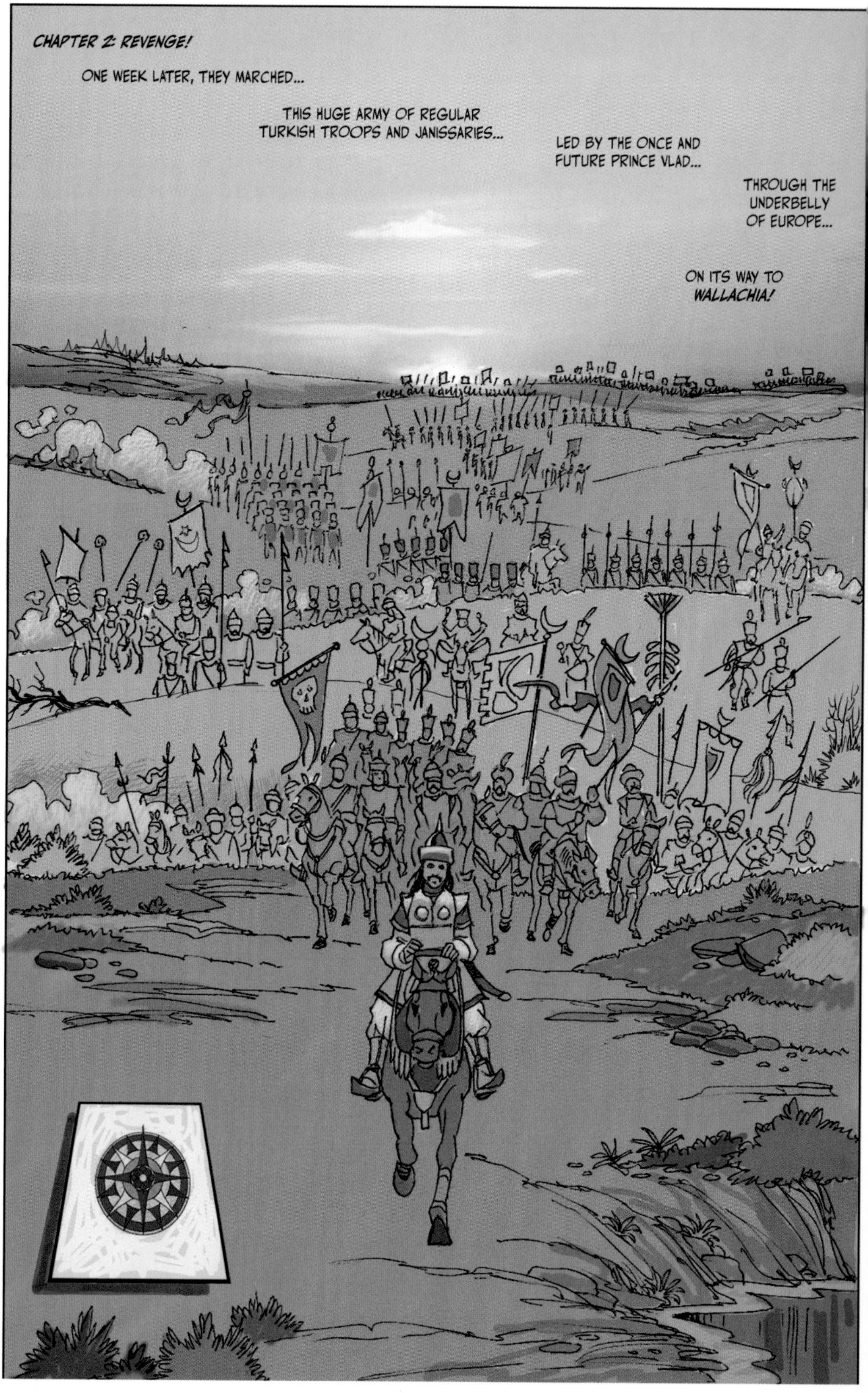
CHAPTER 2: REVENGE!
ONE WEEK LATER, THEY MARCHED...
THIS HUGE ARMY OF REGULAR TURKISH TROOPS AND JANISSARIES...
LED BY THE ONCE AND FUTURE PRINCE VLAD...
THROUGH THE UNDERBELLY OF EUROPE...
ON ITS WAY TO WALLACHIA!

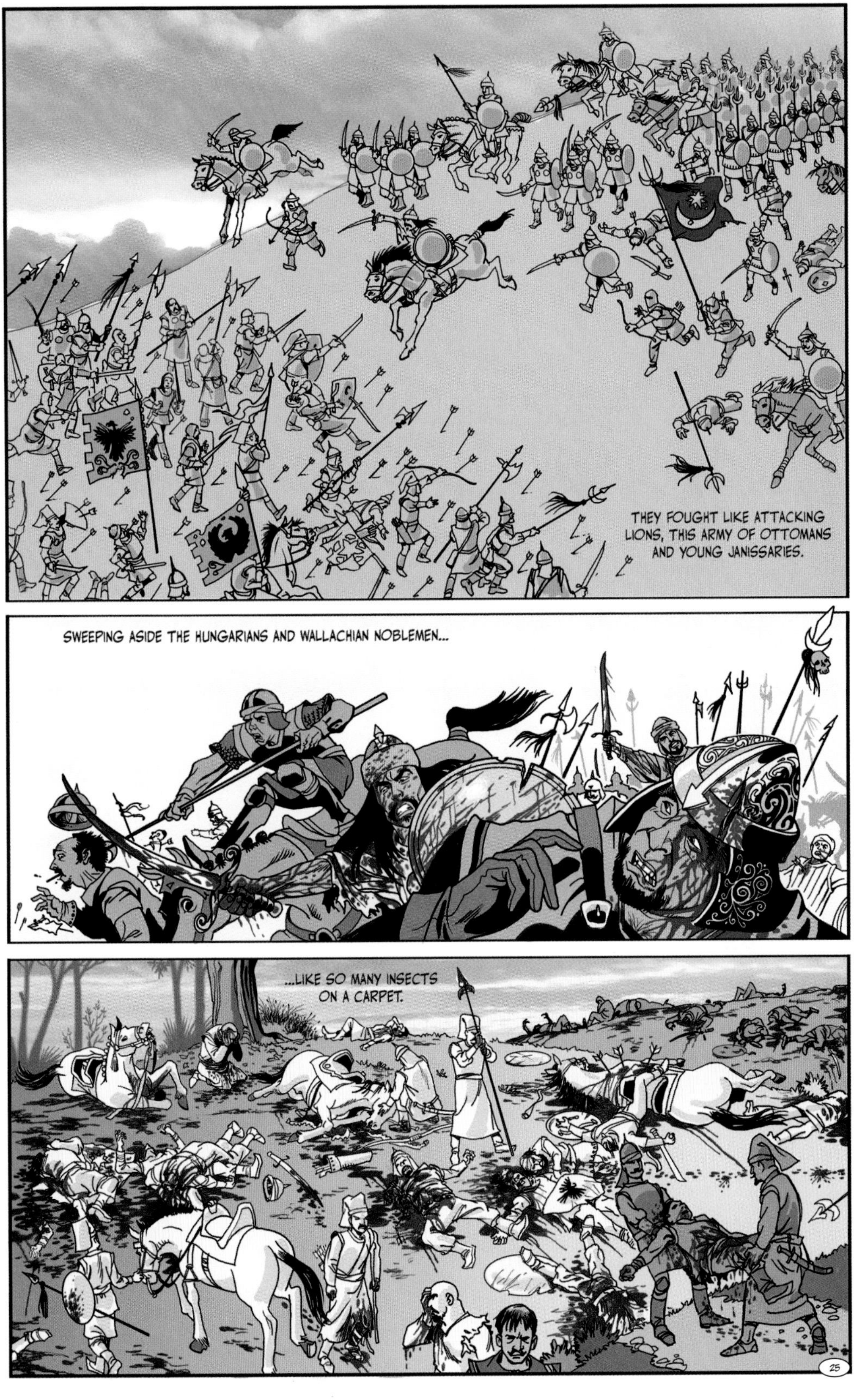
THEY FOUGHT LIKE ATTACKING LIONS, THIS ARMY OF OTTOMANS AND YOUNG JANISSARIES.
SWEEPING ASIDE THE HUNGARIANS AND WALLACHIAN NOBLEMEN...
...LIKE SO MANY INSECTS ON A CARPET.

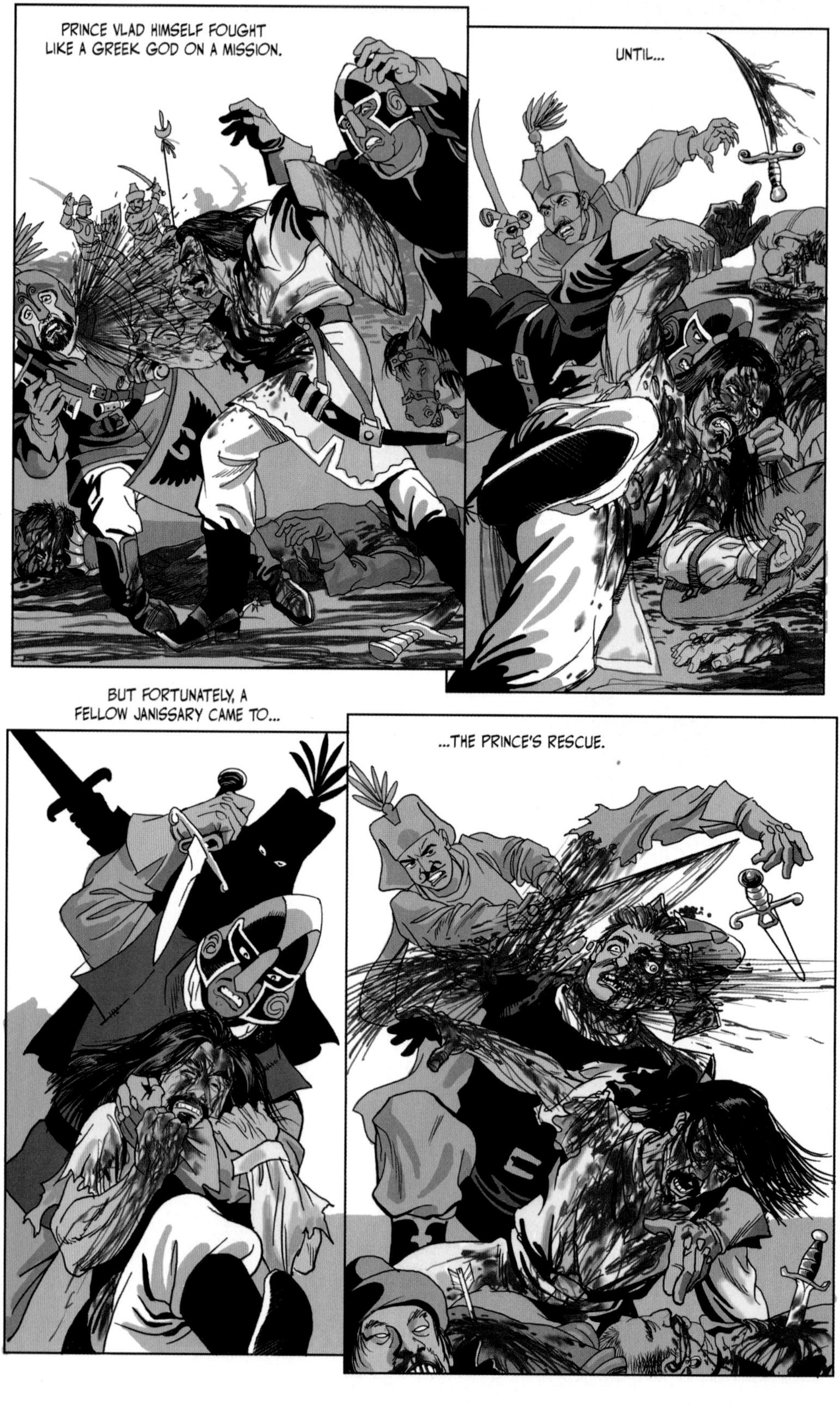
PRINCE VLAD HIMSELF FOUGHT LIKE A GREEK GOD ON A MISSION.
UNTIL...
BUT FORTUNATELY, A FELLOW JANISSARY CAME TO...
...THE PRINCE'S RESCUE.

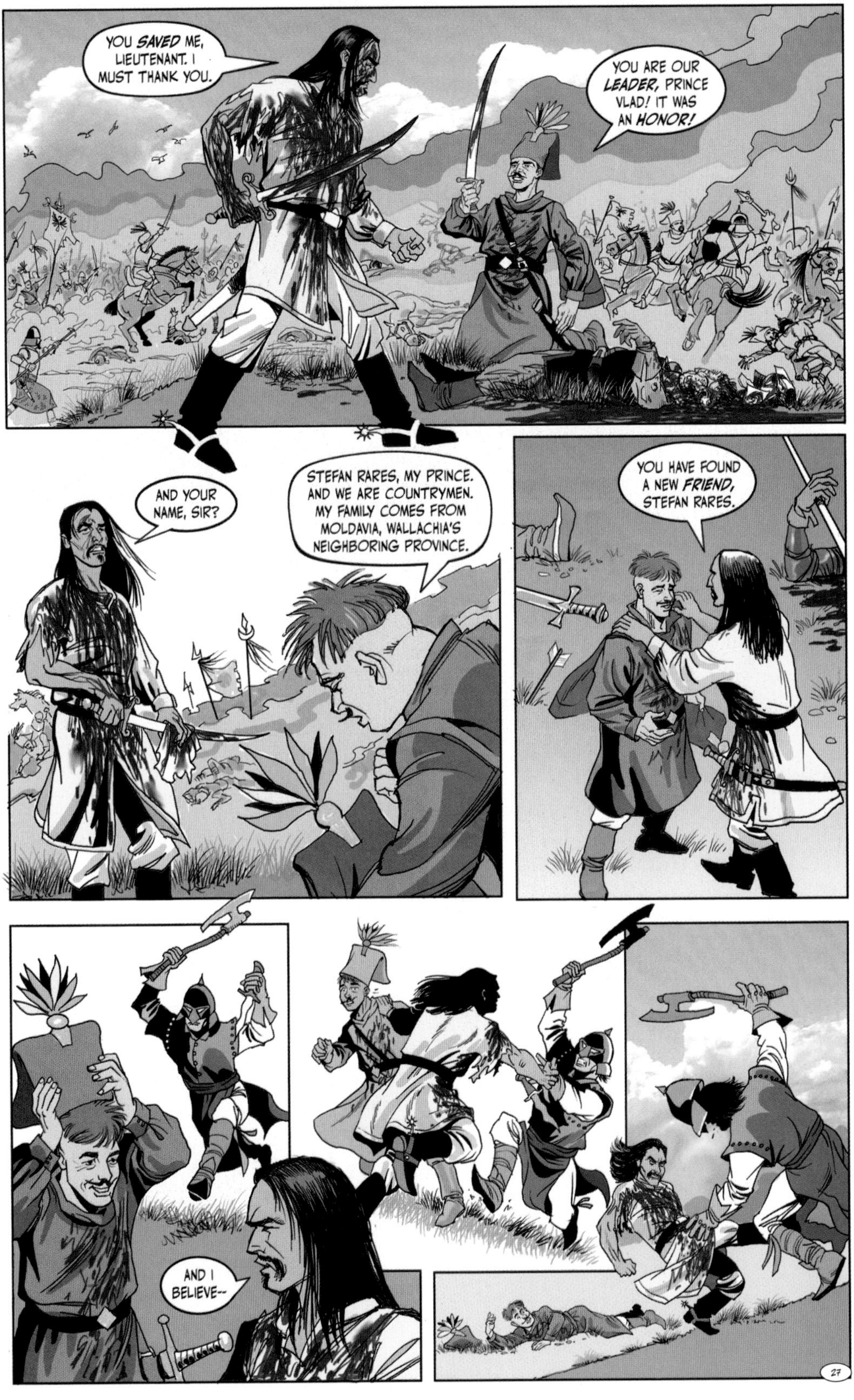
YOU SAVED ME, LIEUTENANT. I MUST THANK YOU.
YOU ARE OUR LEADER, PRINCE VLAD! IT WAS AN HONOR!
AND YOUR NAME, SIR?
STEFAN RARES, MY PRINCE. AND WE ARE COUNTRYMEN. MY FAMILY COMES FROM MOLDAVIA, WALLACHIA'S NEIGHBORING PROVINCE.
YOU HAVE FOUND A NEW FRIEND, STEFAN RARES.
AND I BELIEVE--

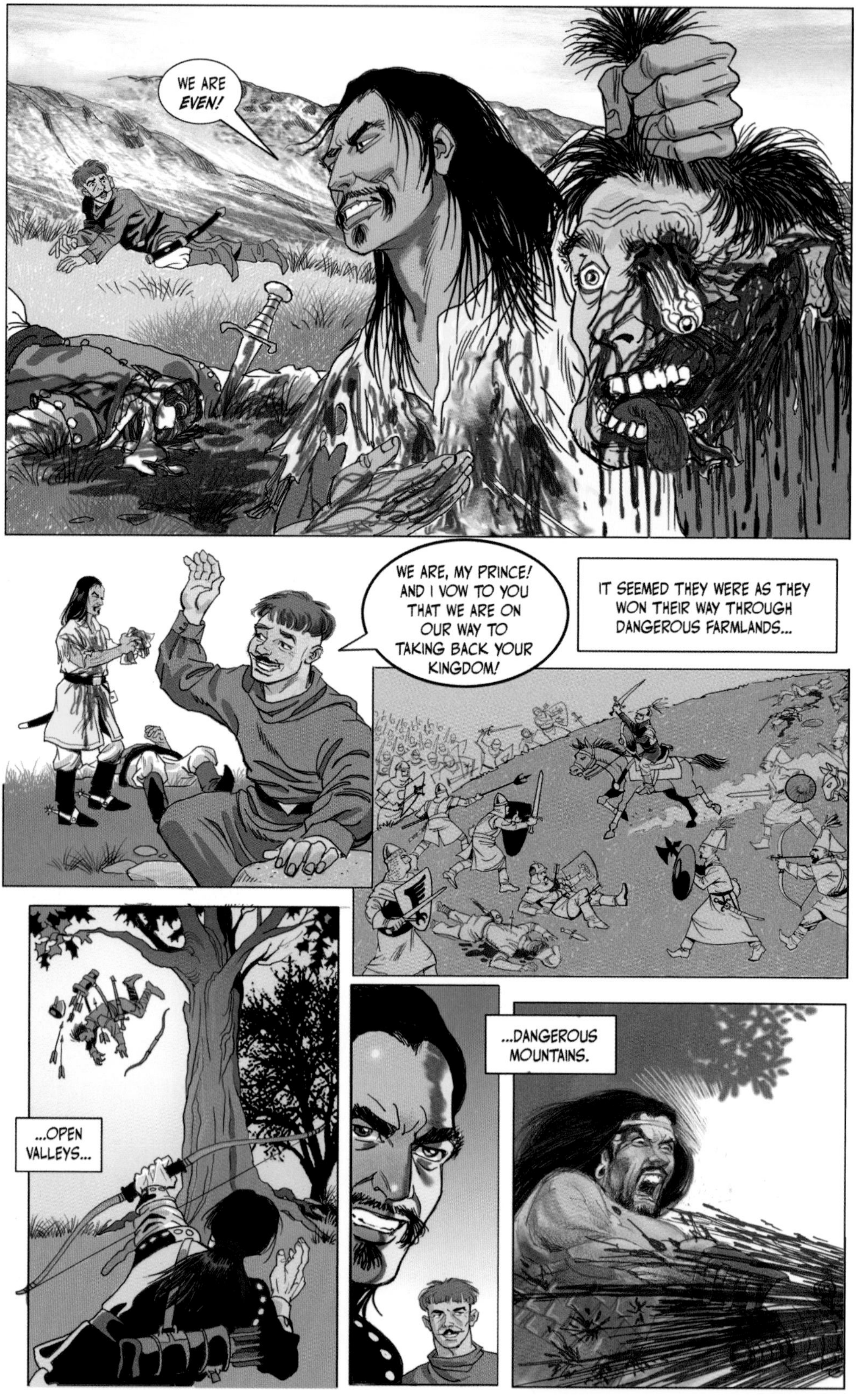
WE ARE EVEN!
WE ARE, MY PRINCE! AND I VOW TO YOU THAT WE ARE ON OUR WAY TO TAKING BACK YOUR KINGDOM!
IT SEEMED THEY WERE AS THEY WON THEIR WAY THROUGH DANGEROUS FARMLANDS...
...OPEN VALLEYS...
...DANGEROUS MOUNTAINS.

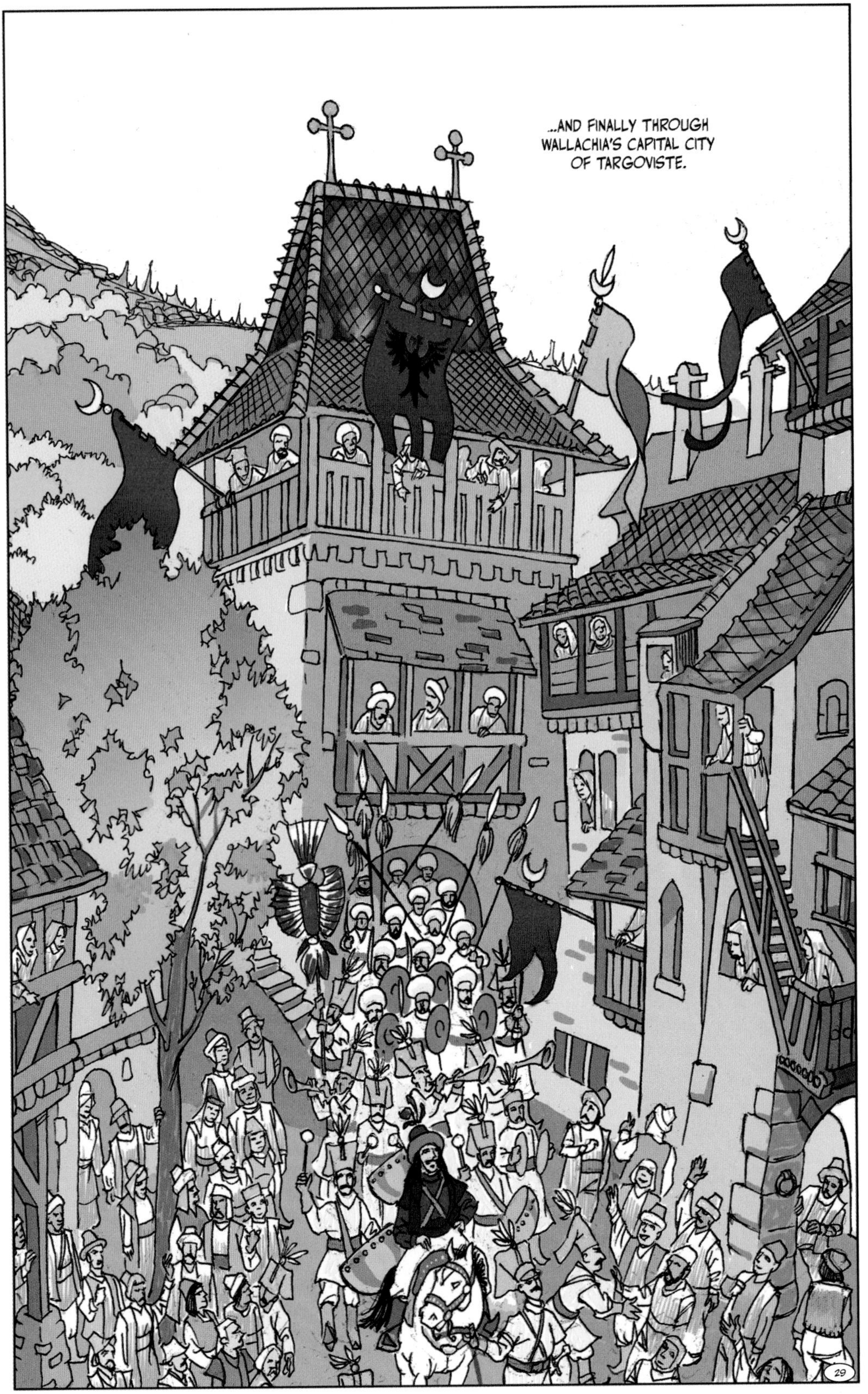
...AND FINALLY THROUGH WALLACHIA'S CAPITAL CITY OF TARGOVISTE.

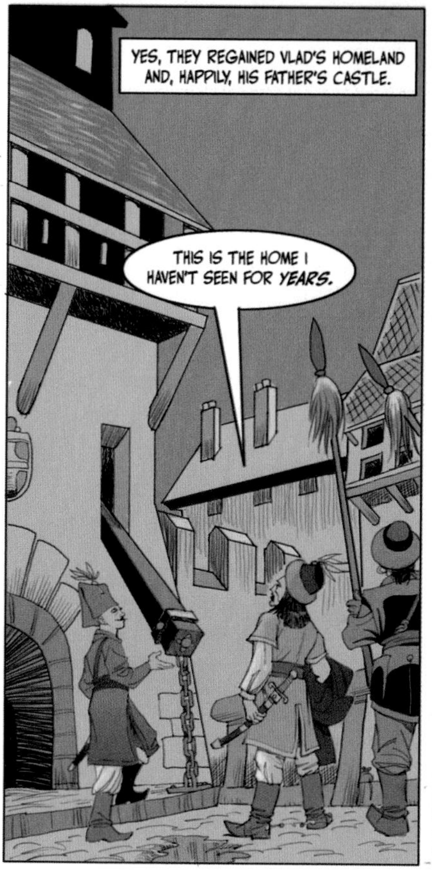
YES, THEY REGAINED VLAD'S HOMELAND AND, HAPPILY, HIS FATHER'S CASTLE.
THIS IS THE HOME I HAVEN'T SEEN FOR *YEARS.*

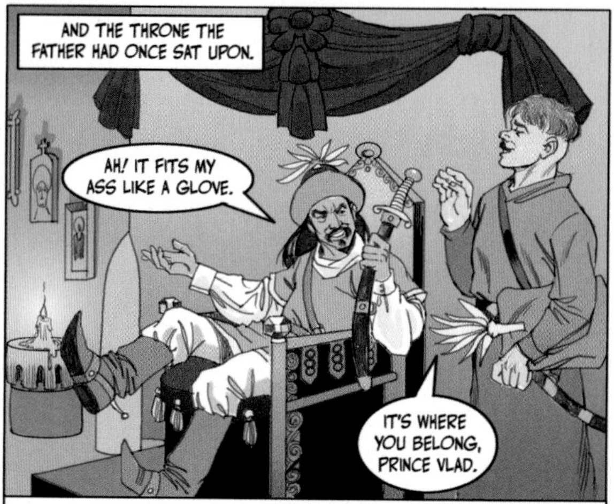
AND THE THRONE THE FATHER HAD ONCE SAT UPON.
AH! IT FITS MY ASS LIKE A GLOVE.
IT'S WHERE YOU BELONG, PRINCE VLAD.

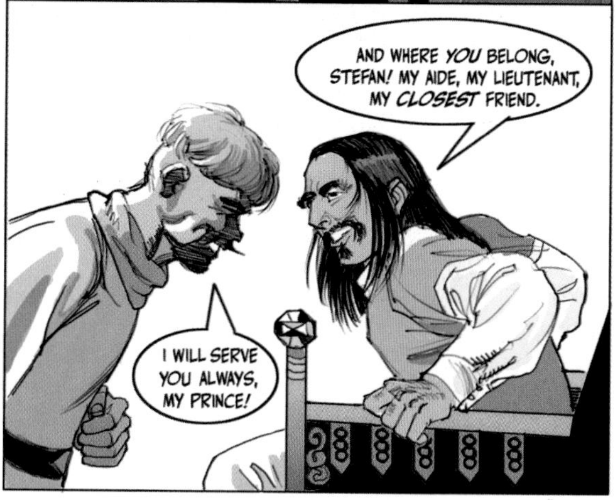
AND WHERE *YOU* BELONG, STEFAN! MY AIDE, MY LIEUTENANT, MY *CLOSEST* FRIEND.
I WILL SERVE YOU ALWAYS, MY PRINCE!

AT LAST, WALLACHIA WAS VLAD'S...YES, BUT FOR THE MERE EXHALING OF A BREATH.

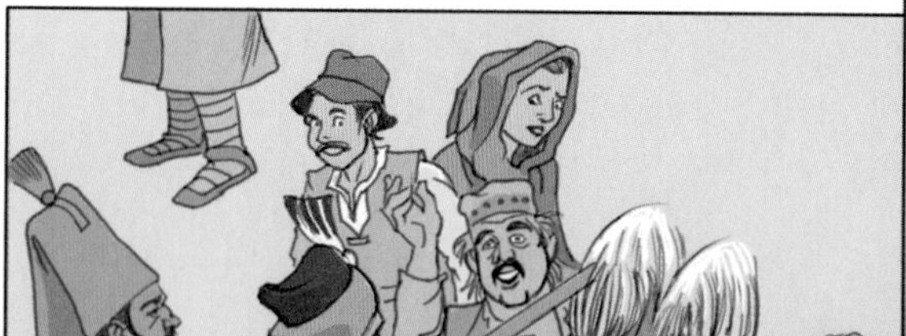

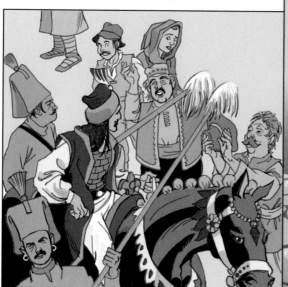

TWO MONTHS LATER, HUNGARIAN SOLDIERS SCALED THE WALLS OF THE CASTLE.

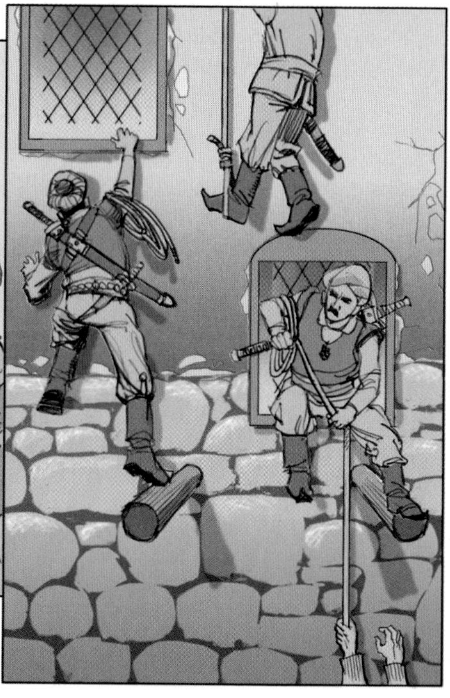

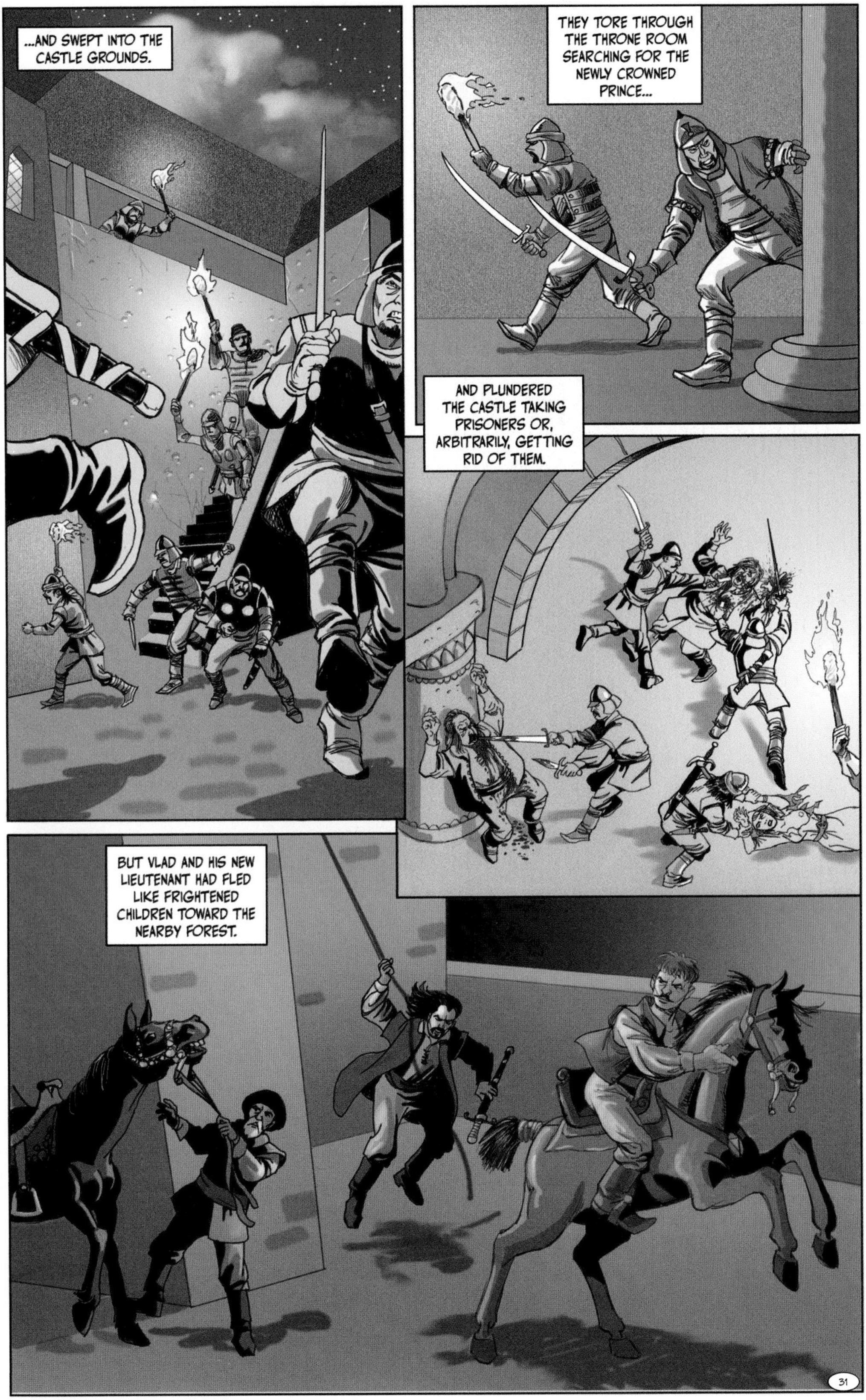
...AND SWEPT INTO THE CASTLE GROUNDS.
THEY TORE THROUGH THE THRONE ROOM SEARCHING FOR THE NEWLY CROWNED PRINCE...
AND PLUNDERED THE CASTLE TAKING PRISONERS OR, ARBITRARILY, GETTING RID OF THEM.
BUT VLAD AND HIS NEW LIEUTENANT HAD FLED LIKE FRIGHTENED CHILDREN TOWARD THE NEARBY FOREST.

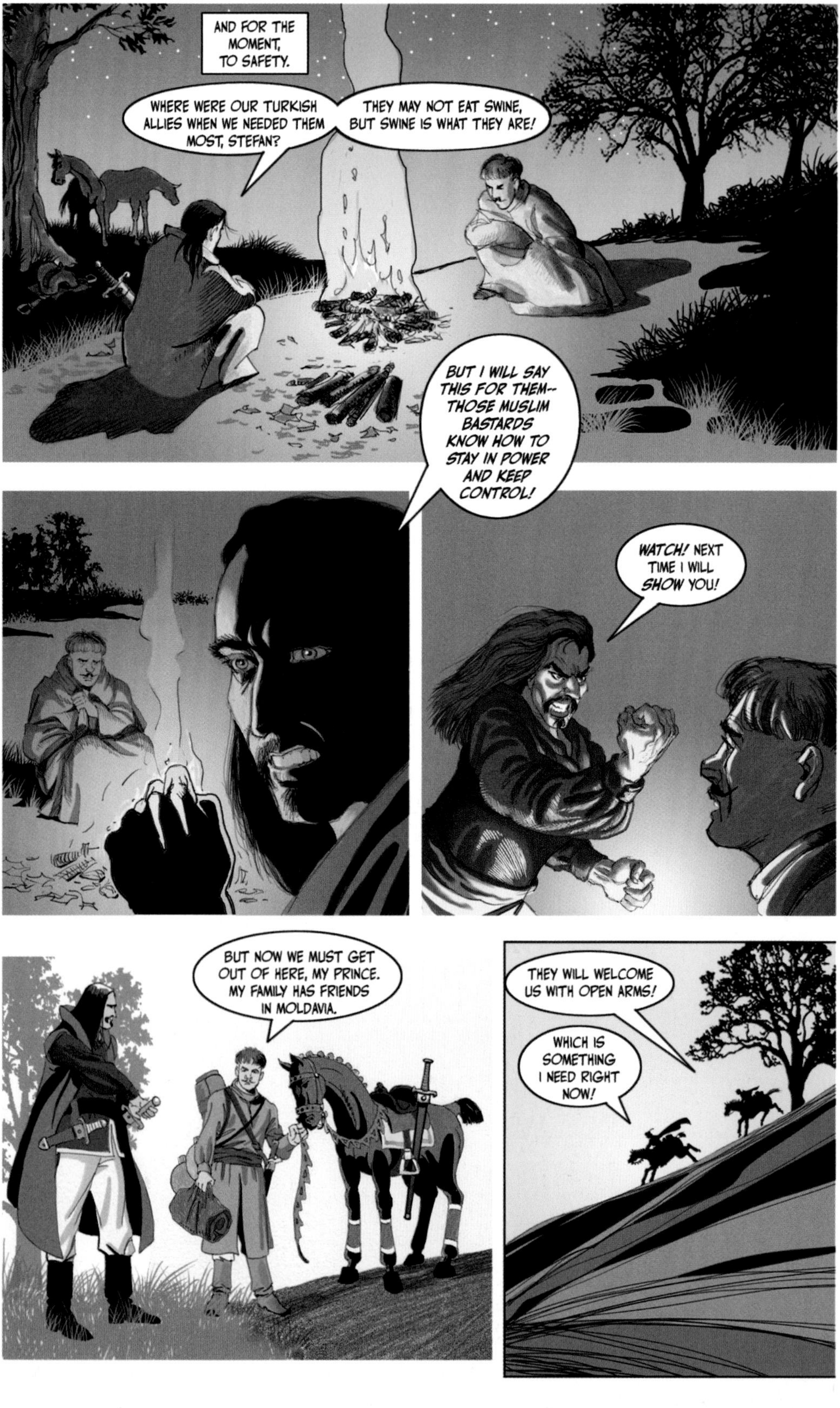
AND FOR THE MOMENT, TO SAFETY.
WHERE WERE OUR TURKISH ALLIES WHEN WE NEEDED THEM MOST, STEFAN?
THEY MAY NOT EAT SWINE, BUT SWINE IS WHAT THEY ARE!
BUT I WILL SAY THIS FOR THEM-- THOSE MUSLIM BASTARDS KNOW HOW TO STAY IN POWER AND KEEP CONTROL!
WATCH! NEXT TIME I WILL SHOW YOU!
BUT NOW WE MUST GET OUT OF HERE, MY PRINCE. MY FAMILY HAS FRIENDS IN MOLDAVIA.
THEY WILL WELCOME US WITH OPEN ARMS!
WHICH IS SOMETHING I NEED RIGHT NOW!

CHAPTER 3: MOLDAVIA

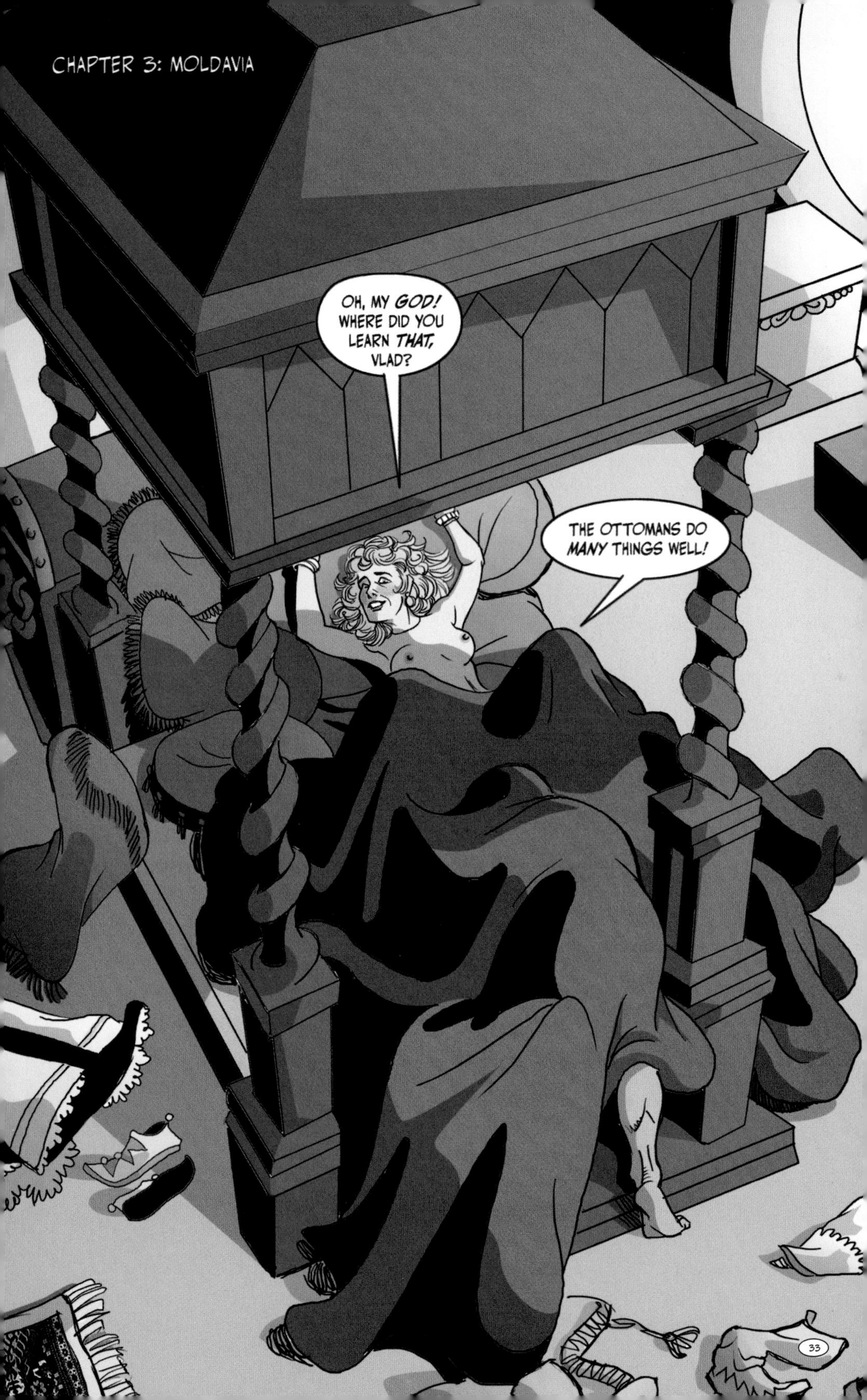
OH, MY *GOD!* WHERE DID YOU LEARN *THAT,* VLAD?
THE OTTOMANS DO *MANY* THINGS WELL!

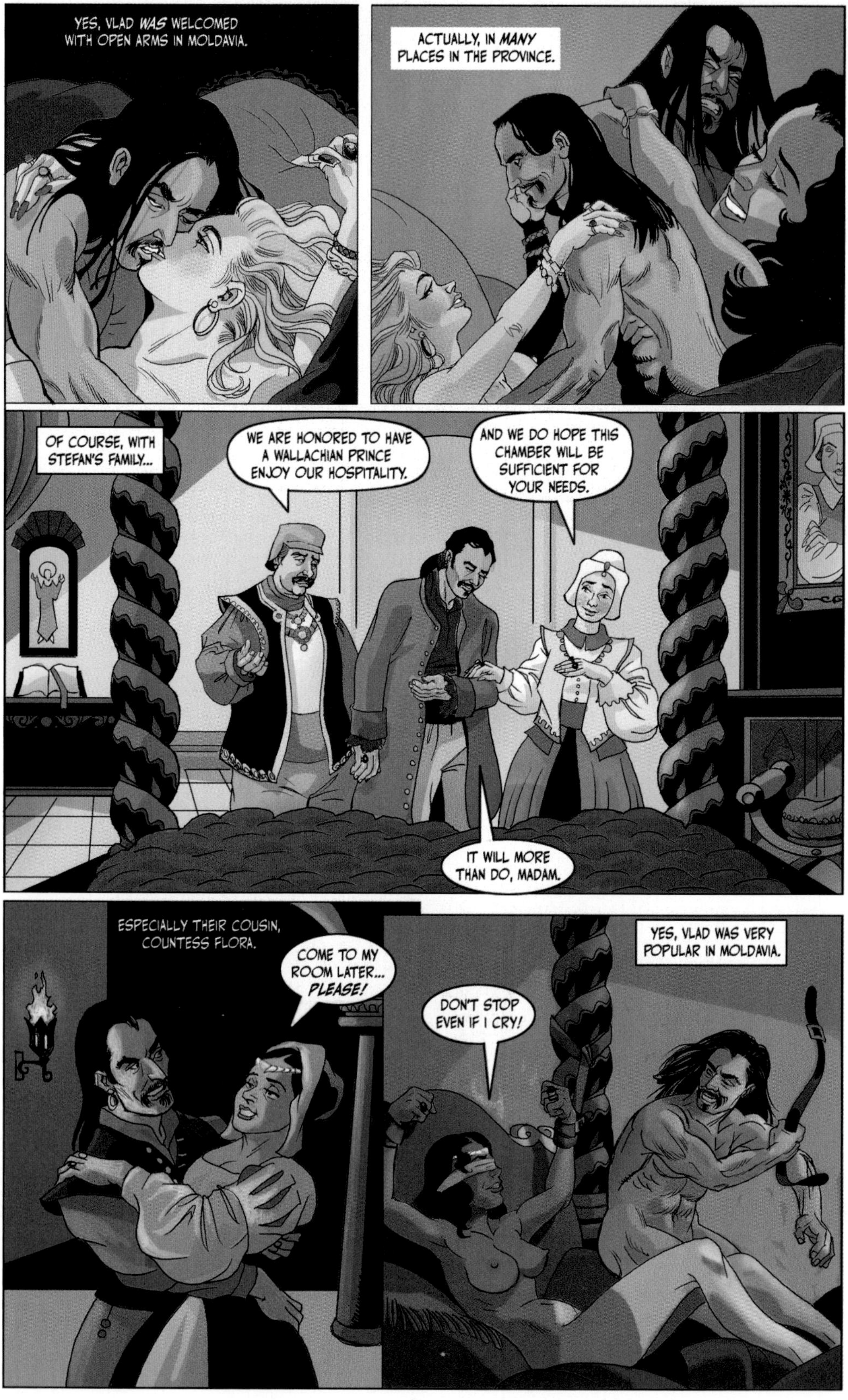
YES, VLAD *WAS* WELCOMED WITH OPEN ARMS IN MOLDAVIA.
ACTUALLY, IN *MANY* PLACES IN THE PROVINCE.
OF COURSE, WITH STEFAN'S FAMILY...
WE ARE HONORED TO HAVE A WALLACHIAN PRINCE ENJOY OUR HOSPITALITY.
AND WE DO HOPE THIS CHAMBER WILL BE SUFFICIENT FOR YOUR NEEDS.
IT WILL MORE THAN DO, MADAM.
ESPECIALLY THEIR COUSIN, COUNTESS FLORA.
COME TO MY ROOM LATER... *PLEASE!*
YES, VLAD WAS VERY POPULAR IN MOLDAVIA.
DON'T STOP EVEN IF I CRY!

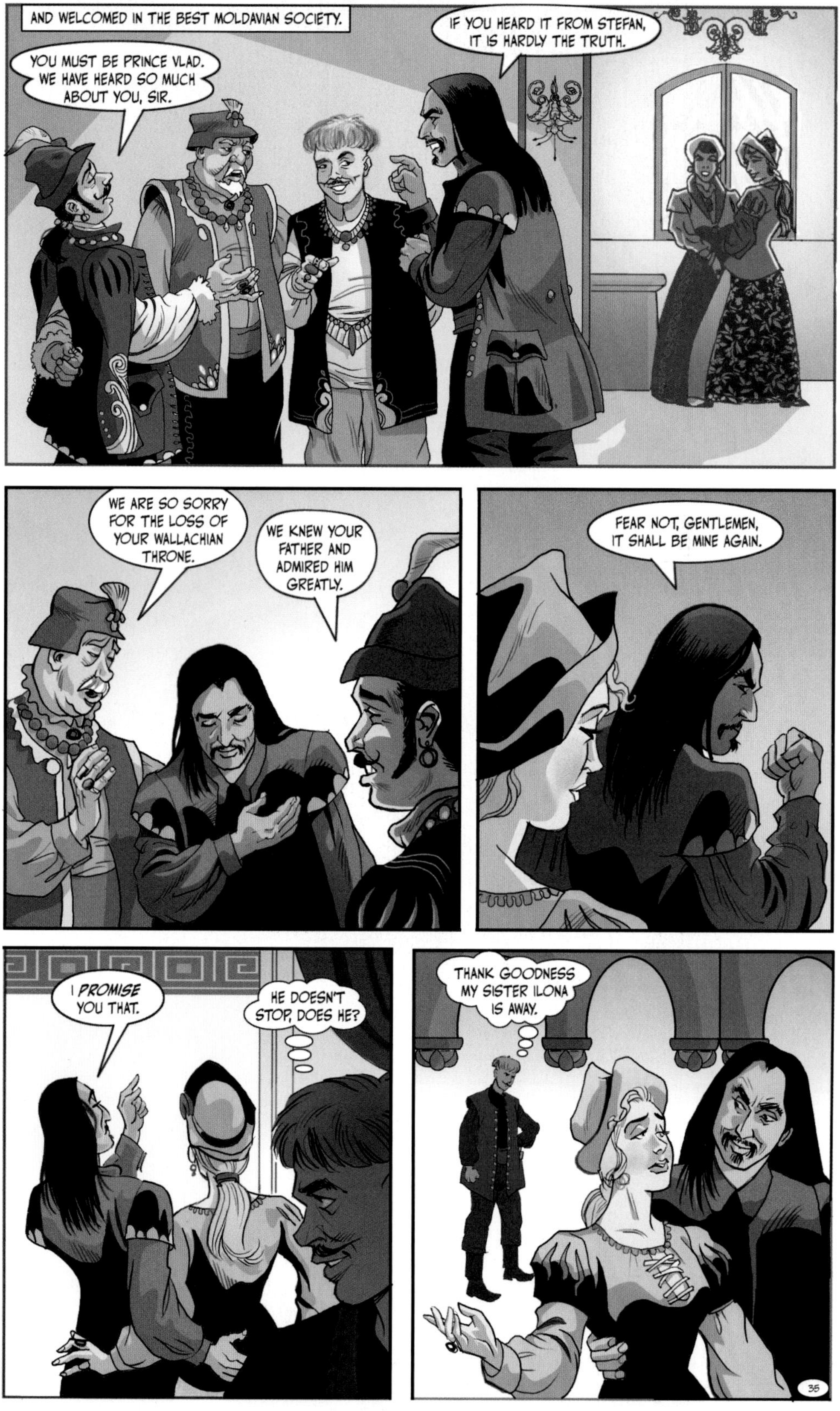
AND WELCOMED IN THE BEST MOLDAVIAN SOCIETY.
YOU MUST BE PRINCE VLAD. WE HAVE HEARD SO MUCH ABOUT YOU, SIR.
IF YOU HEARD IT FROM STEFAN, IT IS HARDLY THE TRUTH.
WE ARE SO SORRY FOR THE LOSS OF YOUR WALLACHIAN THRONE.
WE KNEW YOUR FATHER AND ADMIRED HIM GREATLY.
FEAR NOT, GENTLEMEN, IT SHALL BE MINE AGAIN.
I *PROMISE* YOU THAT.
HE DOESN'T STOP, DOES HE?
THANK GOODNESS MY SISTER ILONA IS AWAY.
35

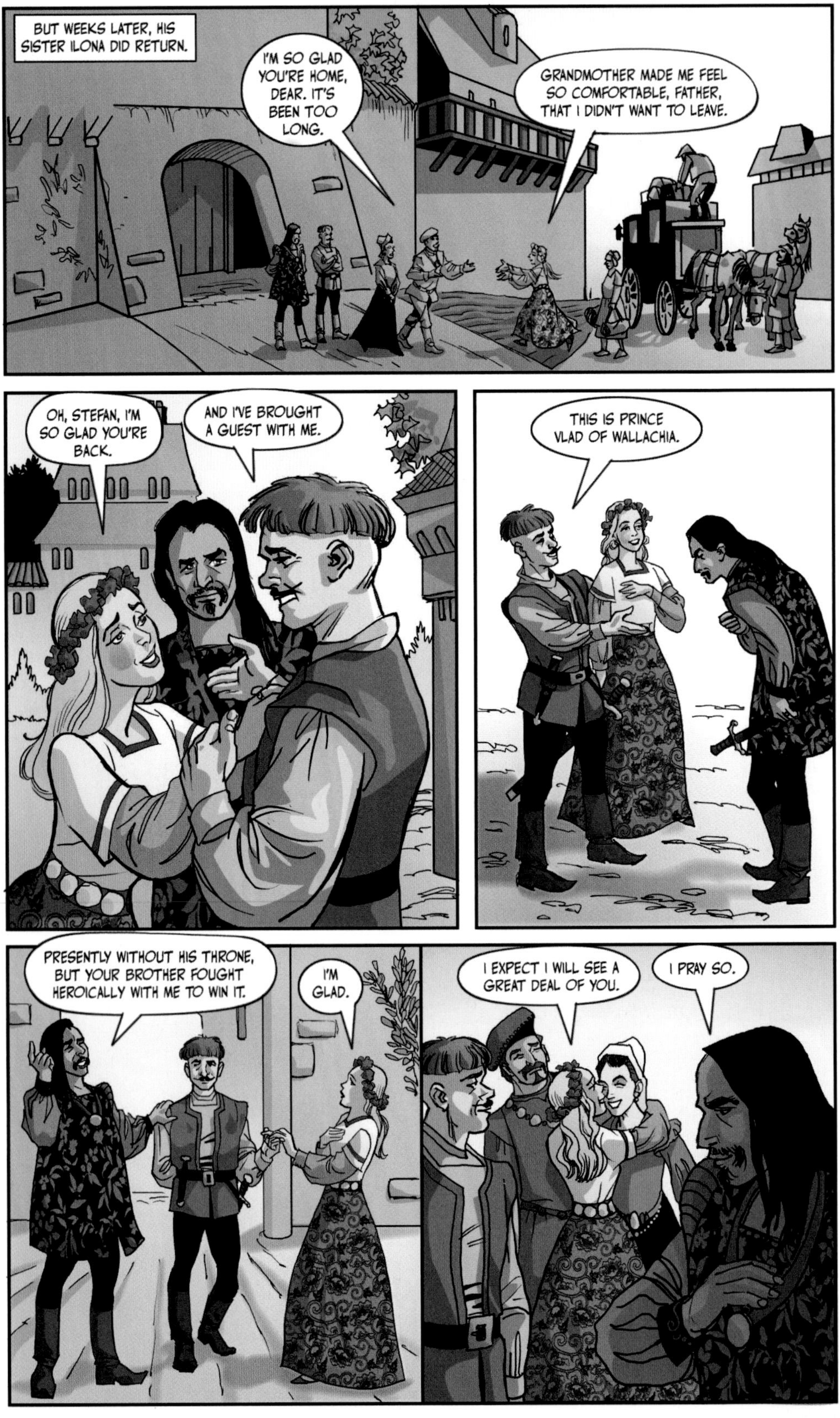
BUT WEEKS LATER, HIS SISTER ILONA DID RETURN.
I'M SO GLAD YOU'RE HOME, DEAR. IT'S BEEN TOO LONG.
GRANDMOTHER MADE ME FEEL SO COMFORTABLE, FATHER, THAT I DIDN'T WANT TO LEAVE.
OH, STEFAN, I'M SO GLAD YOU'RE BACK.
AND I'VE BROUGHT A GUEST WITH ME.
THIS IS PRINCE VLAD OF WALLACHIA.
PRESENTLY WITHOUT HIS THRONE, BUT YOUR BROTHER FOUGHT HEROICALLY WITH ME TO WIN IT.
I'M GLAD.
I EXPECT I WILL SEE A GREAT DEAL OF YOU.
I PRAY SO.

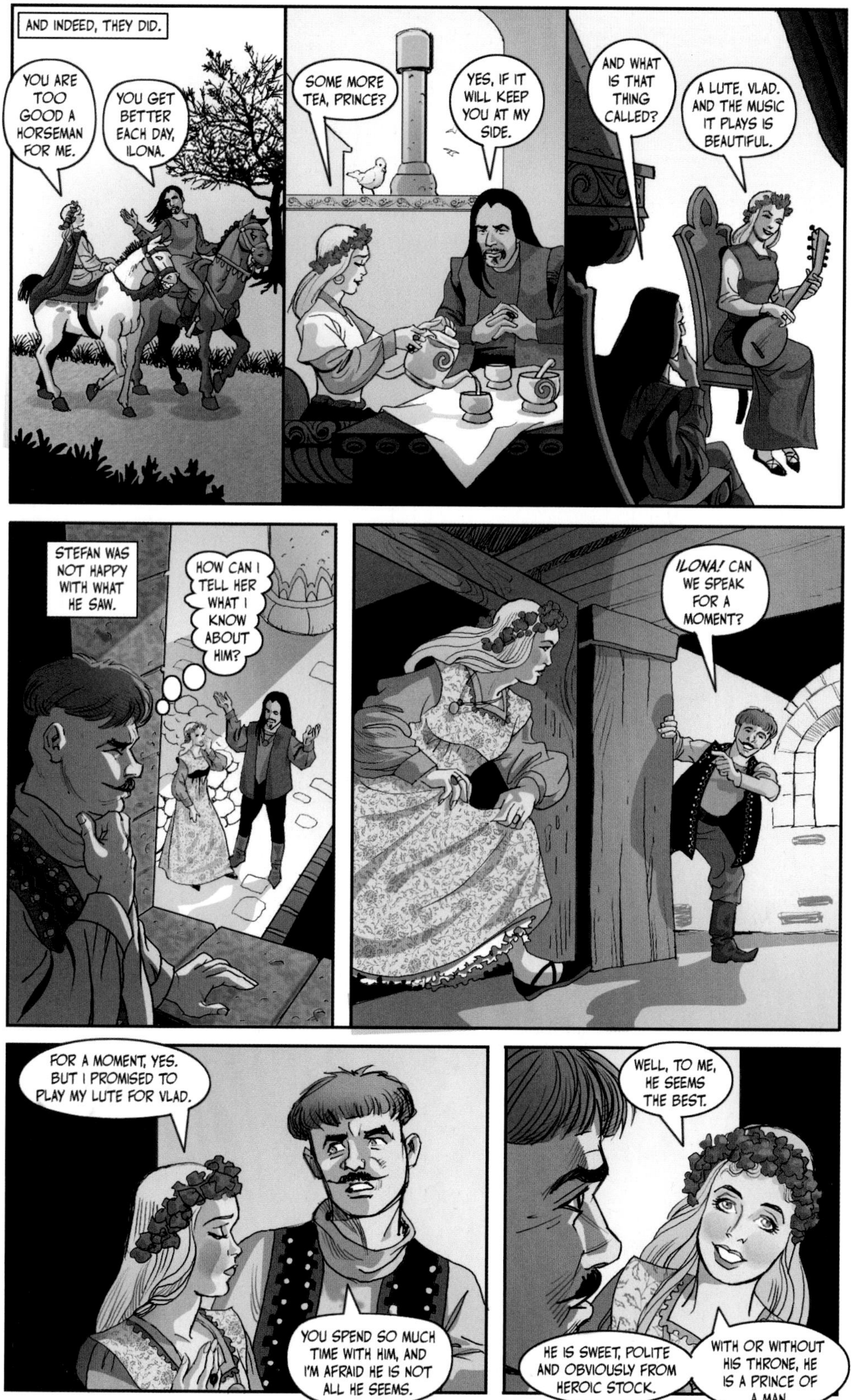
AND INDEED, THEY DID.
YOU ARE TOO GOOD A HORSEMAN FOR ME.
YOU GET BETTER EACH DAY, ILONA.
SOME MORE TEA, PRINCE?
YES, IF IT WILL KEEP YOU AT MY SIDE.
AND WHAT IS THAT THING CALLED?
A LUTE, VLAD. AND THE MUSIC IT PLAYS IS BEAUTIFUL.
STEFAN WAS NOT HAPPY WITH WHAT HE SAW.
HOW CAN I TELL HER WHAT I KNOW ABOUT HIM?
ILONA! CAN WE SPEAK FOR A MOMENT?
FOR A MOMENT, YES. BUT I PROMISED TO PLAY MY LUTE FOR VLAD.
YOU SPEND SO MUCH TIME WITH HIM, AND I'M AFRAID HE IS NOT ALL HE SEEMS.
WELL, TO ME, HE SEEMS THE BEST.
HE IS SWEET, POLITE AND OBVIOUSLY FROM HEROIC STOCK.
WITH OR WITHOUT HIS THRONE, HE IS A PRINCE OF A MAN.

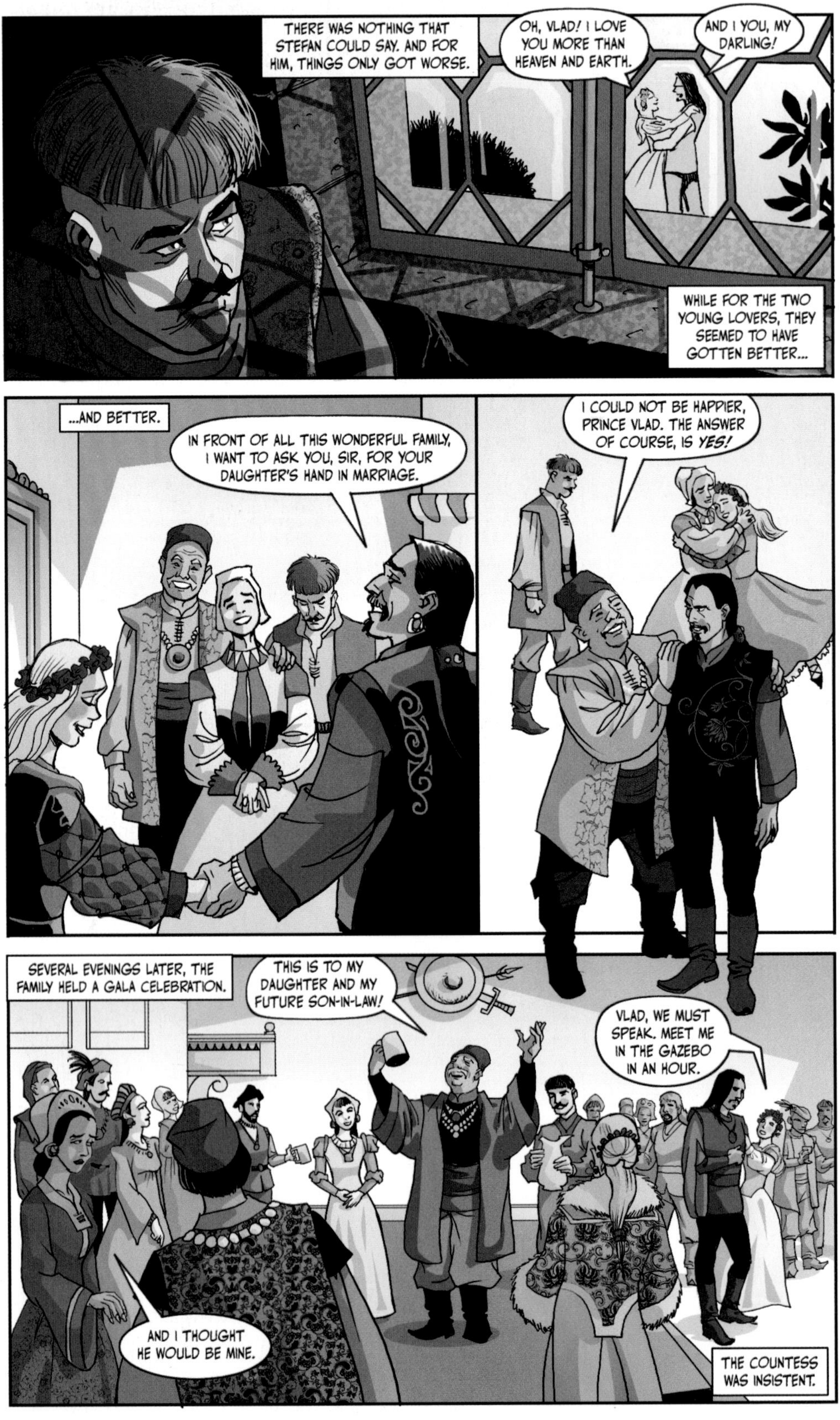
THERE WAS NOTHING THAT STEFAN COULD SAY. AND FOR HIM, THINGS ONLY GOT WORSE.
OH, VLAD! I LOVE YOU MORE THAN HEAVEN AND EARTH.
AND I YOU, MY DARLING!
WHILE FOR THE TWO YOUNG LOVERS, THEY SEEMED TO HAVE GOTTEN BETTER...
...AND BETTER.
IN FRONT OF ALL THIS WONDERFUL FAMILY, I WANT TO ASK YOU, SIR, FOR YOUR DAUGHTER'S HAND IN MARRIAGE.
I COULD NOT BE HAPPIER, PRINCE VLAD. THE ANSWER OF COURSE, IS *YES!*
SEVERAL EVENINGS LATER, THE FAMILY HELD A GALA CELEBRATION.
THIS IS TO MY DAUGHTER AND MY FUTURE SON-IN-LAW!
VLAD, WE MUST SPEAK. MEET ME IN THE GAZEBO IN AN HOUR.
AND I THOUGHT HE WOULD BE MINE.
THE COUNTESS WAS INSISTENT.

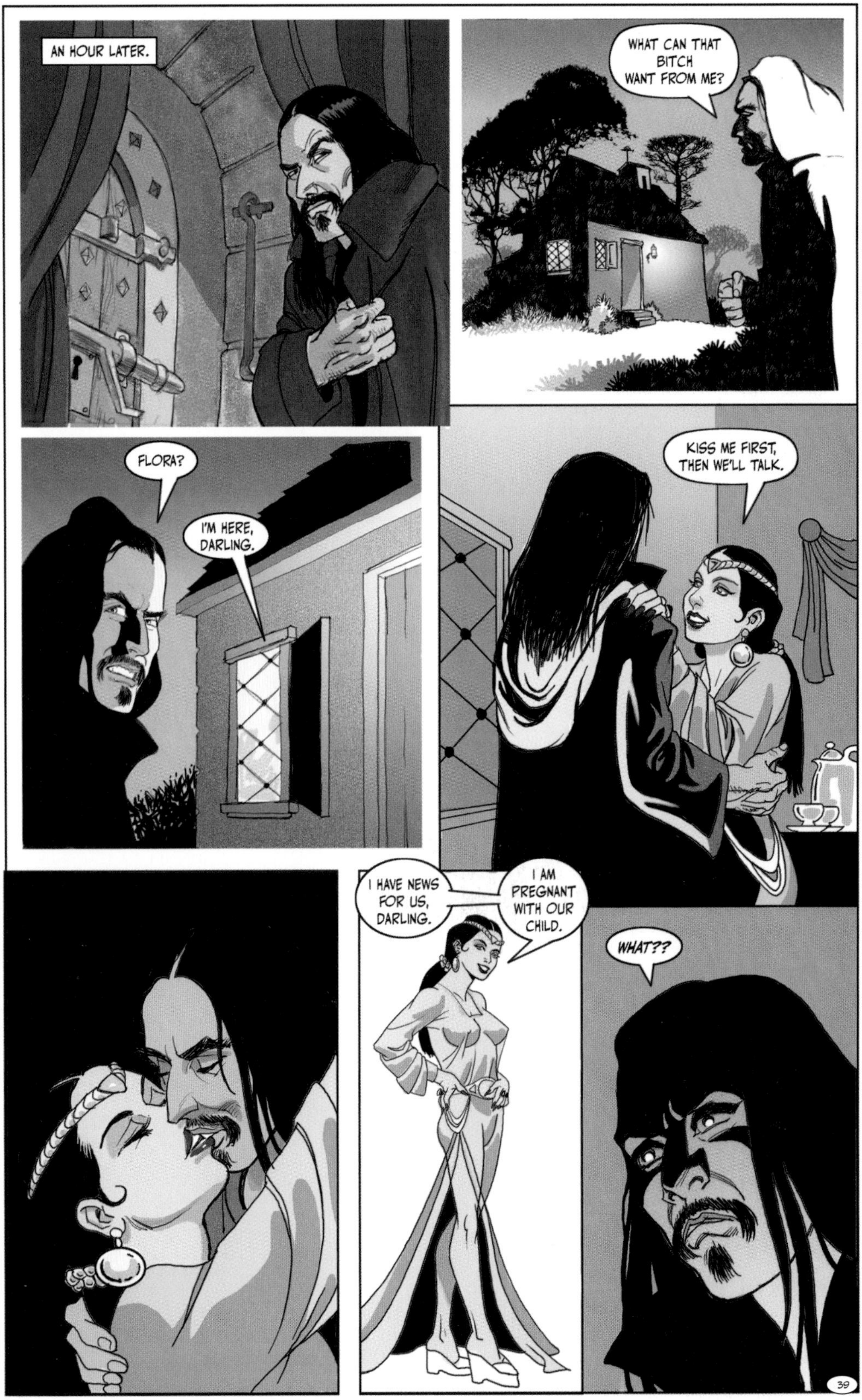
AN HOUR LATER.
WHAT CAN THAT BITCH WANT FROM ME?
FLORA?
I'M HERE, DARLING.
KISS ME FIRST, THEN WE'LL TALK.
I HAVE NEWS FOR US, DARLING.
I AM PREGNANT WITH OUR CHILD.
WHAT??

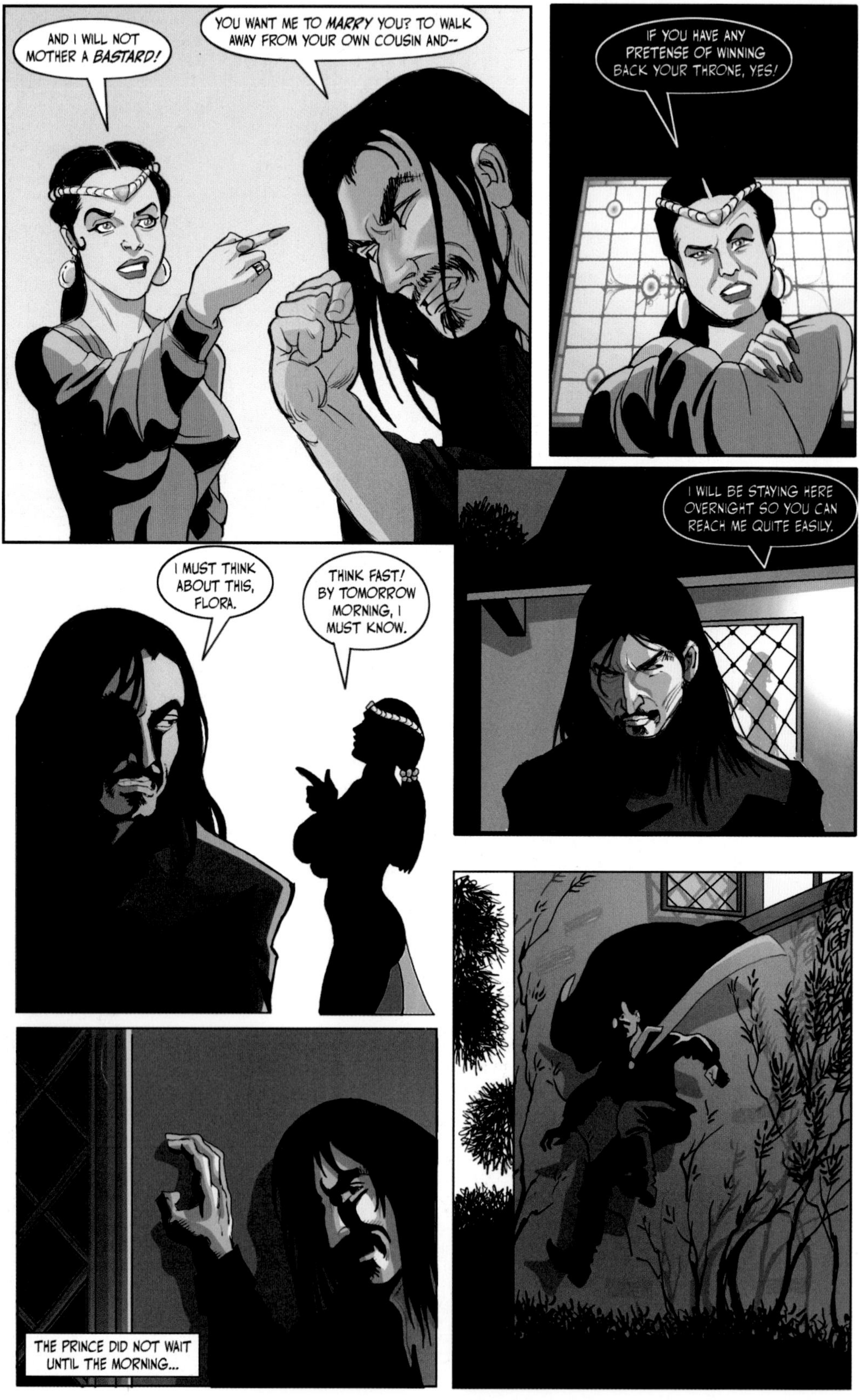
AND I WILL NOT MOTHER A *BASTARD!*
YOU WANT ME TO *MARRY* YOU? TO WALK AWAY FROM YOUR OWN COUSIN AND--
IF YOU HAVE ANY PRETENSE OF WINNING BACK YOUR THRONE, YES!
I WILL BE STAYING HERE OVERNIGHT SO YOU CAN REACH ME QUITE EASILY.
I MUST THINK ABOUT THIS, FLORA.
THINK FAST! BY TOMORROW MORNING, I MUST KNOW.
THE PRINCE DID NOT WAIT UNTIL THE MORNING...

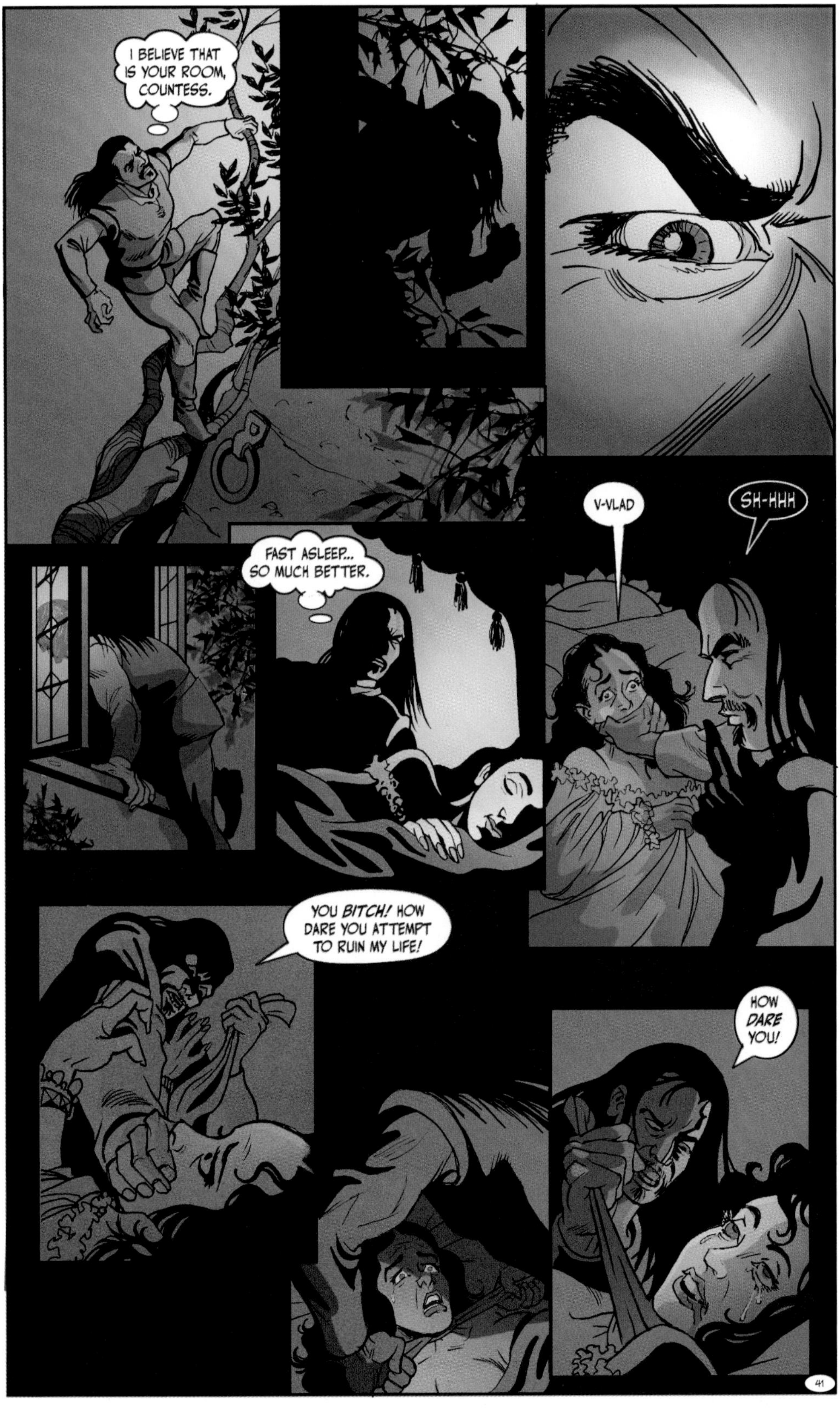

I BELIEVE THAT IS YOUR ROOM, COUNTESS.
FAST ASLEEP... SO MUCH BETTER.
V-VLAD
SH-HHH
YOU *BITCH!* HOW DARE YOU ATTEMPT TO RUIN MY LIFE!
HOW *DARE* YOU!

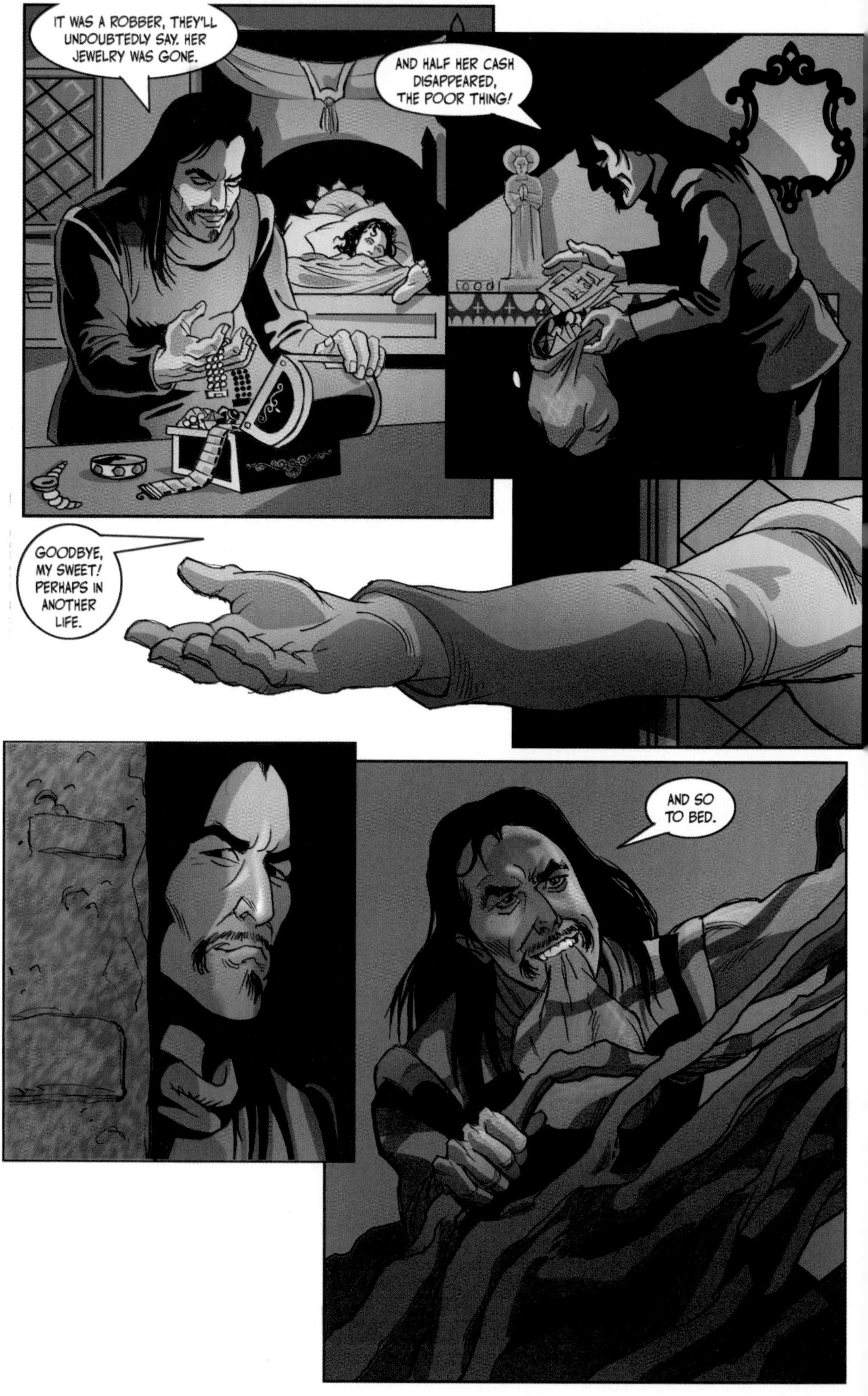
IT WAS A ROBBER, THEY'LL UNDOUBTEDLY SAY. HER JEWELRY WAS GONE.
AND HALF HER CASH DISAPPEARED, THE POOR THING!
GOODBYE, MY SWEET! PERHAPS IN ANOTHER LIFE.
AND SO TO BED.

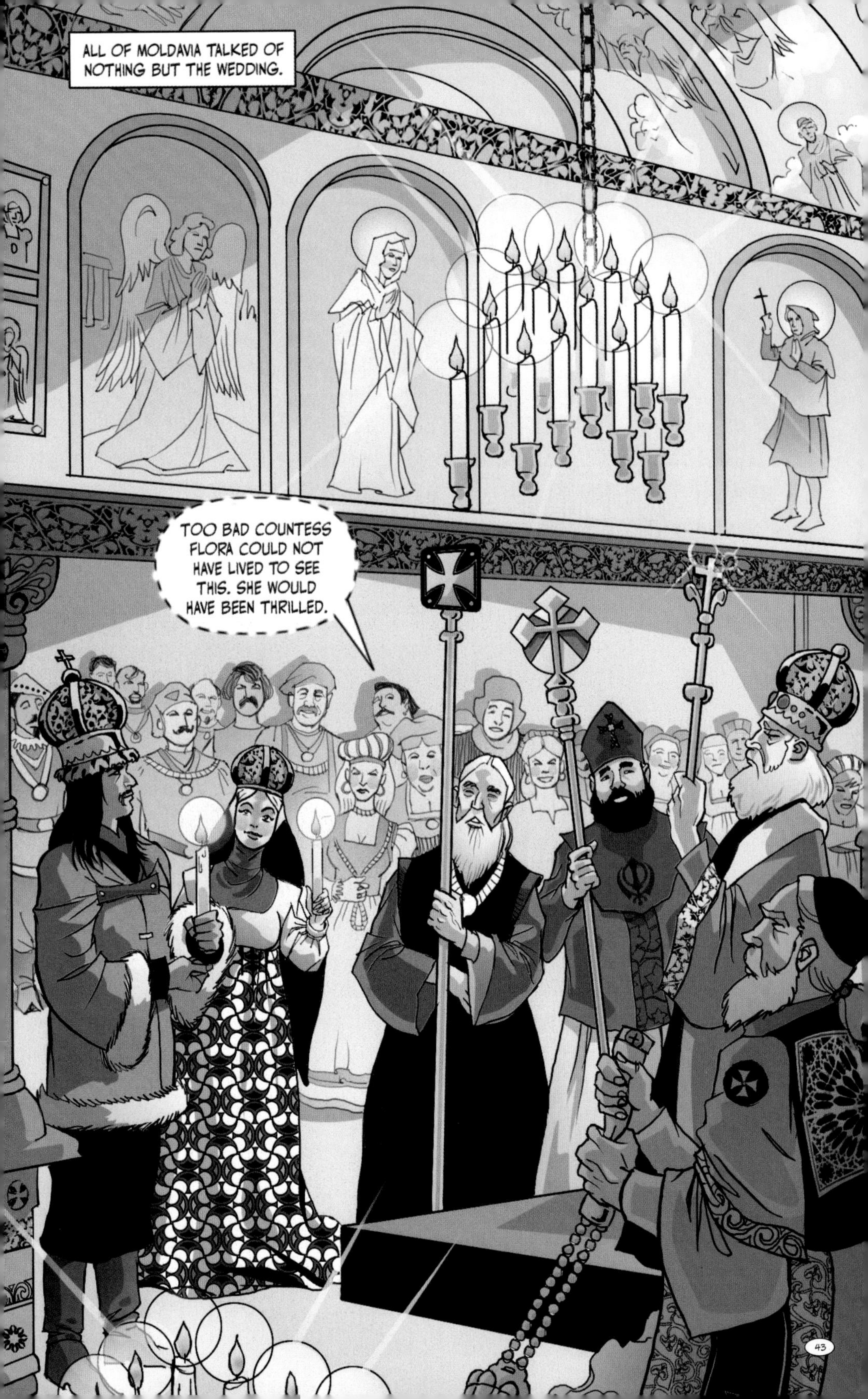
ALL OF MOLDAVIA TALKED OF NOTHING BUT THE WEDDING.
TOO BAD COUNTESS FLORA COULD NOT HAVE LIVED TO SEE THIS. SHE WOULD HAVE BEEN THRILLED.

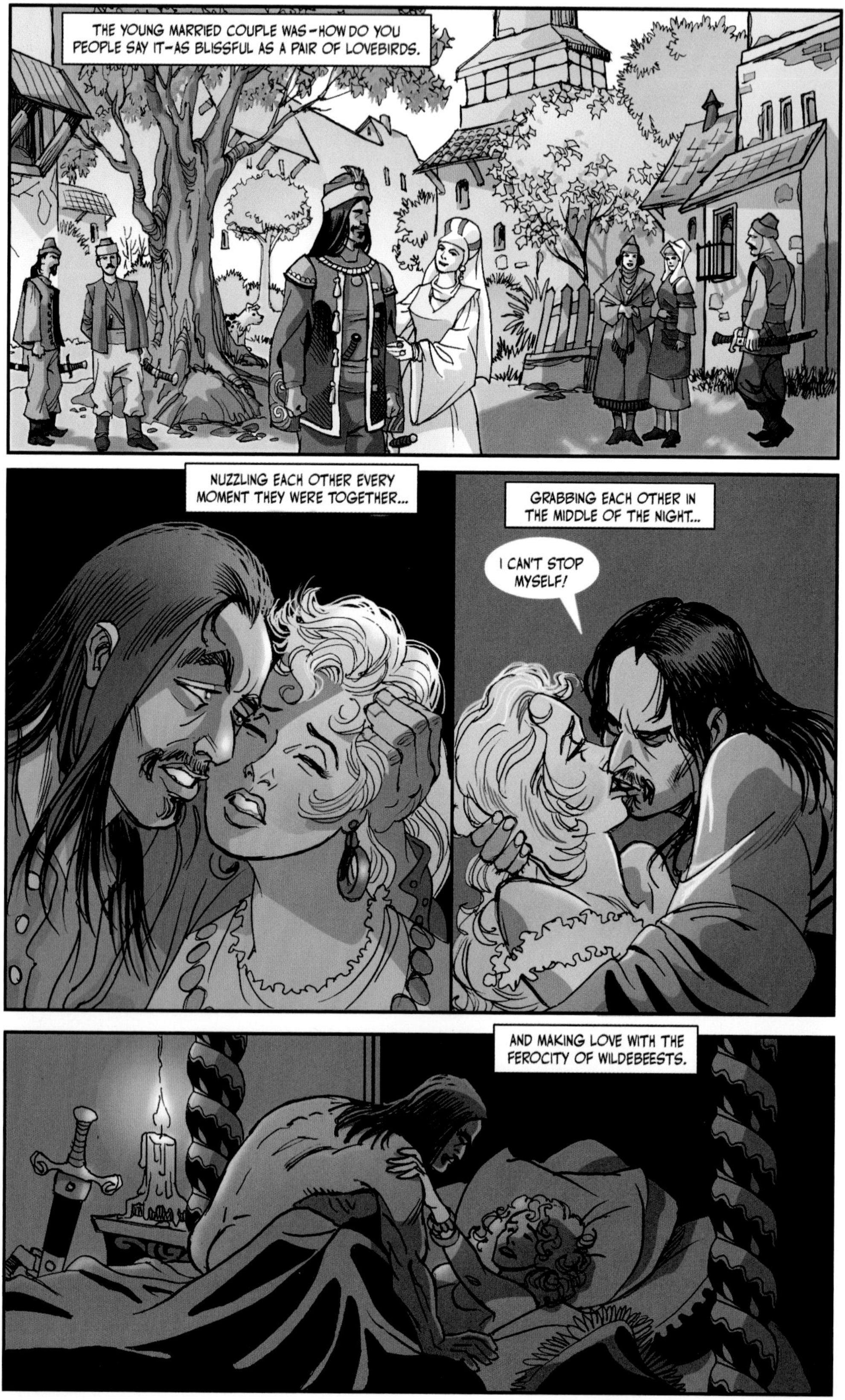
THE YOUNG MARRIED COUPLE WAS—HOW DO YOU PEOPLE SAY IT—AS BLISSFUL AS A PAIR OF LOVEBIRDS.
NUZZLING EACH OTHER EVERY MOMENT THEY WERE TOGETHER...
GRABBING EACH OTHER IN THE MIDDLE OF THE NIGHT...
I CAN'T STOP MYSELF!
AND MAKING LOVE WITH THE FEROCITY OF WILDEBEESTS.

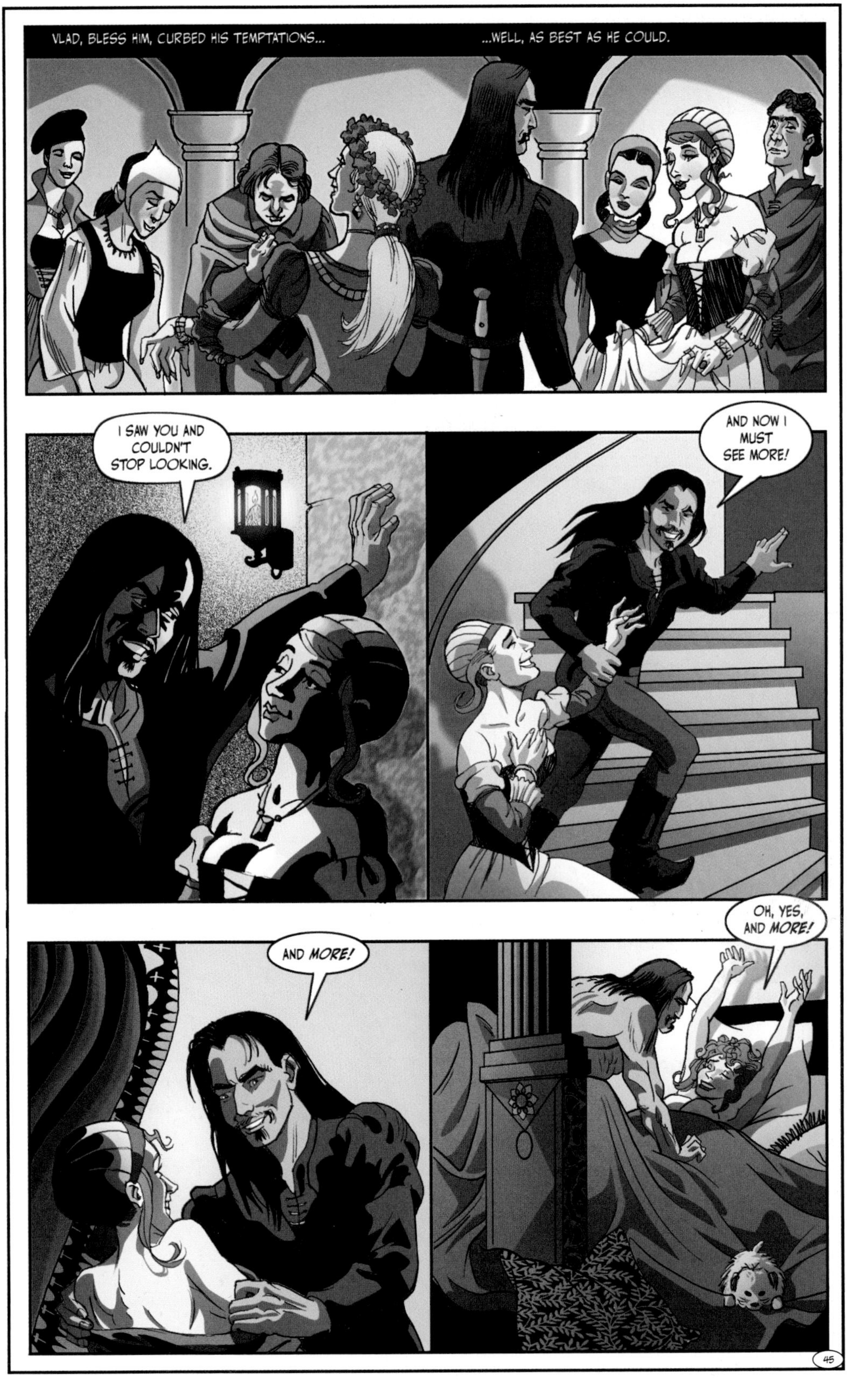
VLAD, BLESS HIM, CURBED HIS TEMPTATIONS...
...WELL, AS BEST AS HE COULD.
I SAW YOU AND COULDN'T STOP LOOKING.
AND NOW I MUST SEE MORE!
AND MORE!
OH, YES, AND MORE!

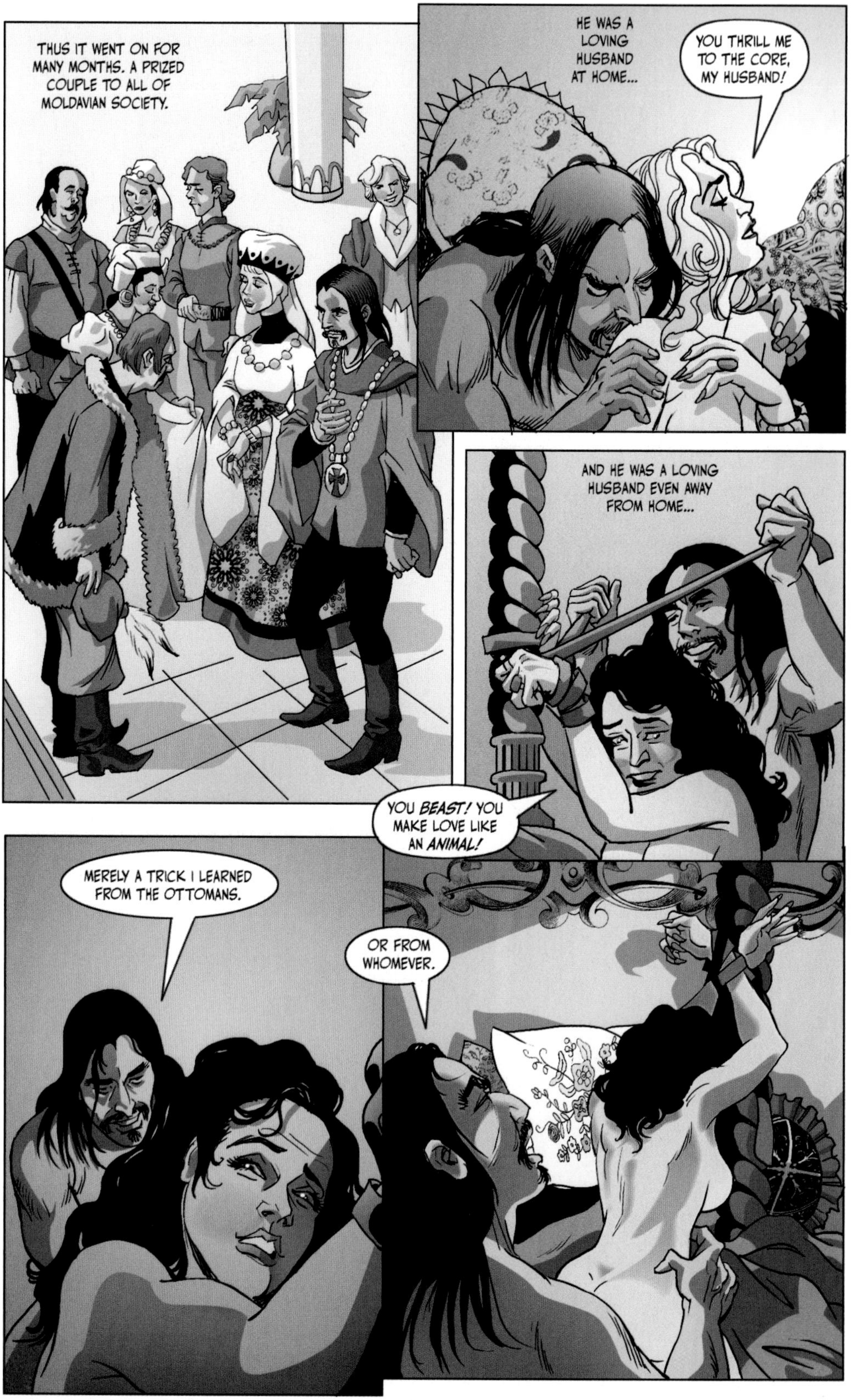
THUS IT WENT ON FOR MANY MONTHS. A PRIZED COUPLE TO ALL OF MOLDAVIAN SOCIETY.
HE WAS A LOVING HUSBAND AT HOME...
YOU THRILL ME TO THE CORE, MY HUSBAND!
AND HE WAS A LOVING HUSBAND EVEN AWAY FROM HOME...
YOU *BEAST!* YOU MAKE LOVE LIKE AN *ANIMAL!*
MERELY A TRICK I LEARNED FROM THE OTTOMANS.
OR FROM WHOMEVER.

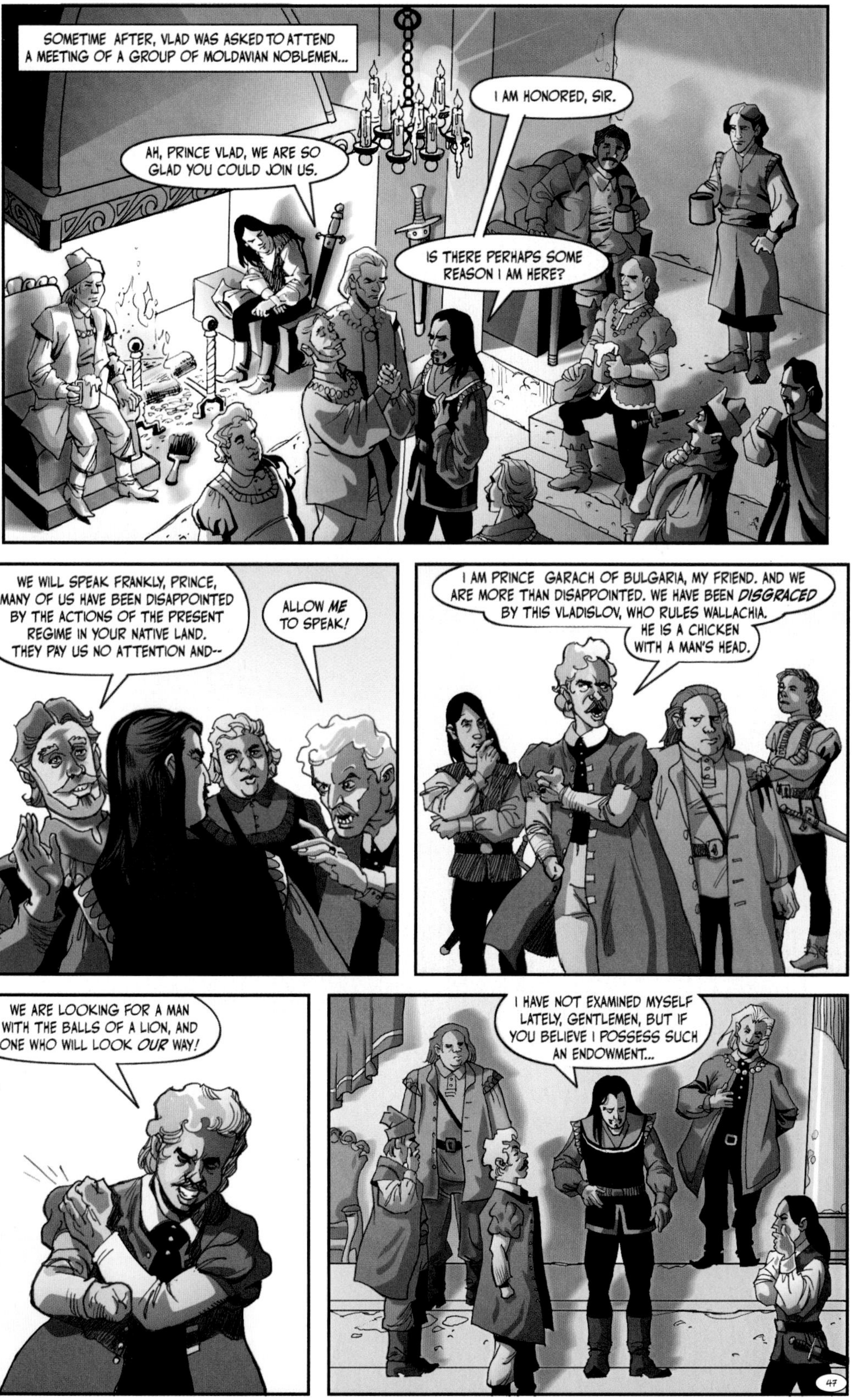

SOMETIME AFTER, VLAD WAS ASKED TO ATTEND A MEETING OF A GROUP OF MOLDAVIAN NOBLEMEN...
AH, PRINCE VLAD, WE ARE SO GLAD YOU COULD JOIN US.
I AM HONORED, SIR.
IS THERE PERHAPS SOME REASON I AM HERE?
WE WILL SPEAK FRANKLY, PRINCE, MANY OF US HAVE BEEN DISAPPOINTED BY THE ACTIONS OF THE PRESENT REGIME IN YOUR NATIVE LAND. THEY PAY US NO ATTENTION AND--
ALLOW *ME* TO SPEAK!
I AM PRINCE GARACH OF BULGARIA, MY FRIEND. AND WE ARE MORE THAN DISAPPOINTED. WE HAVE BEEN *DISGRACED* BY THIS VLADISLOV, WHO RULES WALLACHIA.
HE IS A CHICKEN WITH A MAN'S HEAD.
WE ARE LOOKING FOR A MAN WITH THE BALLS OF A LION, AND ONE WHO WILL LOOK *OUR* WAY!
I HAVE NOT EXAMINED MYSELF LATELY, GENTLEMEN, BUT IF YOU BELIEVE I POSSESS SUCH AN ENDOWMENT...

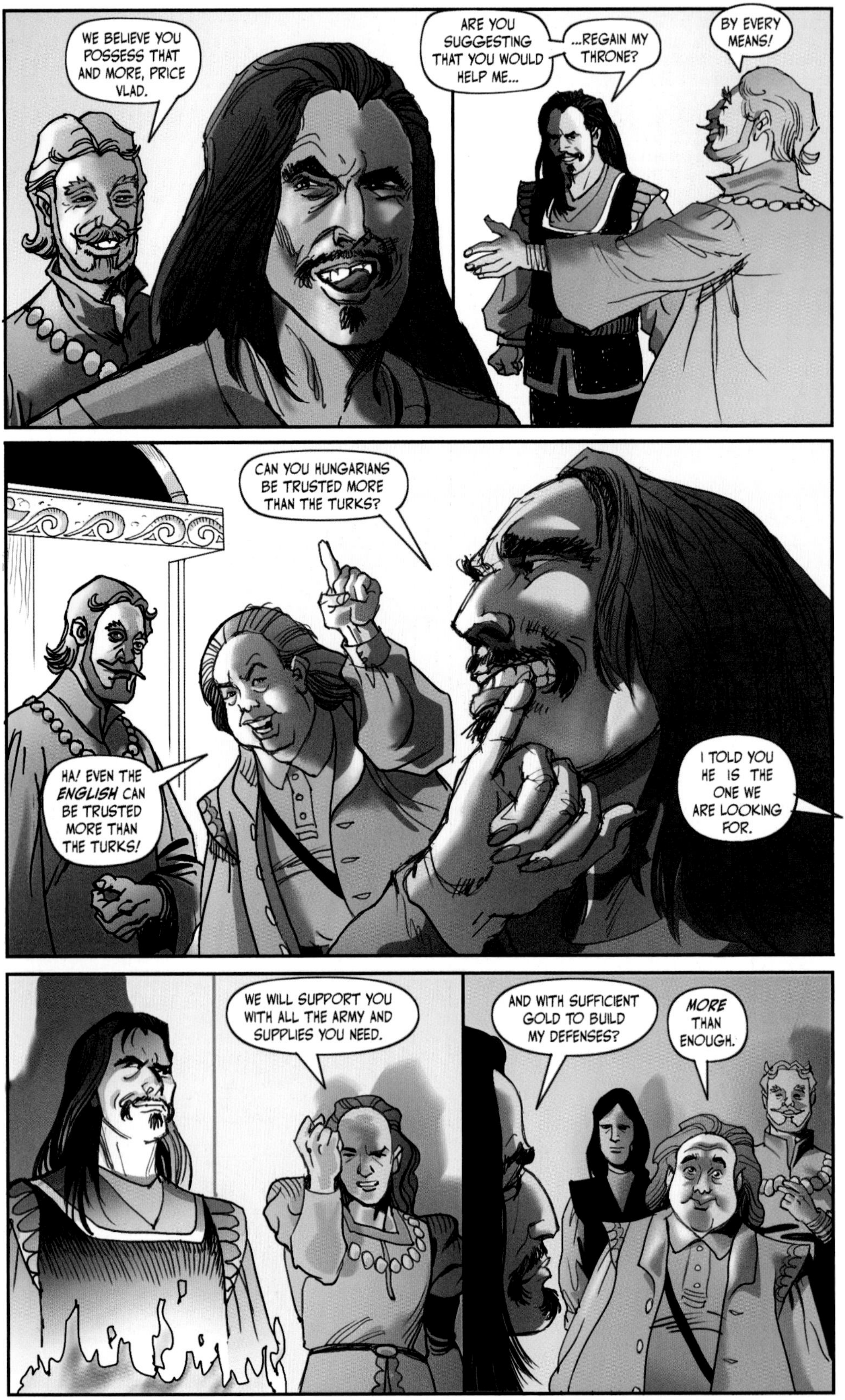
WE BELIEVE YOU POSSESS THAT AND MORE, PRICE VLAD.
ARE YOU SUGGESTING THAT YOU WOULD HELP ME...
...REGAIN MY THRONE?
BY EVERY MEANS!
CAN YOU HUNGARIANS BE TRUSTED MORE THAN THE TURKS?
HA! EVEN THE *ENGLISH* CAN BE TRUSTED MORE THAN THE TURKS!
I TOLD YOU HE IS THE ONE WE ARE LOOKING FOR.
WE WILL SUPPORT YOU WITH ALL THE ARMY AND SUPPLIES YOU NEED.
AND WITH SUFFICIENT GOLD TO BUILD MY DEFENSES?
MORE THAN ENOUGH.

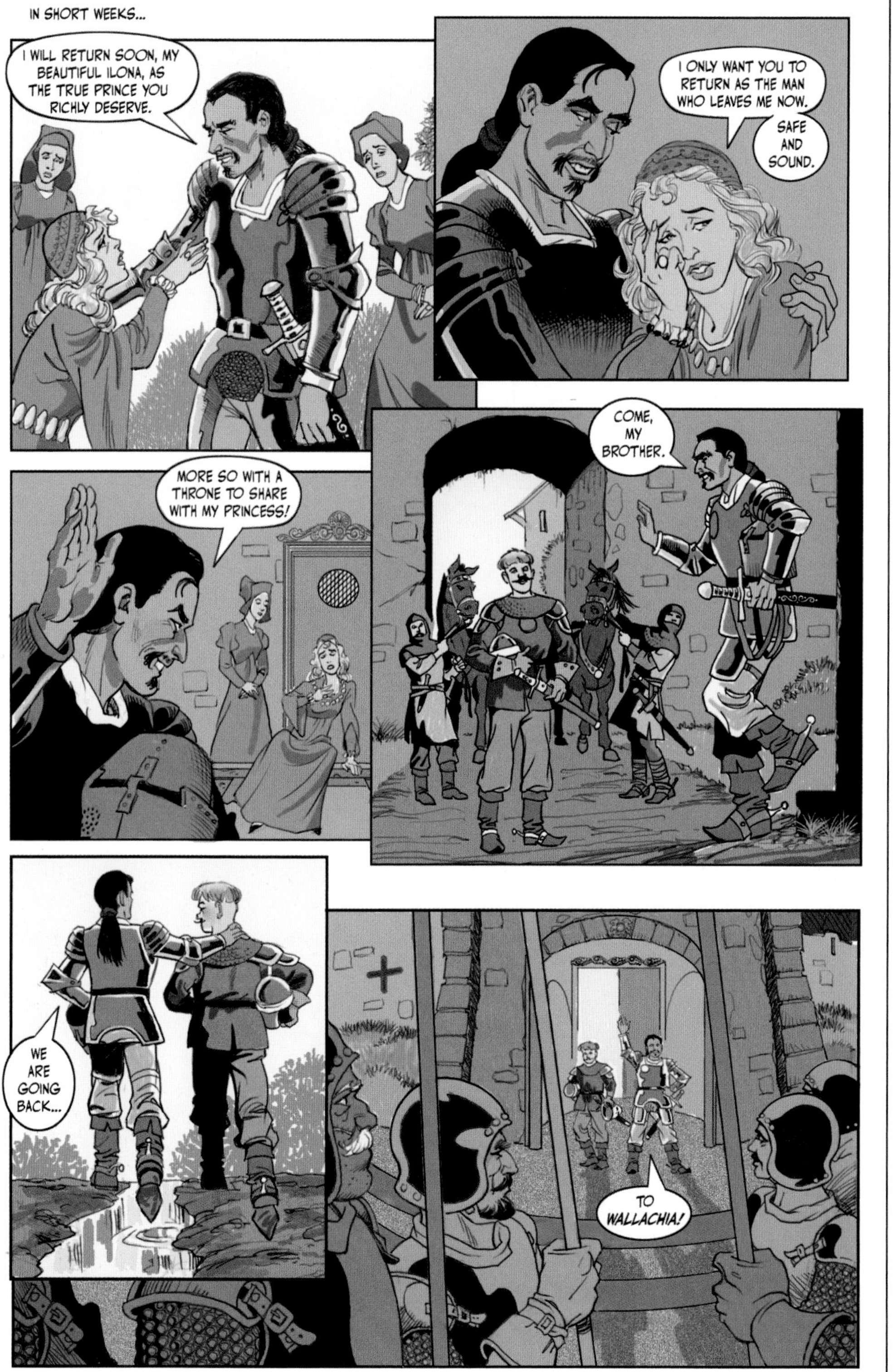

IN SHORT WEEKS...
I WILL RETURN SOON, MY BEAUTIFUL ILONA, AS THE TRUE PRINCE YOU RICHLY DESERVE.
I ONLY WANT YOU TO RETURN AS THE MAN WHO LEAVES ME NOW.
SAFE AND SOUND.
MORE SO WITH A THRONE TO SHARE WITH MY PRINCESS!
COME, MY BROTHER.
WE ARE GOING BACK...
TO *WALLACHIA!*

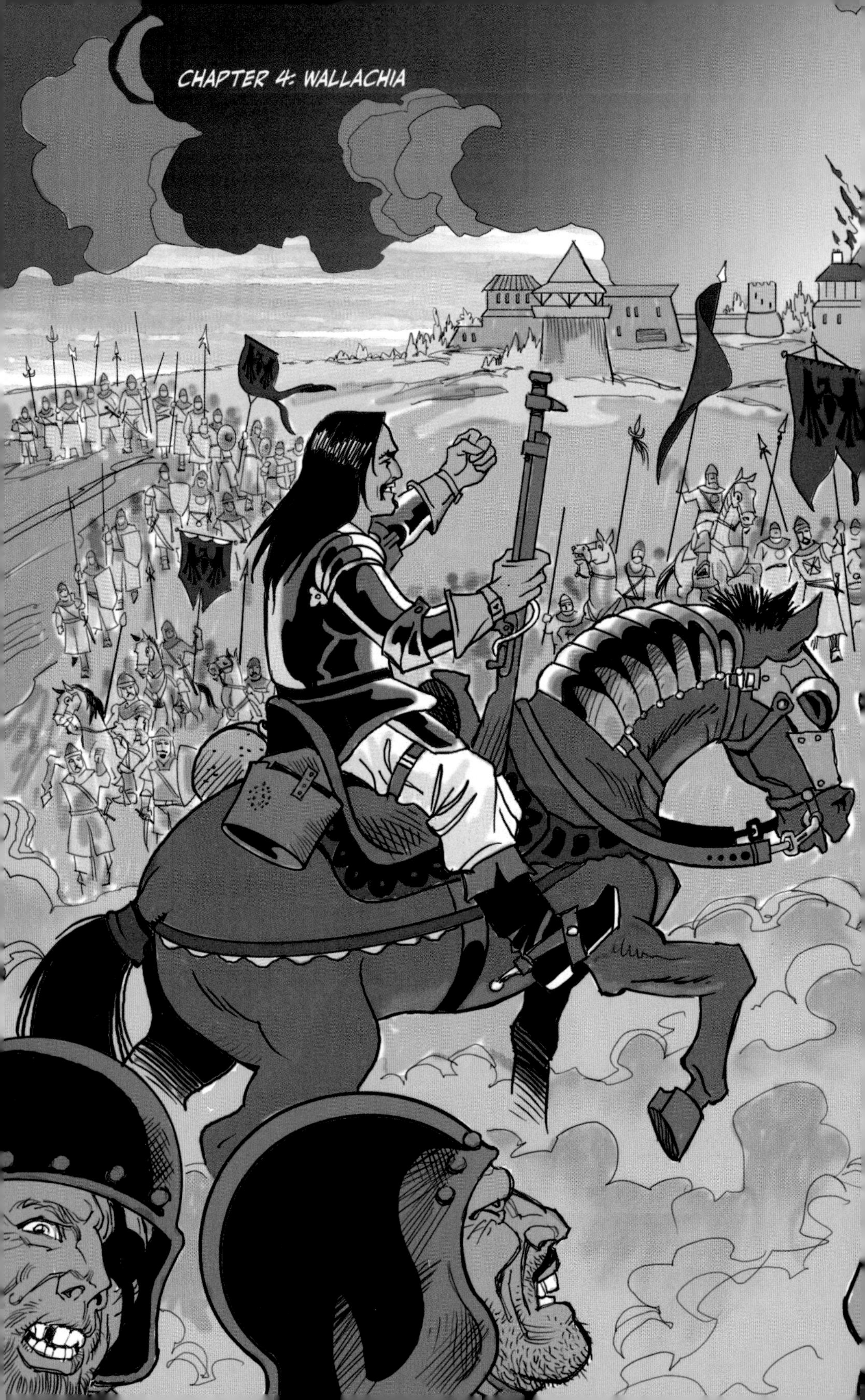
CHAPTER 4: WALLACHIA

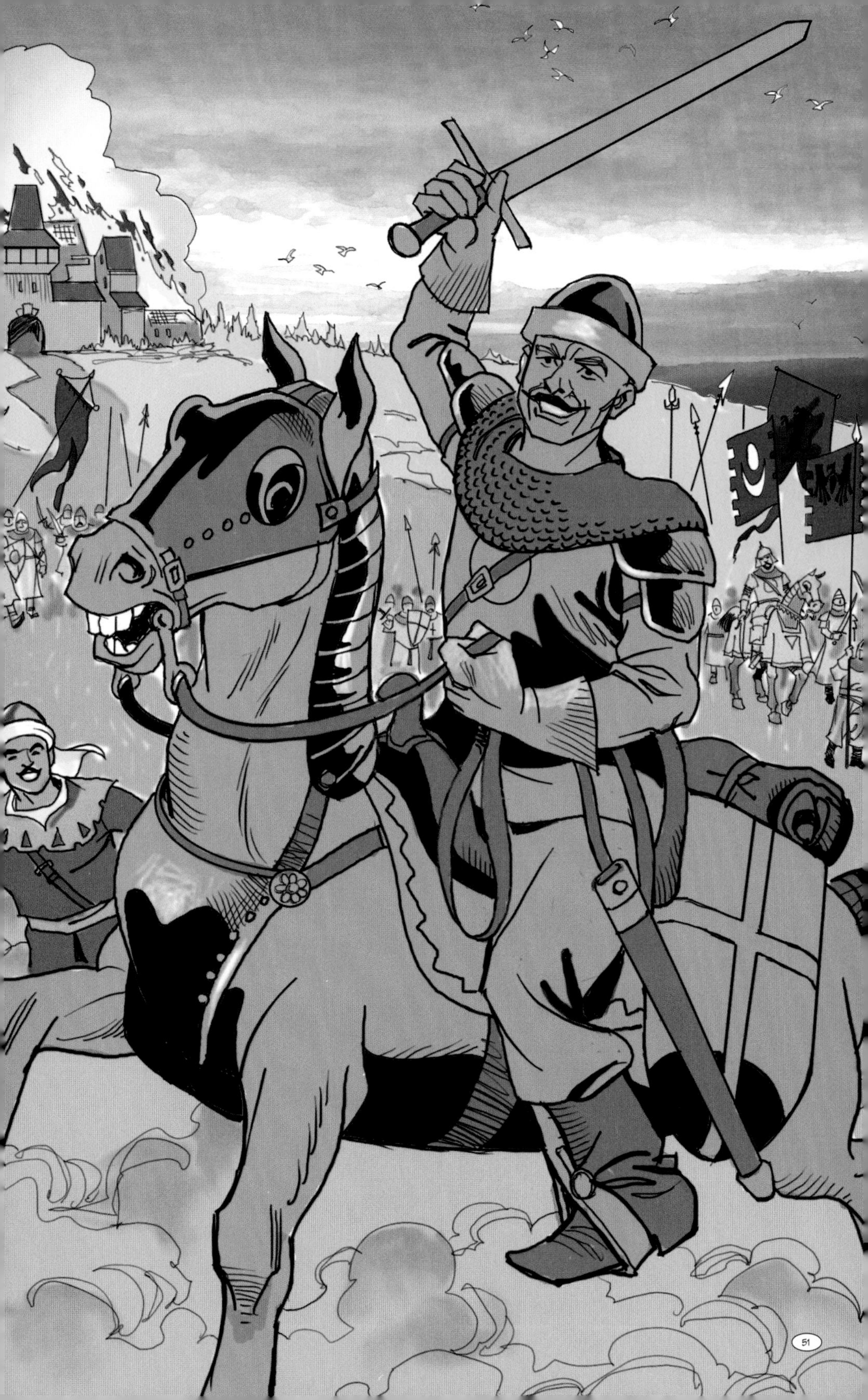

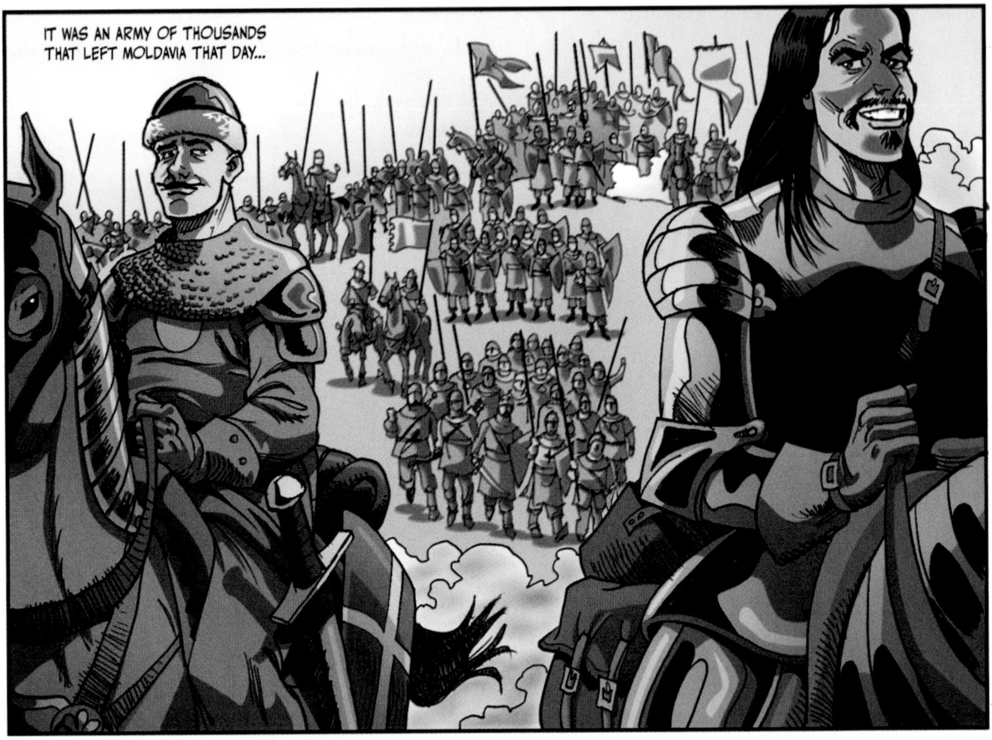
IT WAS AN ARMY OF THOUSANDS THAT LEFT MOLDAVIA THAT DAY...

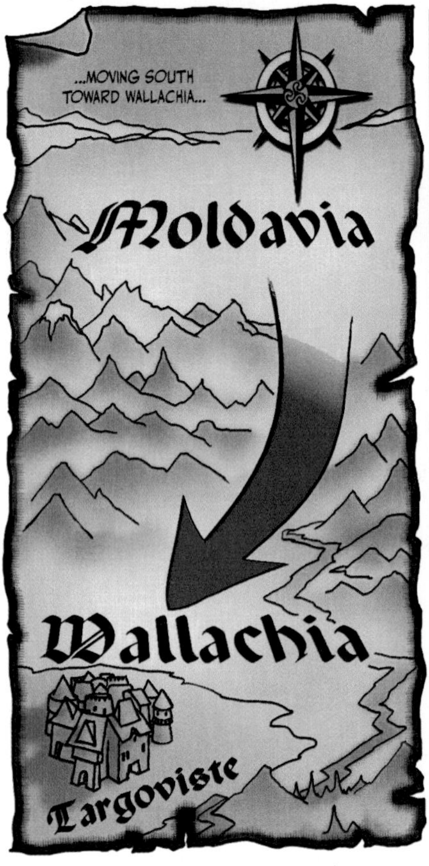
...MOVING SOUTH TOWARD WALLACHIA...
Moldavia
Wallachia
Targoviste

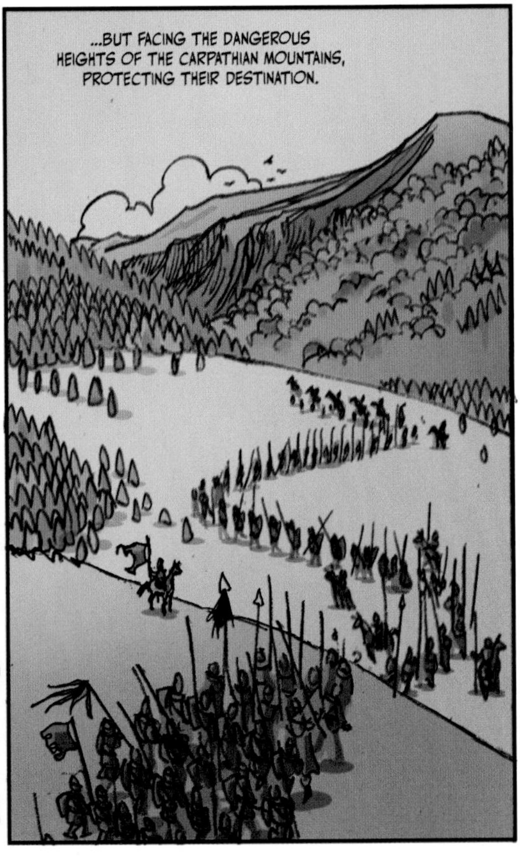
...BUT FACING THE DANGEROUS HEIGHTS OF THE CARPATHIAN MOUNTAINS, PROTECTING THEIR DESTINATION.

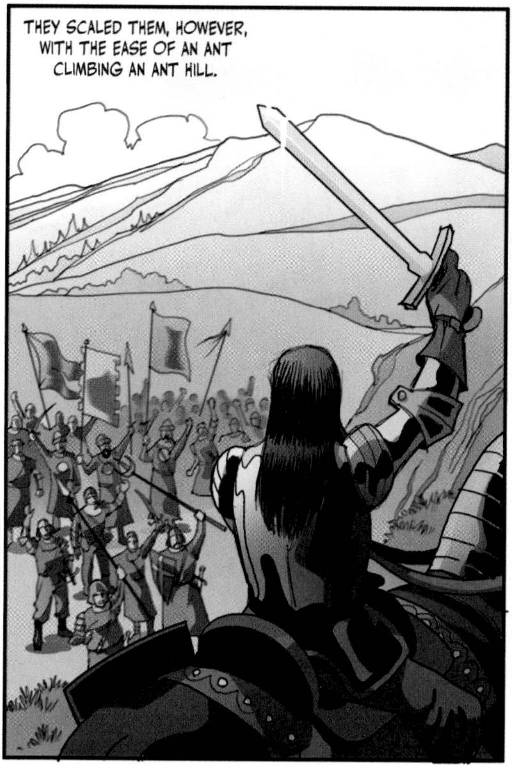
THEY SCALED THEM, HOWEVER, WITH THE EASE OF AN ANT CLIMBING AN ANT HILL.

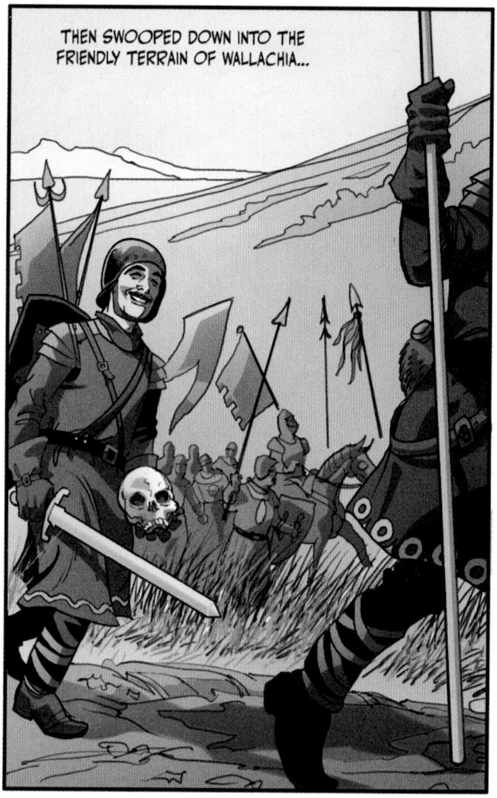
THEN SWOOPED DOWN INTO THE FRIENDLY TERRAIN OF WALLACHIA...

...WHERE THEY SWEPT THROUGH CITY AFTER CITY...

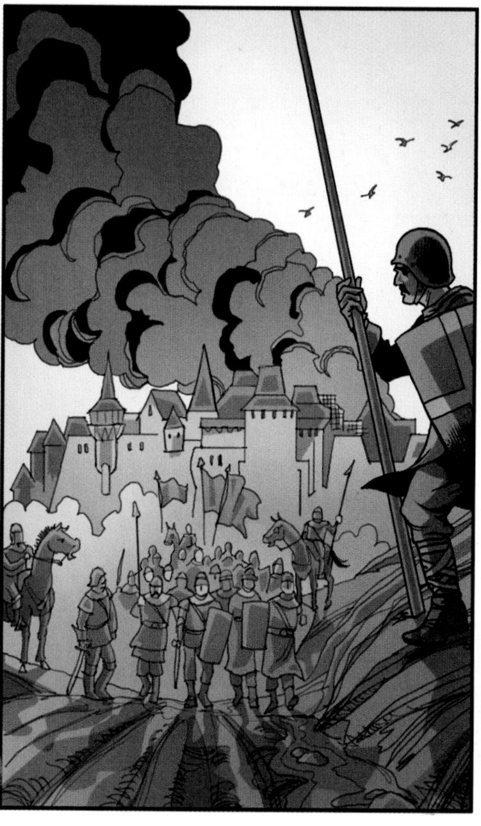

...LEAVING BLOOD IN THEIR TRACKS AND THE SMELL OF VICTORY IN THEIR NOSTRILS.

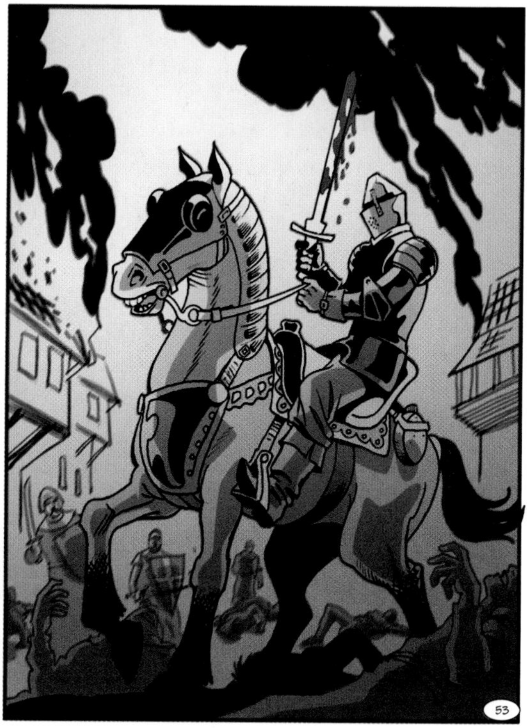

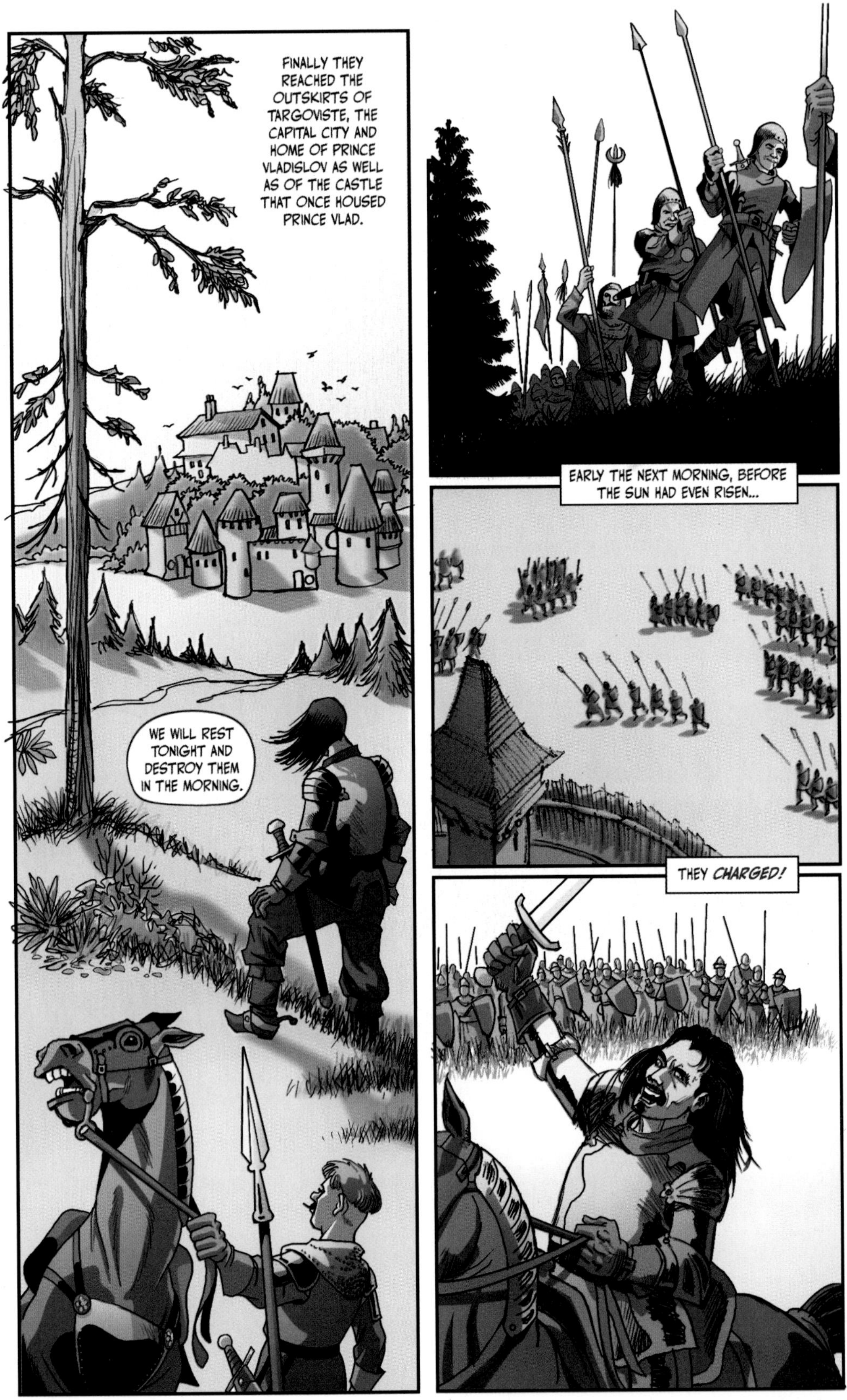
FINALLY THEY REACHED THE OUTSKIRTS OF TARGOVISTE, THE CAPITAL CITY AND HOME OF PRINCE VLADISLOV AS WELL AS OF THE CASTLE THAT ONCE HOUSED PRINCE VLAD.
WE WILL REST TONIGHT AND DESTROY THEM IN THE MORNING.
EARLY THE NEXT MORNING, BEFORE THE SUN HAD EVEN RISEN...
THEY *CHARGED!*

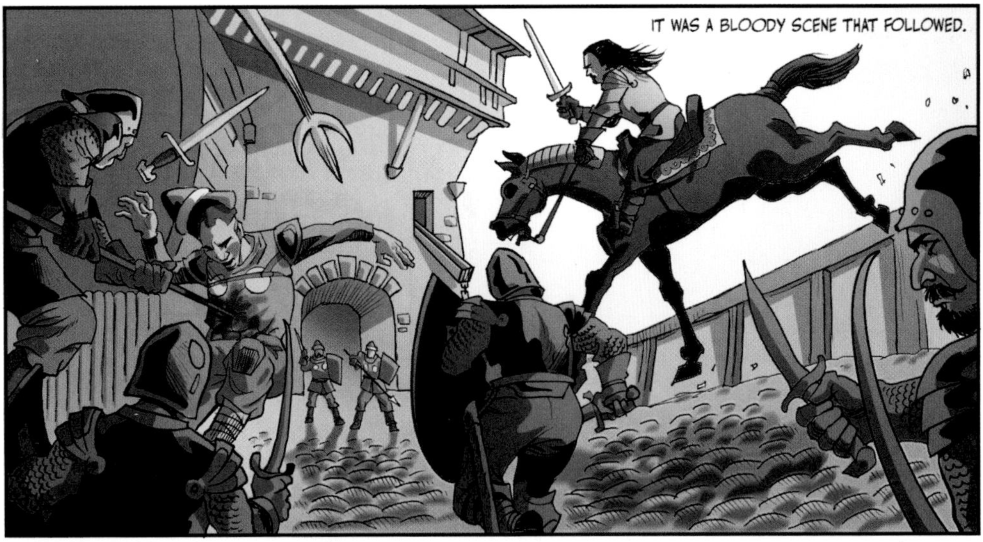
IT WAS A BLOODY SCENE THAT FOLLOWED.

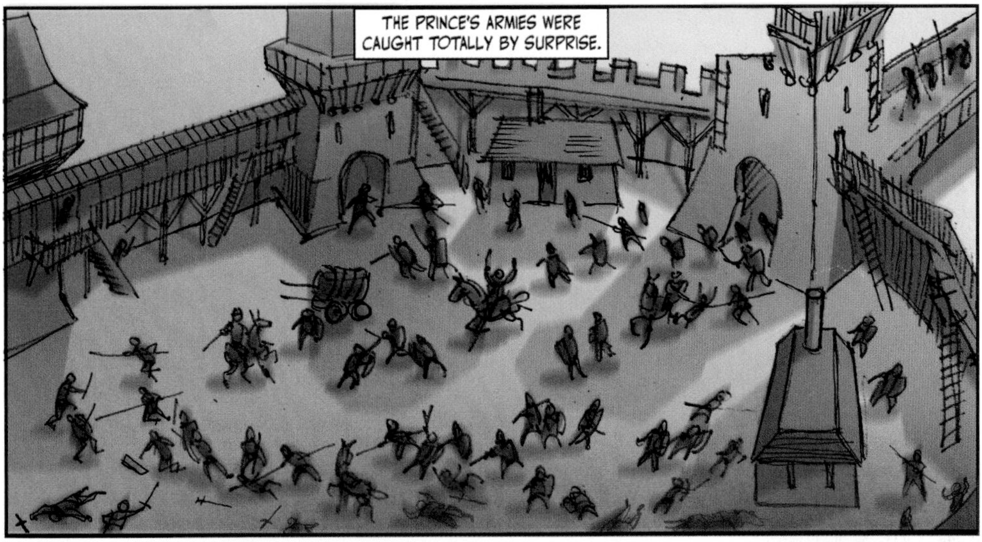
THE PRINCE'S ARMIES WERE CAUGHT TOTALLY BY SURPRISE.

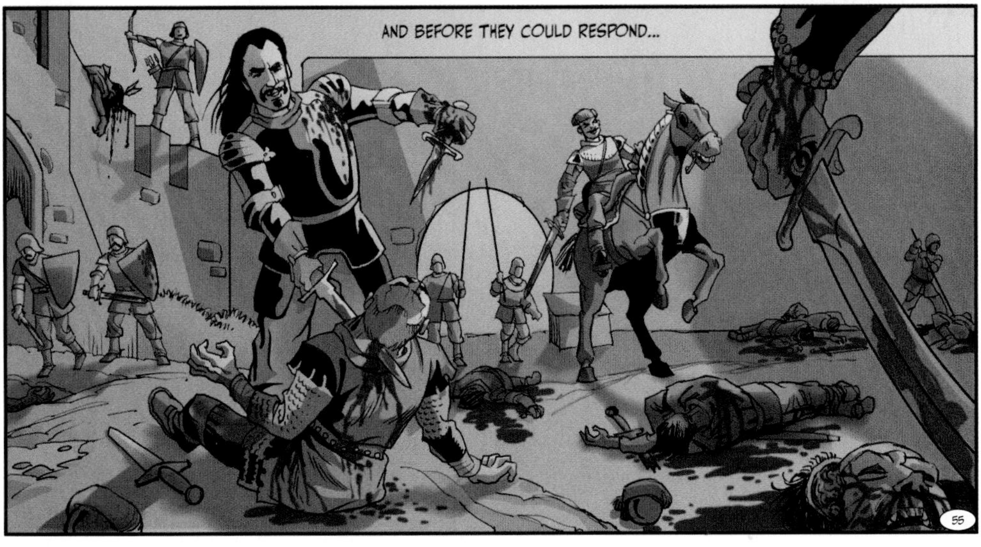
AND BEFORE THEY COULD RESPOND...

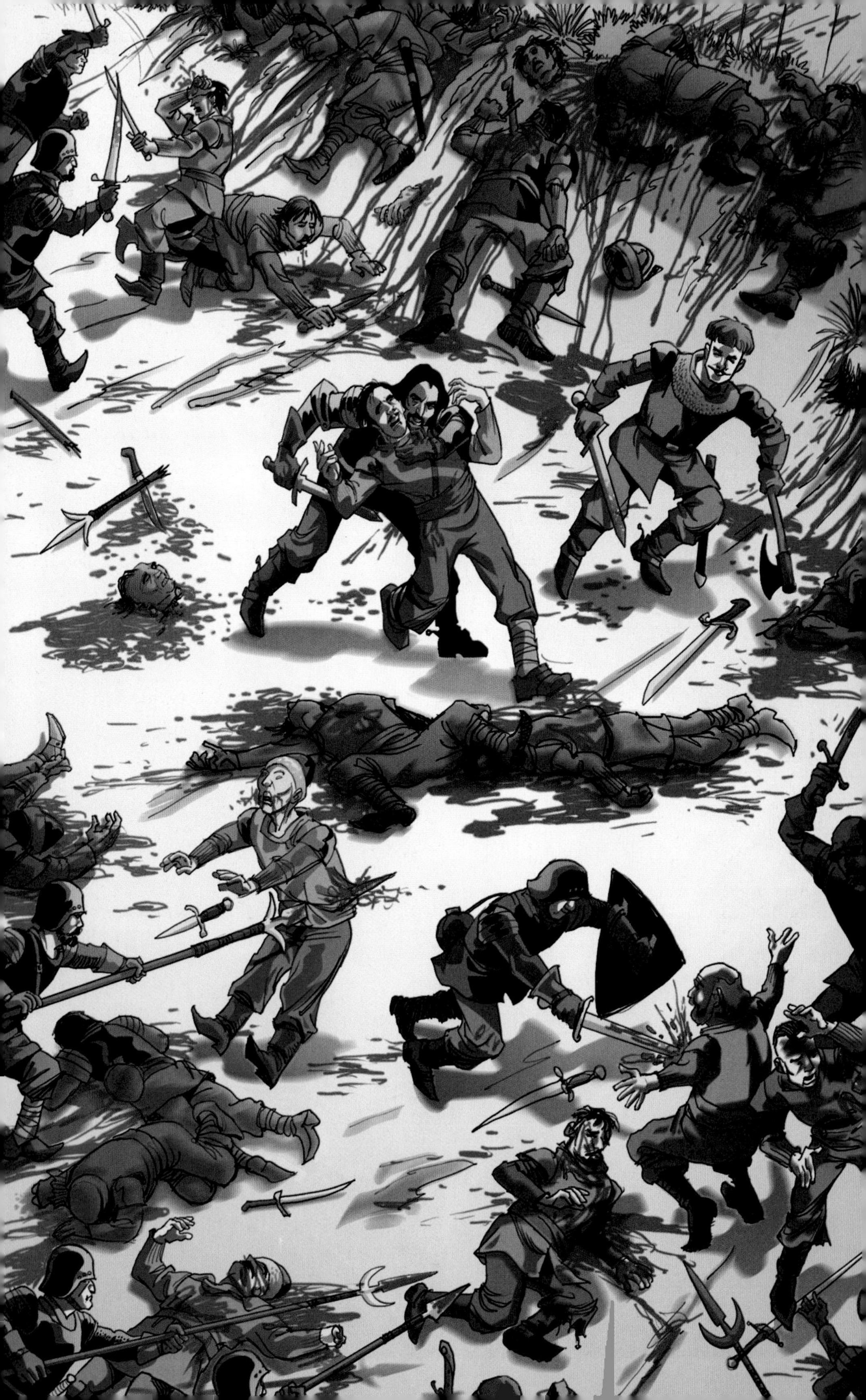

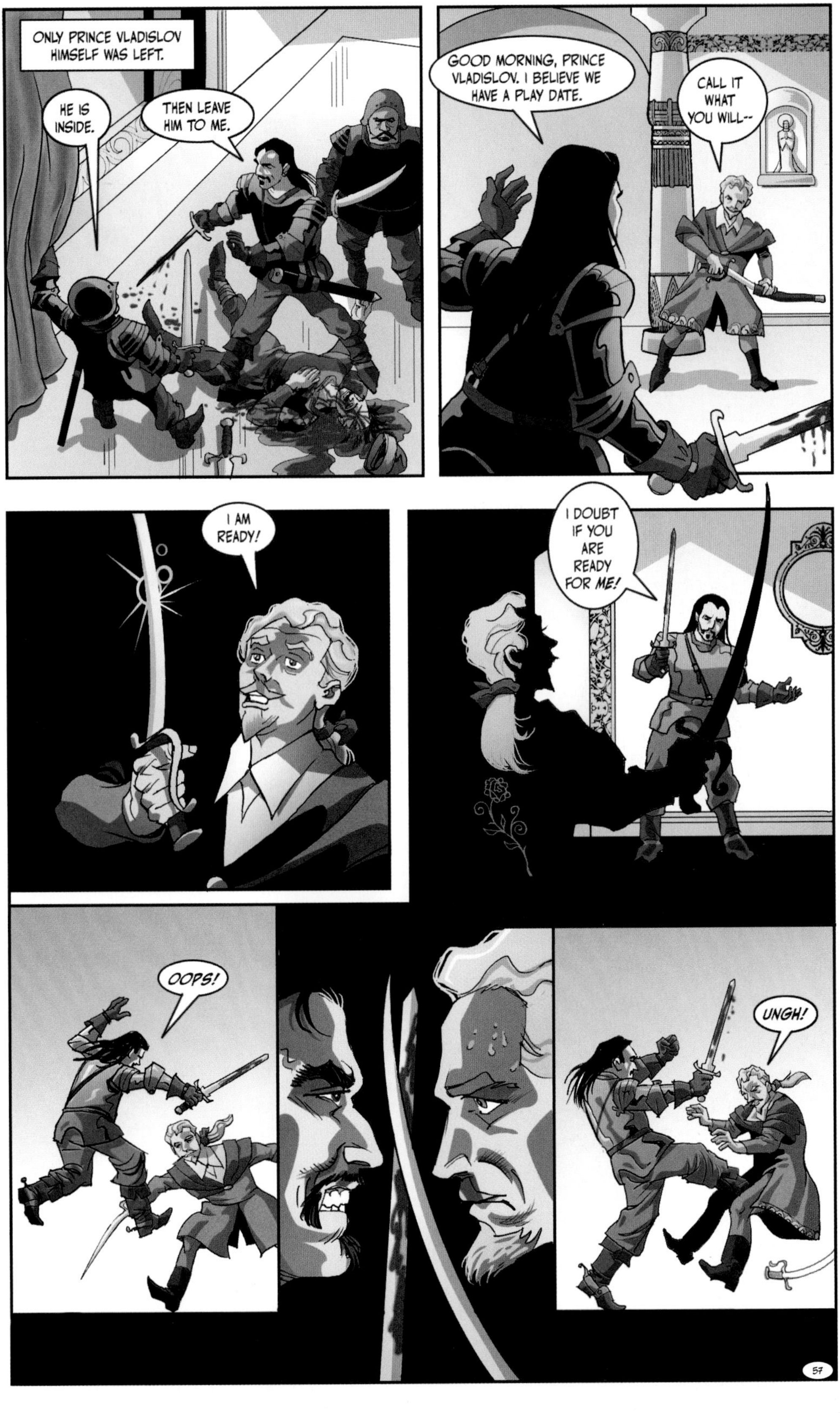
ONLY PRINCE VLADISLOV HIMSELF WAS LEFT.
HE IS INSIDE.
THEN LEAVE HIM TO ME.
GOOD MORNING, PRINCE VLADISLOV. I BELIEVE WE HAVE A PLAY DATE.
CALL IT WHAT YOU WILL--
I AM READY!
I DOUBT IF YOU ARE READY FOR *ME!*
OOPS!
UNGH!

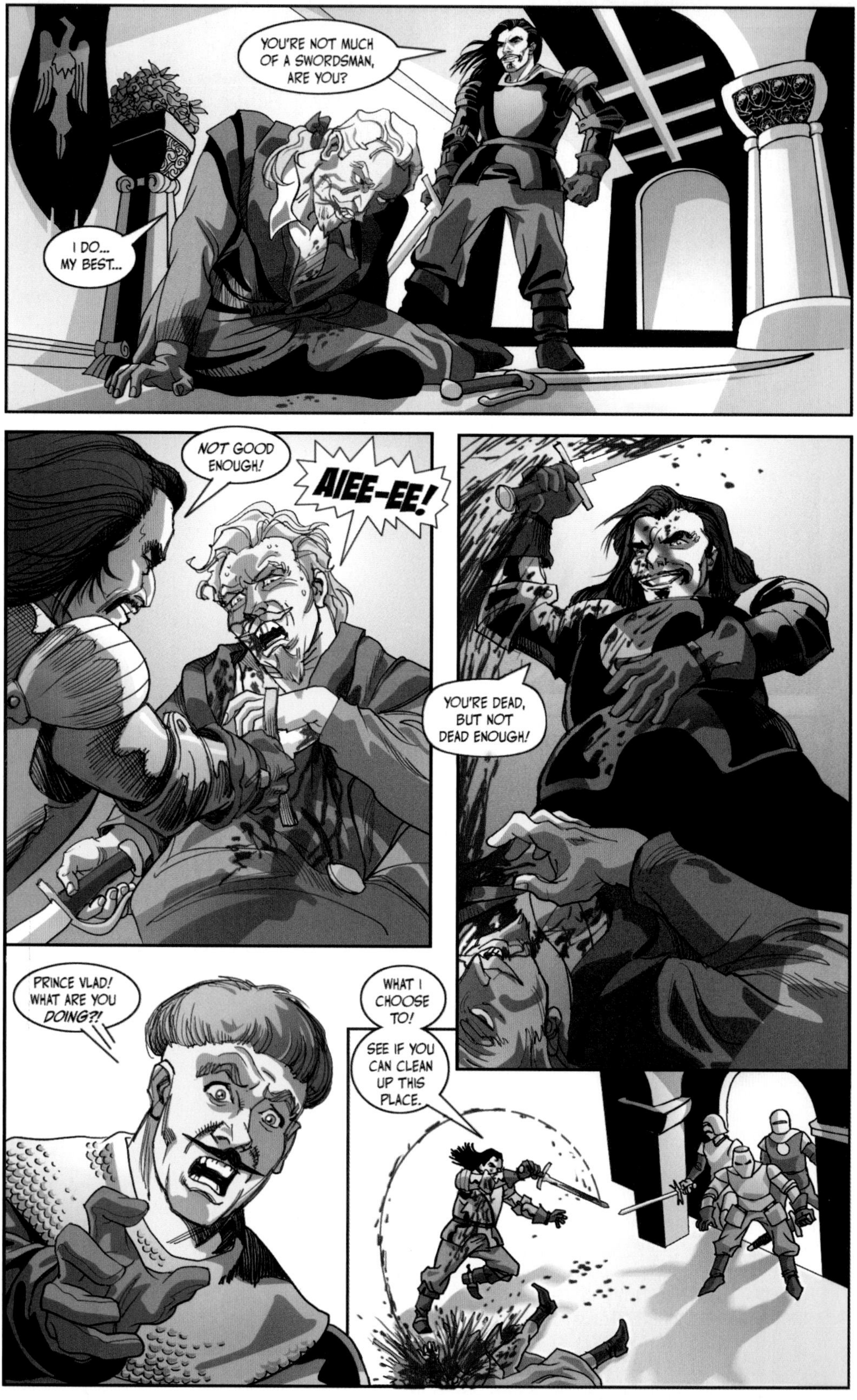

YOU'RE NOT MUCH OF A SWORDSMAN, ARE YOU?
I DO... MY BEST...
NOT GOOD ENOUGH!
AIEE-EE!
YOU'RE DEAD, BUT NOT DEAD ENOUGH!
PRINCE VLAD! WHAT ARE YOU DOING?!
WHAT I CHOOSE TO!
SEE IF YOU CAN CLEAN UP THIS PLACE.

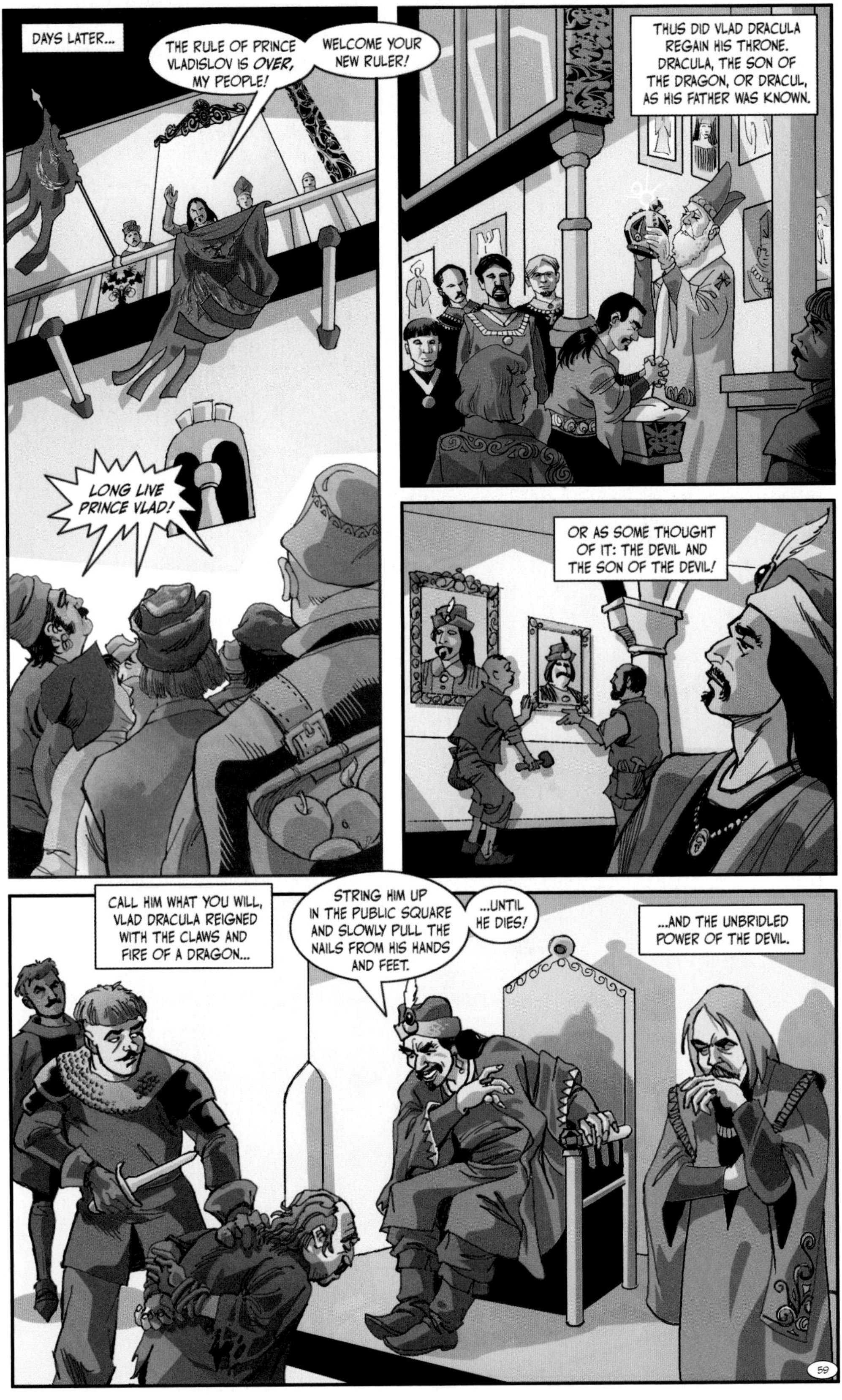
DAYS LATER...
THE RULE OF PRINCE VLADISLOV IS *OVER,* MY PEOPLE!
WELCOME YOUR NEW RULER!
LONG LIVE PRINCE VLAD!
THUS DID VLAD DRACULA REGAIN HIS THRONE. DRACULA, THE SON OF THE DRAGON, OR DRACUL, AS HIS FATHER WAS KNOWN.
OR AS SOME THOUGHT OF IT: THE DEVIL AND THE SON OF THE DEVIL!
CALL HIM WHAT YOU WILL, VLAD DRACULA REIGNED WITH THE CLAWS AND FIRE OF A DRAGON...
STRING HIM UP IN THE PUBLIC SQUARE AND SLOWLY PULL THE NAILS FROM HIS HANDS AND FEET.
...UNTIL HE DIES!
...AND THE UNBRIDLED POWER OF THE DEVIL.

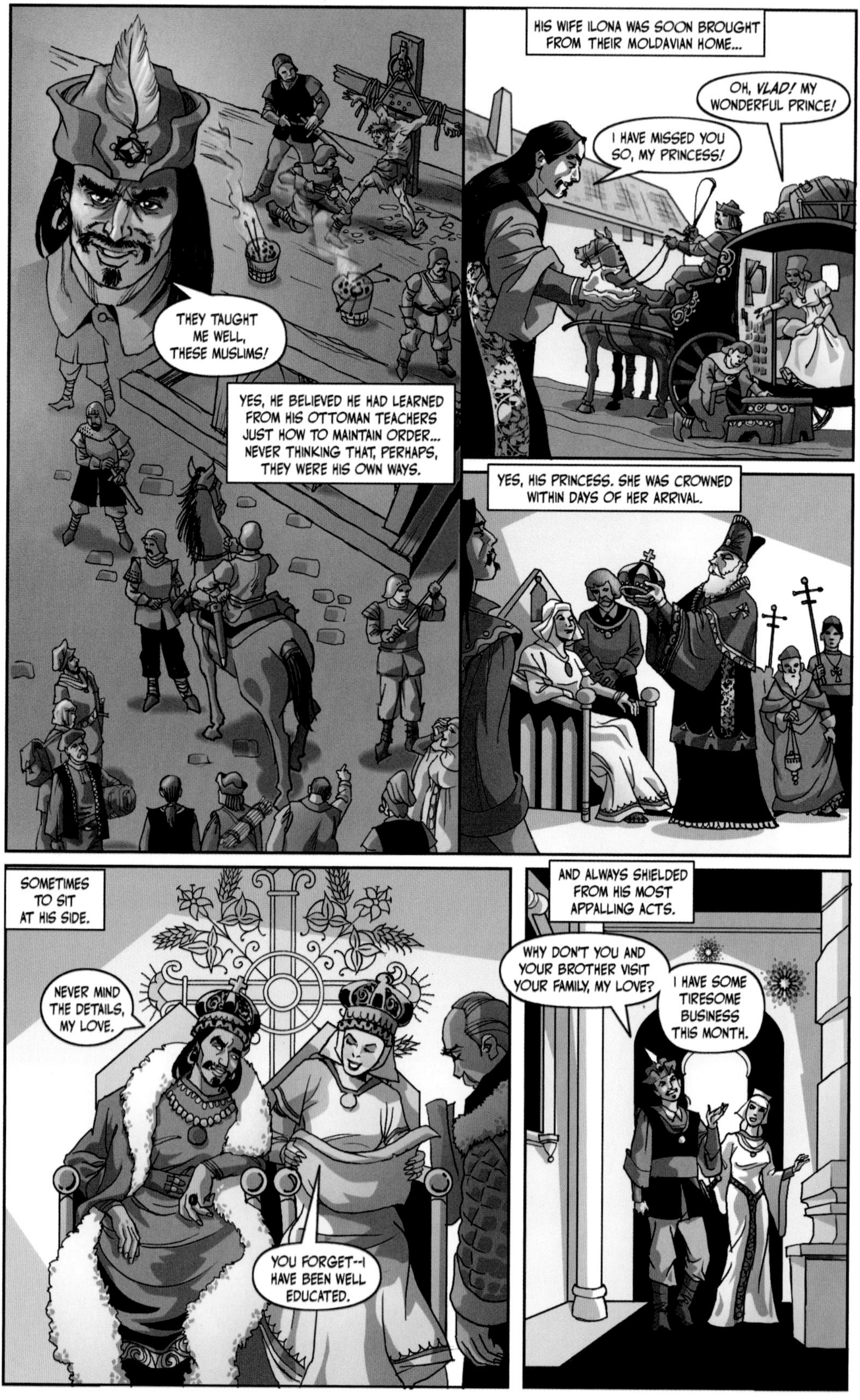
THEY TAUGHT ME WELL, THESE MUSLIMS!
YES, HE BELIEVED HE HAD LEARNED FROM HIS OTTOMAN TEACHERS JUST HOW TO MAINTAIN ORDER... NEVER THINKING THAT, PERHAPS, THEY WERE HIS OWN WAYS.
HIS WIFE ILONA WAS SOON BROUGHT FROM THEIR MOLDAVIAN HOME...
I HAVE MISSED YOU SO, MY PRINCESS!
OH, VLAD! MY WONDERFUL PRINCE!
YES, HIS PRINCESS. SHE WAS CROWNED WITHIN DAYS OF HER ARRIVAL.
SOMETIMES TO SIT AT HIS SIDE.
NEVER MIND THE DETAILS, MY LOVE.
YOU FORGET--I HAVE BEEN WELL EDUCATED.
AND ALWAYS SHIELDED FROM HIS MOST APPALLING ACTS.
WHY DON'T YOU AND YOUR BROTHER VISIT YOUR FAMILY, MY LOVE?
I HAVE SOME TIRESOME BUSINESS THIS MONTH.

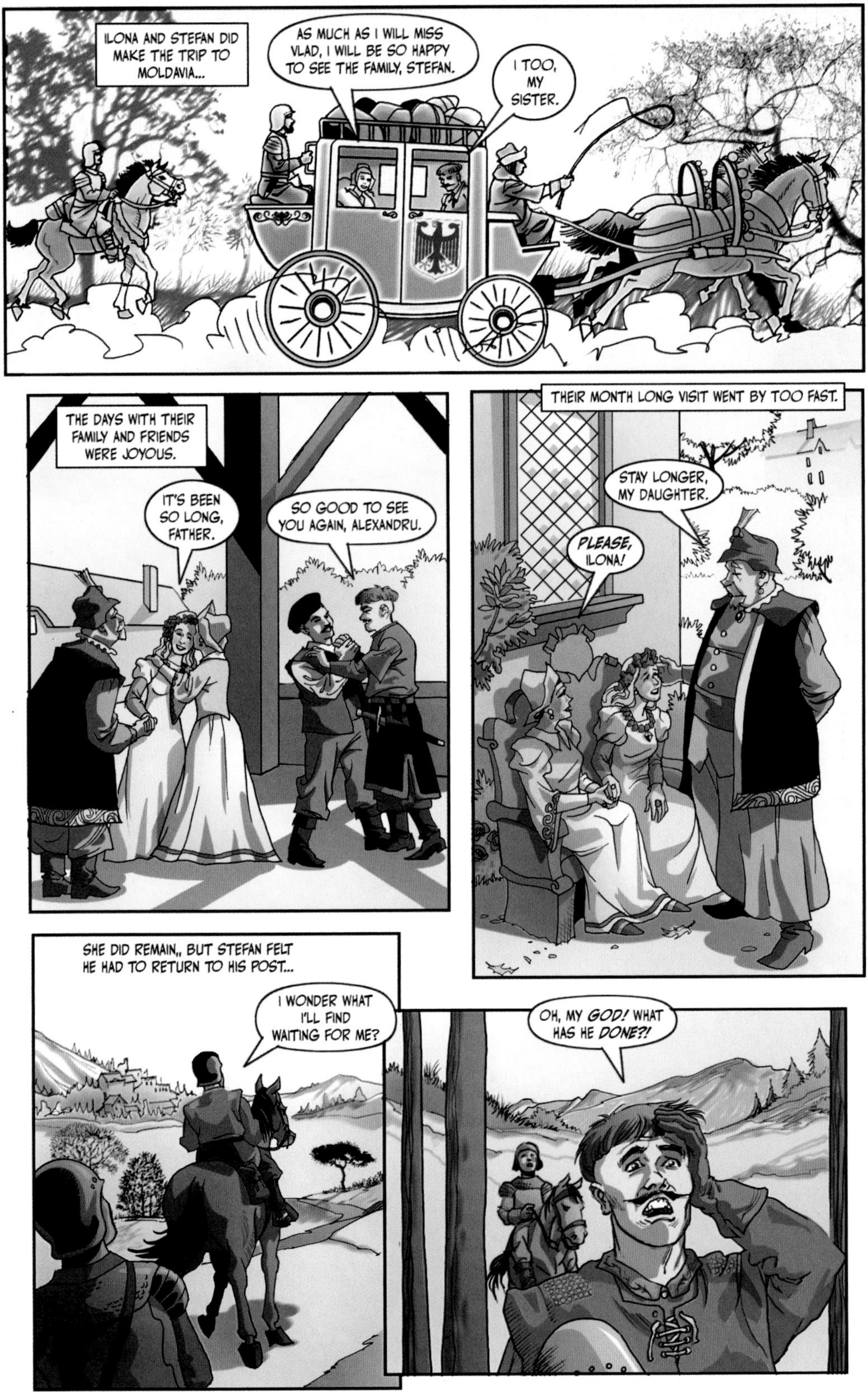

ILONA AND STEFAN DID MAKE THE TRIP TO MOLDAVIA...
AS MUCH AS I WILL MISS VLAD, I WILL BE SO HAPPY TO SEE THE FAMILY, STEFAN.
I TOO, MY SISTER.
THE DAYS WITH THEIR FAMILY AND FRIENDS WERE JOYOUS.
IT'S BEEN SO LONG, FATHER.
SO GOOD TO SEE YOU AGAIN, ALEXANDRU.
THEIR MONTH LONG VISIT WENT BY TOO FAST.
STAY LONGER, MY DAUGHTER.
PLEASE, ILONA!
SHE DID REMAIN,, BUT STEFAN FELT HE HAD TO RETURN TO HIS POST...
I WONDER WHAT I'LL FIND WAITING FOR ME?
OH, MY GOD! WHAT HAS HE DONE?!

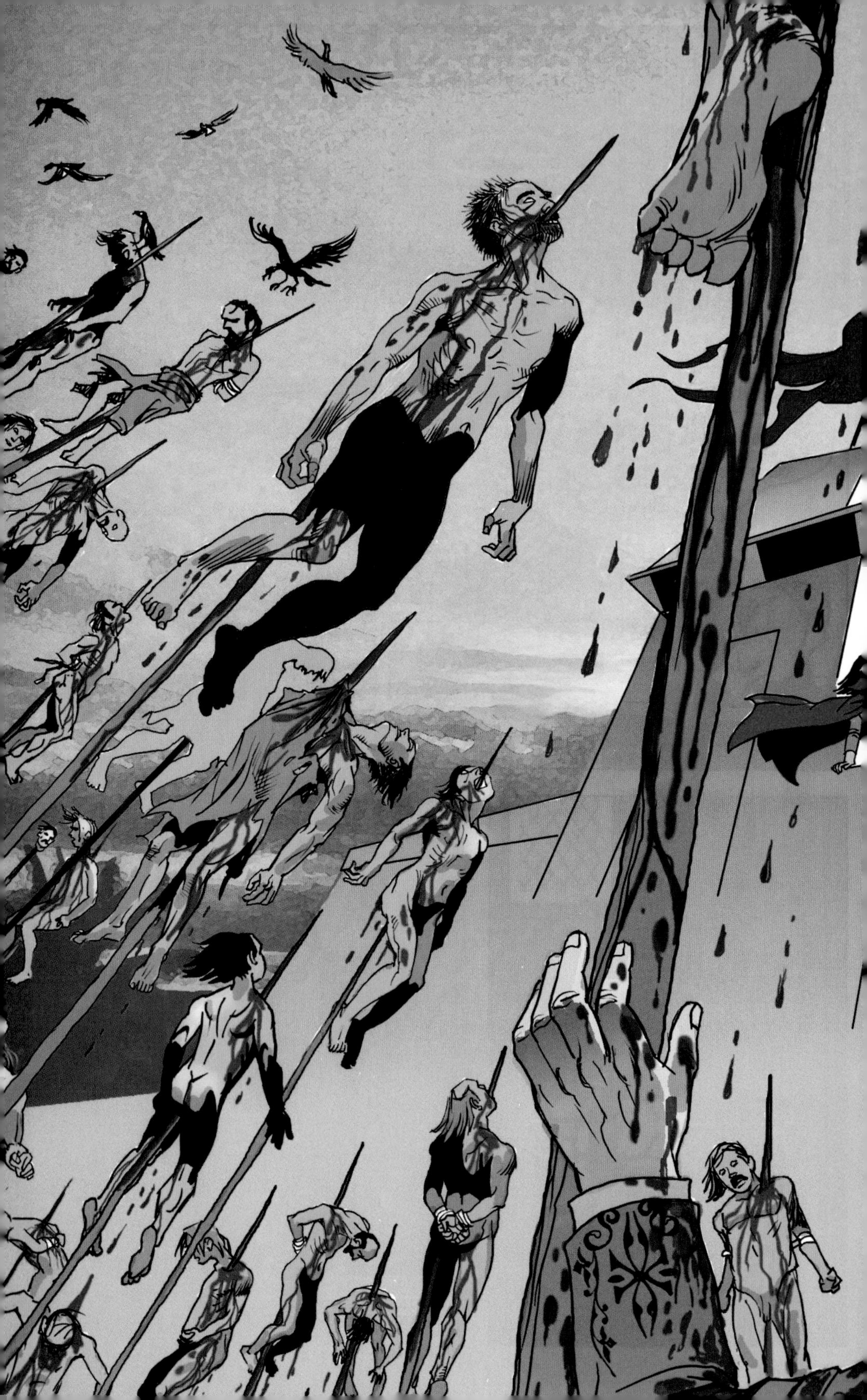

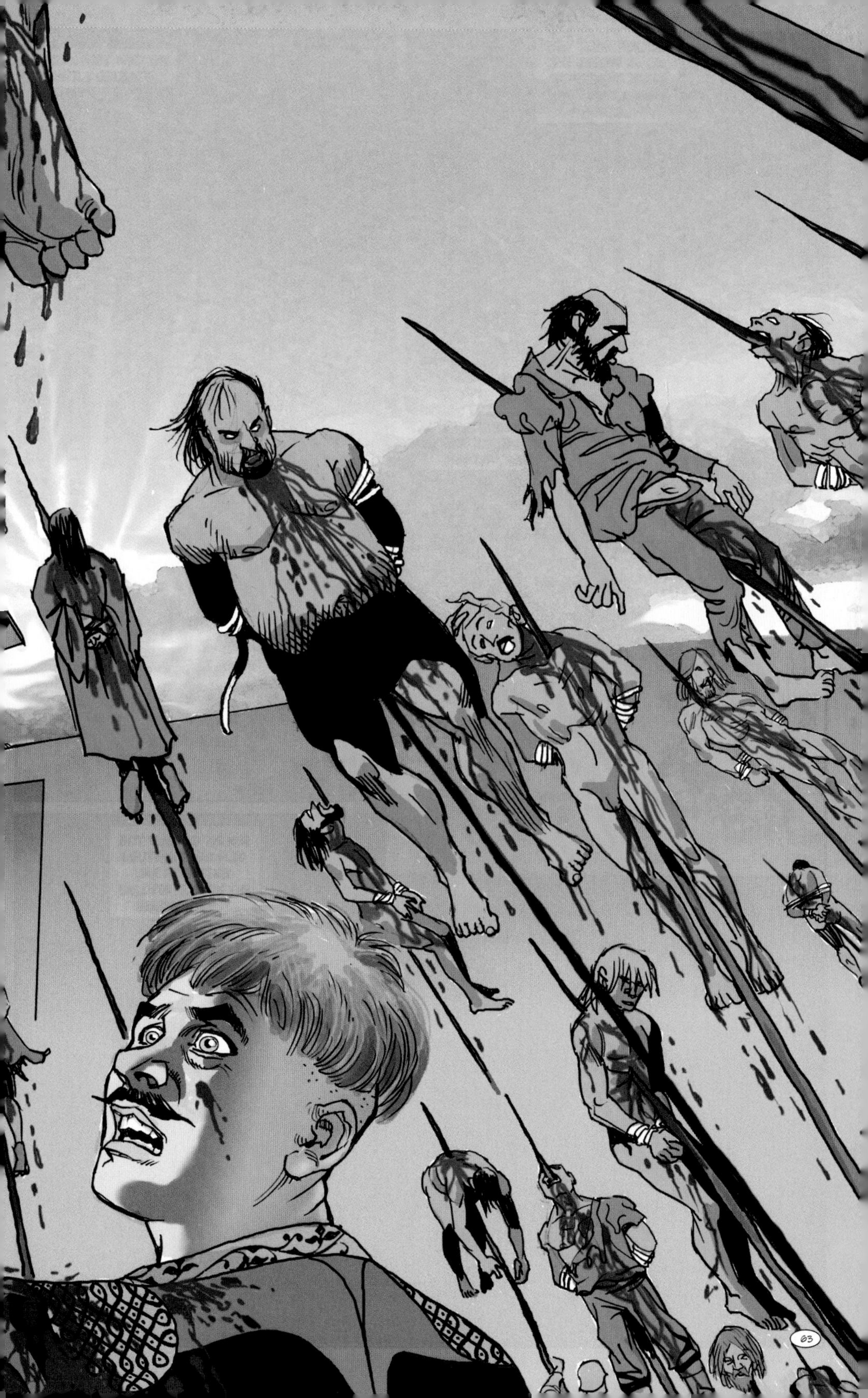

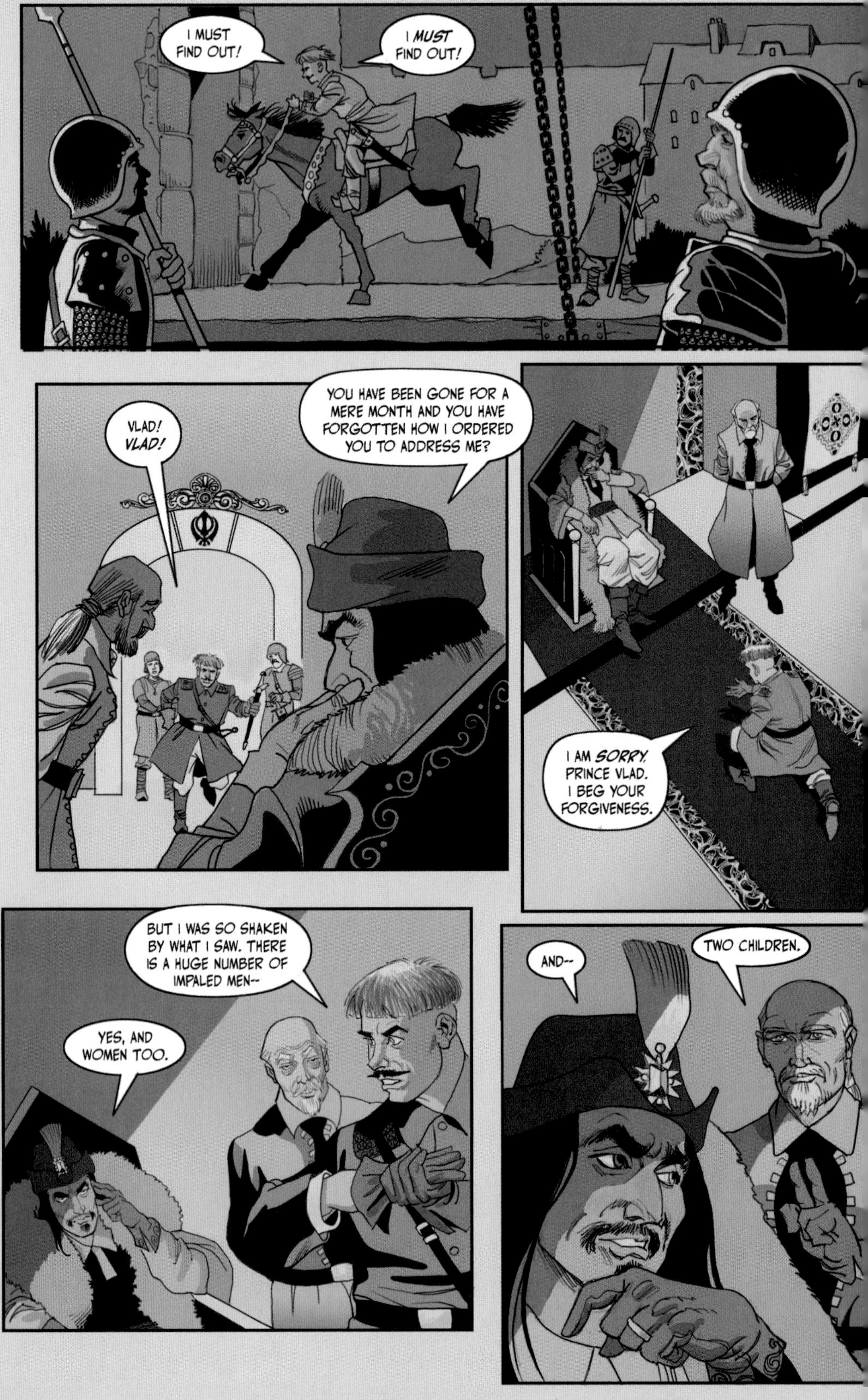
I MUST FIND OUT!
I MUST FIND OUT!
VLAD! VLAD!
YOU HAVE BEEN GONE FOR A MERE MONTH AND YOU HAVE FORGOTTEN HOW I ORDERED YOU TO ADDRESS ME?
I AM SORRY, PRINCE VLAD. I BEG YOUR FORGIVENESS.
BUT I WAS SO SHAKEN BY WHAT I SAW. THERE IS A HUGE NUMBER OF IMPALED MEN--
YES, AND WOMEN TOO.
AND--
TWO CHILDREN.

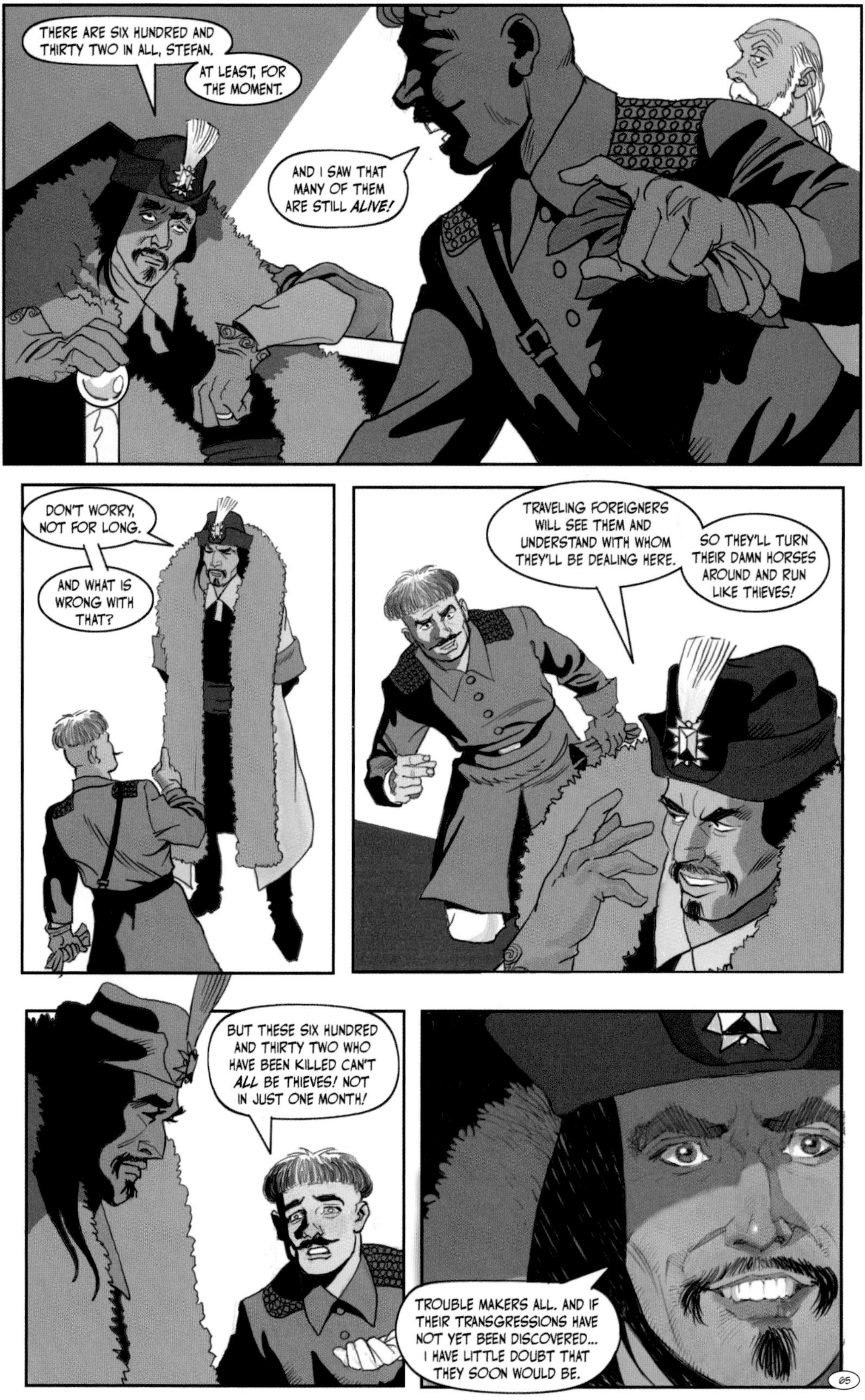
THERE ARE SIX HUNDRED AND THIRTY TWO IN ALL, STEFAN.
AT LEAST, FOR THE MOMENT.
AND I SAW THAT MANY OF THEM ARE STILL *ALIVE!*
DON'T WORRY, NOT FOR LONG.
AND WHAT IS WRONG WITH THAT?
TRAVELING FOREIGNERS WILL SEE THEM AND UNDERSTAND WITH WHOM THEY'LL BE DEALING HERE.
SO THEY'LL TURN THEIR DAMN HORSES AROUND AND RUN LIKE THIEVES!
BUT THESE SIX HUNDRED AND THIRTY TWO WHO HAVE BEEN KILLED CAN'T *ALL* BE THIEVES! NOT IN JUST ONE MONTH!
TROUBLE MAKERS ALL. AND IF THEIR TRANSGRESSIONS HAVE NOT YET BEEN DISCOVERED... I HAVE LITTLE DOUBT THAT THEY SOON WOULD BE.

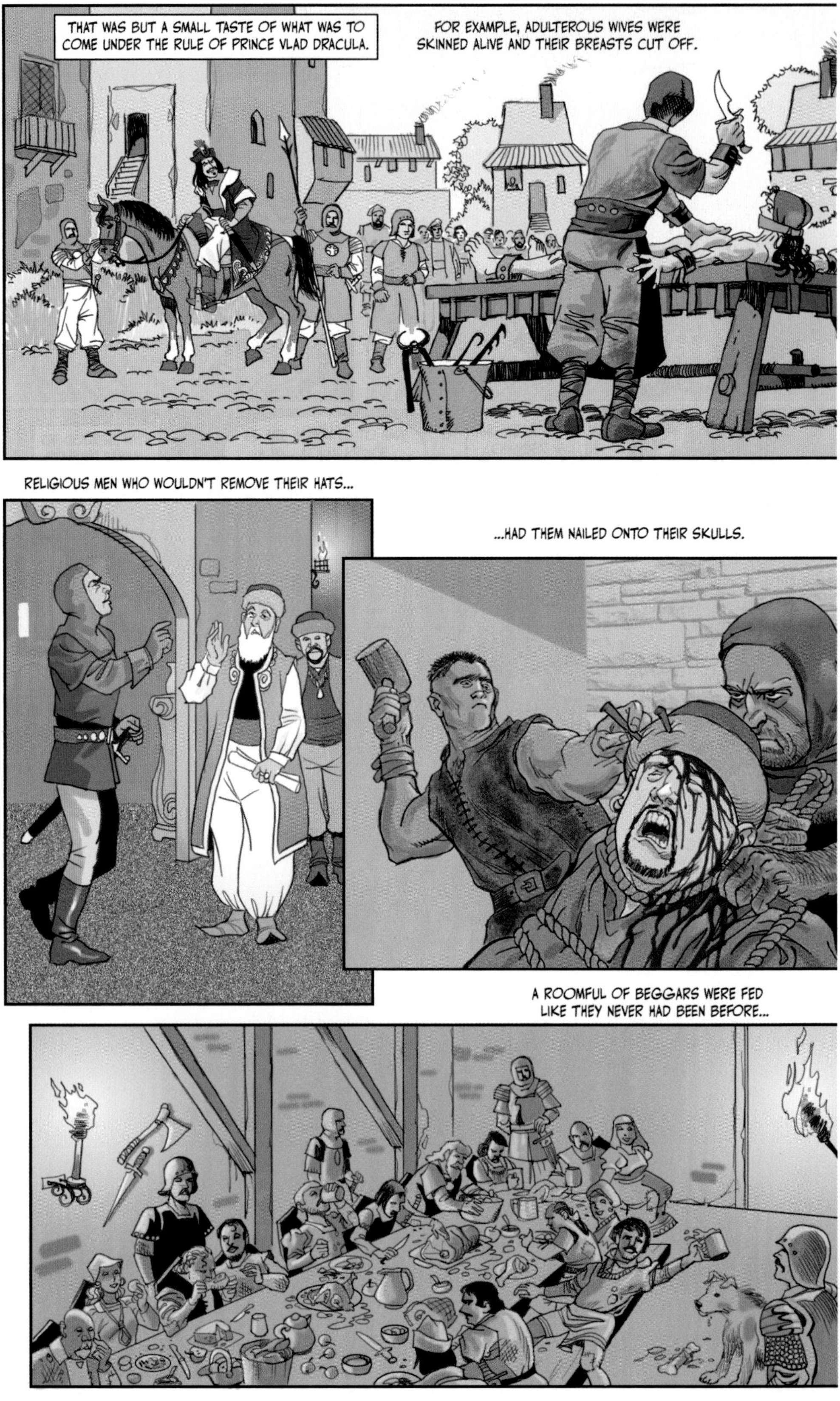
THAT WAS BUT A SMALL TASTE OF WHAT WAS TO COME UNDER THE RULE OF PRINCE VLAD DRACULA.
FOR EXAMPLE, ADULTEROUS WIVES WERE SKINNED ALIVE AND THEIR BREASTS CUT OFF.
RELIGIOUS MEN WHO WOULDN'T REMOVE THEIR HATS...
...HAD THEM NAILED ONTO THEIR SKULLS.
A ROOMFUL OF BEGGARS WERE FED LIKE THEY NEVER HAD BEEN BEFORE...

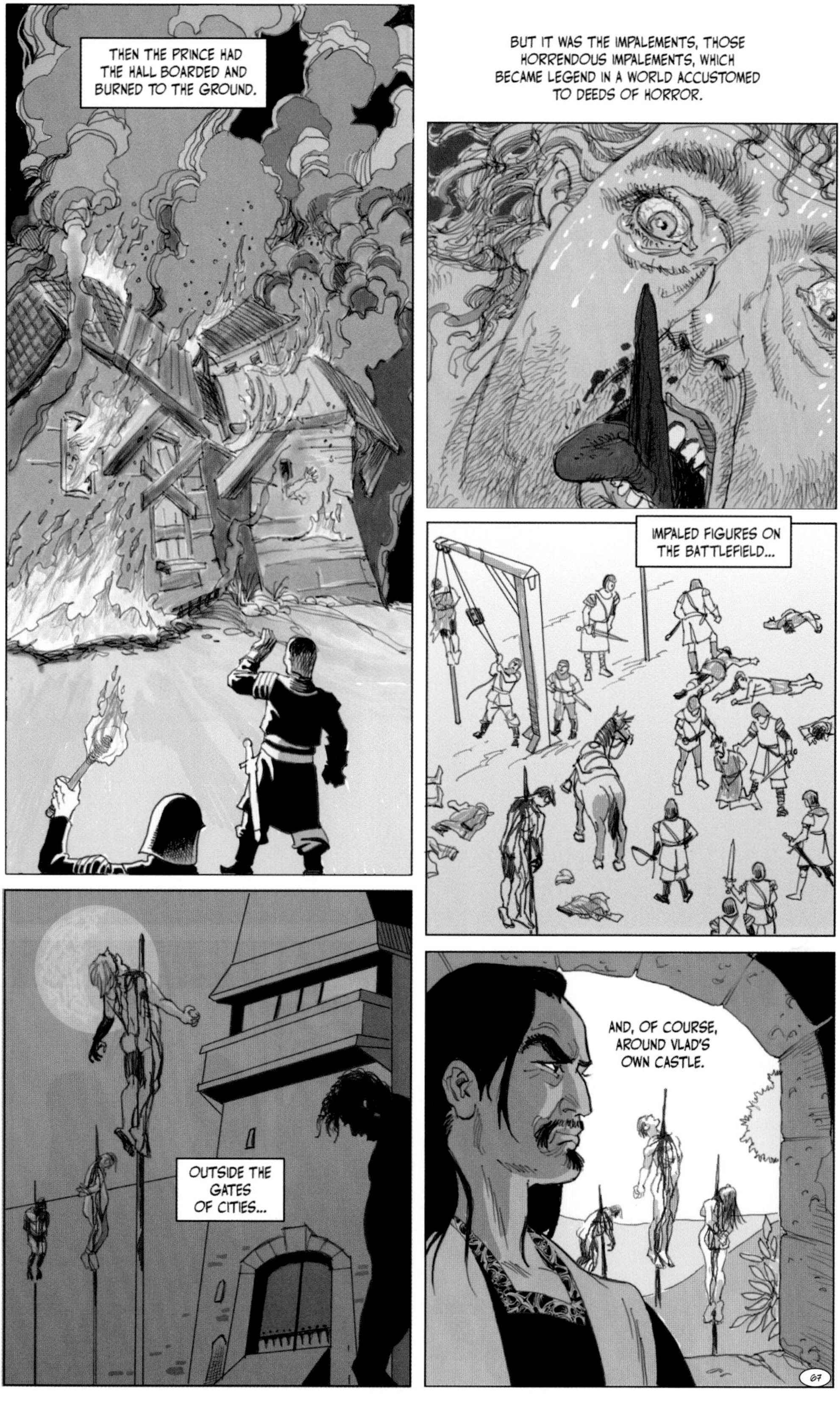
THEN THE PRINCE HAD THE HALL BOARDED AND BURNED TO THE GROUND.
BUT IT WAS THE IMPALEMENTS, THOSE HORRENDOUS IMPALEMENTS, WHICH BECAME LEGEND IN A WORLD ACCUSTOMED TO DEEDS OF HORROR.
IMPALED FIGURES ON THE BATTLEFIELD...
OUTSIDE THE GATES OF CITIES...
AND, OF COURSE, AROUND VLAD'S OWN CASTLE.

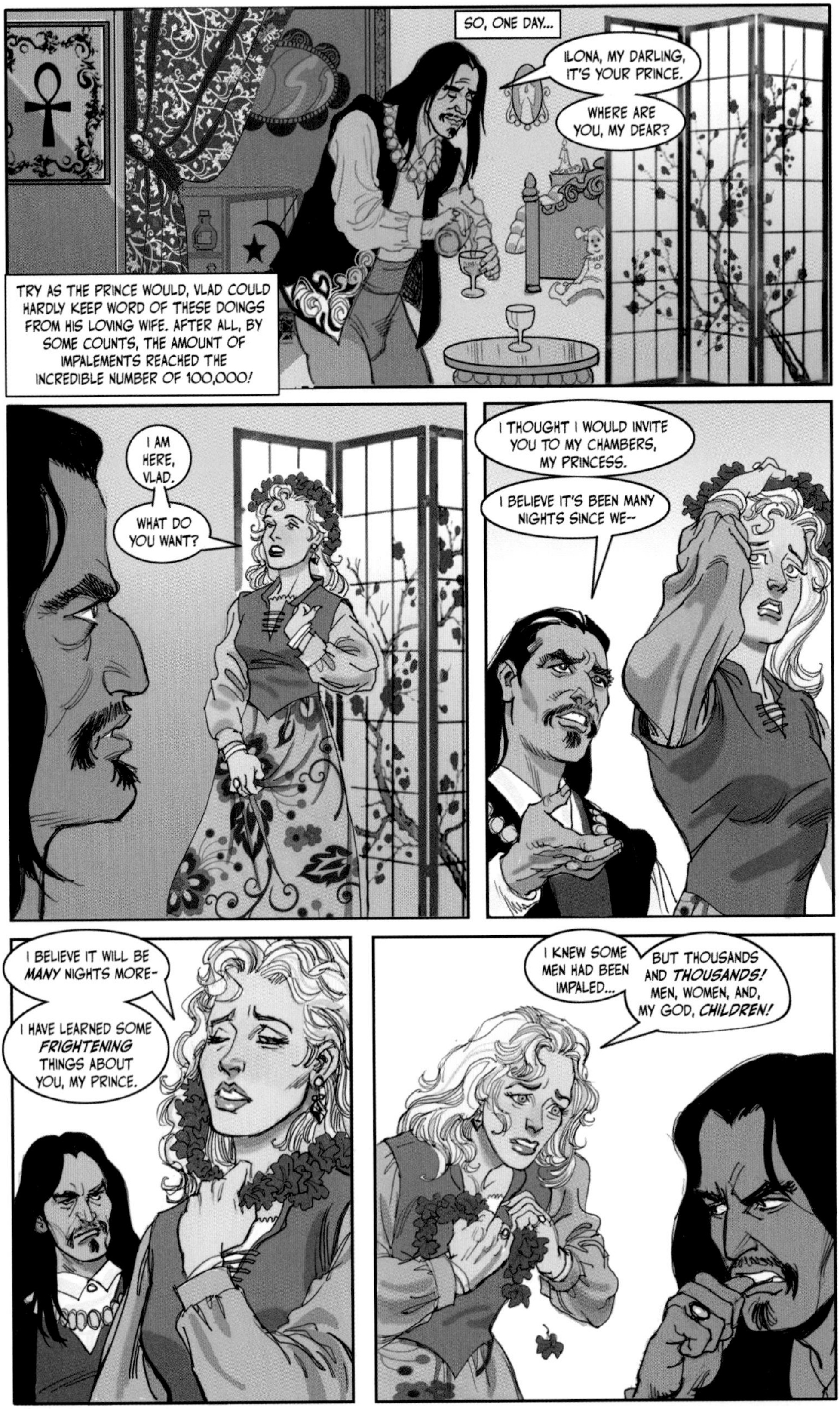
SO, ONE DAY...
ILONA, MY DARLING, IT'S YOUR PRINCE.
WHERE ARE YOU, MY DEAR?
TRY AS THE PRINCE WOULD, VLAD COULD HARDLY KEEP WORD OF THESE DOINGS FROM HIS LOVING WIFE. AFTER ALL, BY SOME COUNTS, THE AMOUNT OF IMPALEMENTS REACHED THE INCREDIBLE NUMBER OF 100,000!
I AM HERE, VLAD.
WHAT DO YOU WANT?
I THOUGHT I WOULD INVITE YOU TO MY CHAMBERS, MY PRINCESS.
I BELIEVE IT'S BEEN MANY NIGHTS SINCE WE--
I BELIEVE IT WILL BE *MANY* NIGHTS MORE-
I HAVE LEARNED SOME ***FRIGHTENING*** THINGS ABOUT YOU, MY PRINCE.
I KNEW SOME MEN HAD BEEN IMPALED...
BUT THOUSANDS AND ***THOUSANDS!*** MEN, WOMEN, AND, MY GOD, ***CHILDREN!***

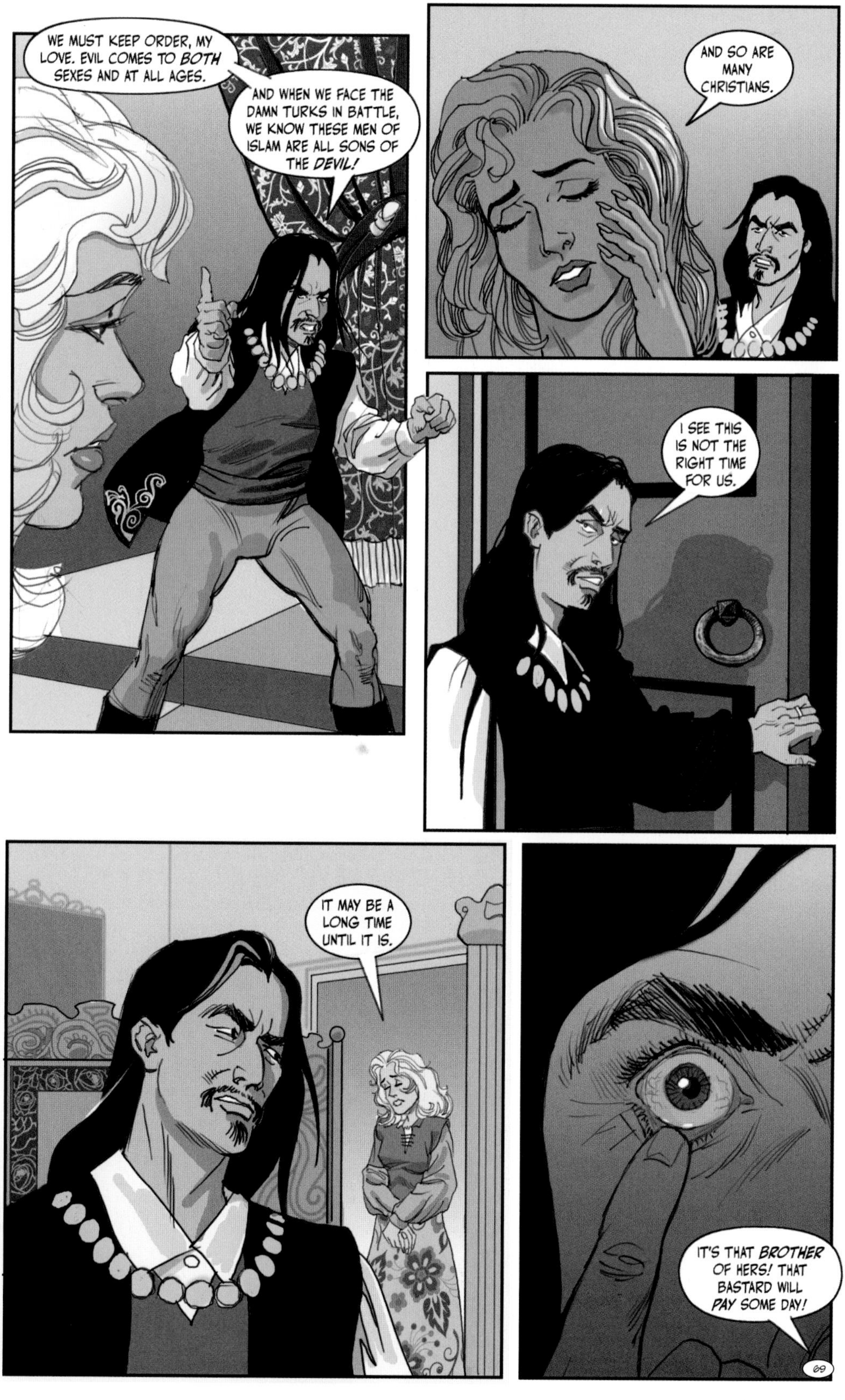
WE MUST KEEP ORDER, MY LOVE. EVIL COMES TO *BOTH* SEXES AND AT ALL AGES.
AND WHEN WE FACE THE DAMN TURKS IN BATTLE, WE KNOW THESE MEN OF ISLAM ARE ALL SONS OF THE *DEVIL!*
AND SO ARE MANY CHRISTIANS.
I SEE THIS IS NOT THE RIGHT TIME FOR US.
IT MAY BE A LONG TIME UNTIL IT IS.
IT'S THAT *BROTHER* OF HERS! THAT BASTARD WILL *PAY* SOME DAY!

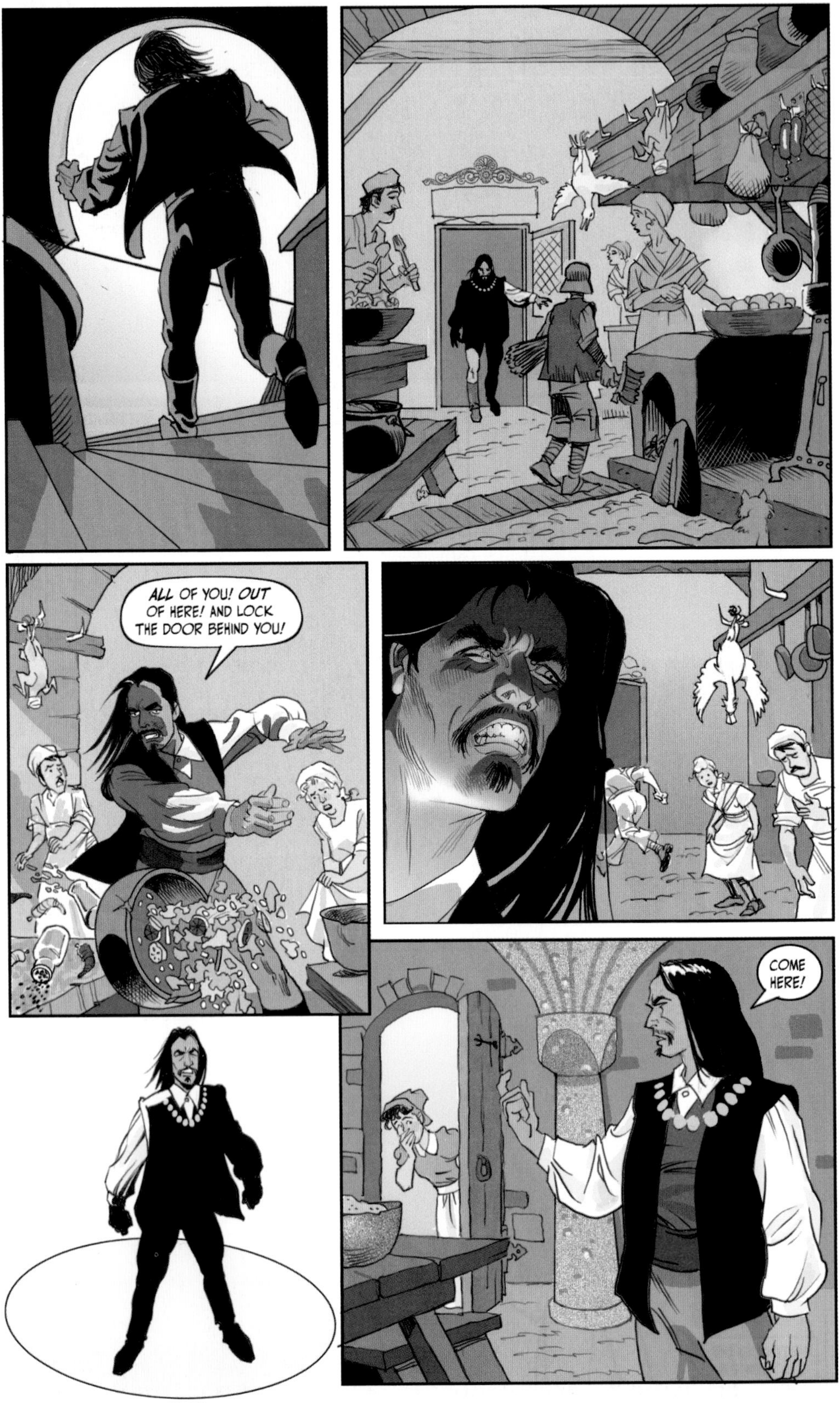
ALL OF YOU! OUT OF HERE! AND LOCK THE DOOR BEHIND YOU!
COME HERE!

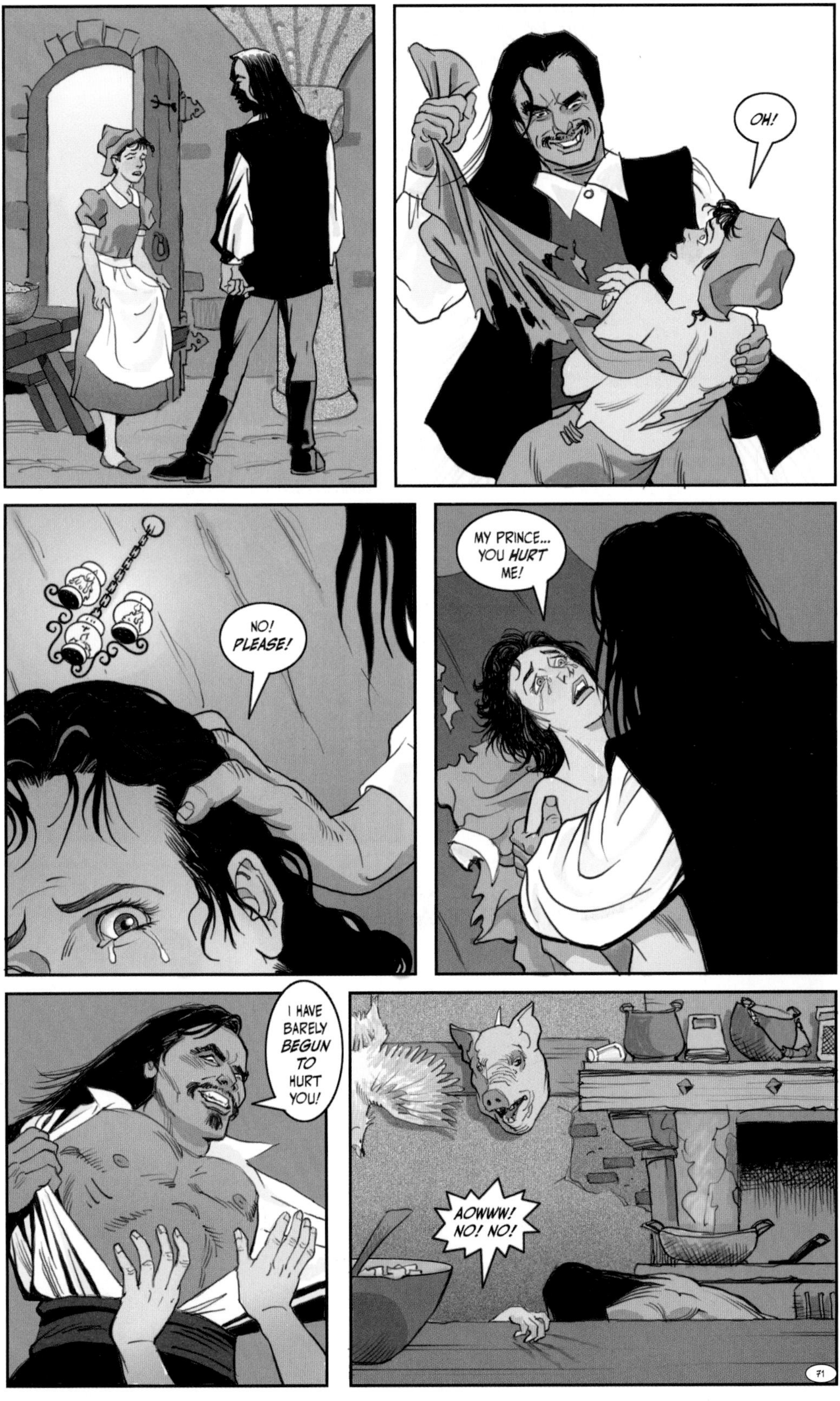
OH!
NO! PLEASE!
MY PRINCE... YOU HURT ME!
I HAVE BARELY BEGUN TO HURT YOU!
AOWWW! NO! NO!

IN THE FIFTH YEAR OF VLAD'S RULE, THE PRINCE DID SOMETHING EVEN MORE DANGEROUS TO HIS REIGN.

THIS IS *TOO MUCH!* WE WILL CEASE PAYING TRIBUTE TO THE OTTOMANS!

THEY HELPED BRING YOU THIS THRONE.

BUT PRINCE, THAT WAS YOUR BARGAIN WITH THEM.

LET THEM *DARE* TAKE IT FROM ME!

HE CAN'T BE REASONED WITH WHEN HE GETS LIKE THIS.

IT'S MUCH BECAUSE OF YOUR *SISTER!*

SHE HAS REFUSED TO BE WITH HIM FOR TOO LONG.

I KNOW...

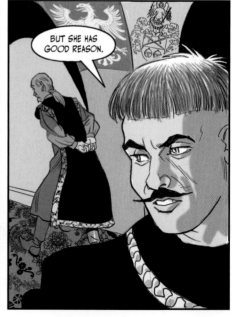

BUT SHE HAS GOOD REASON.

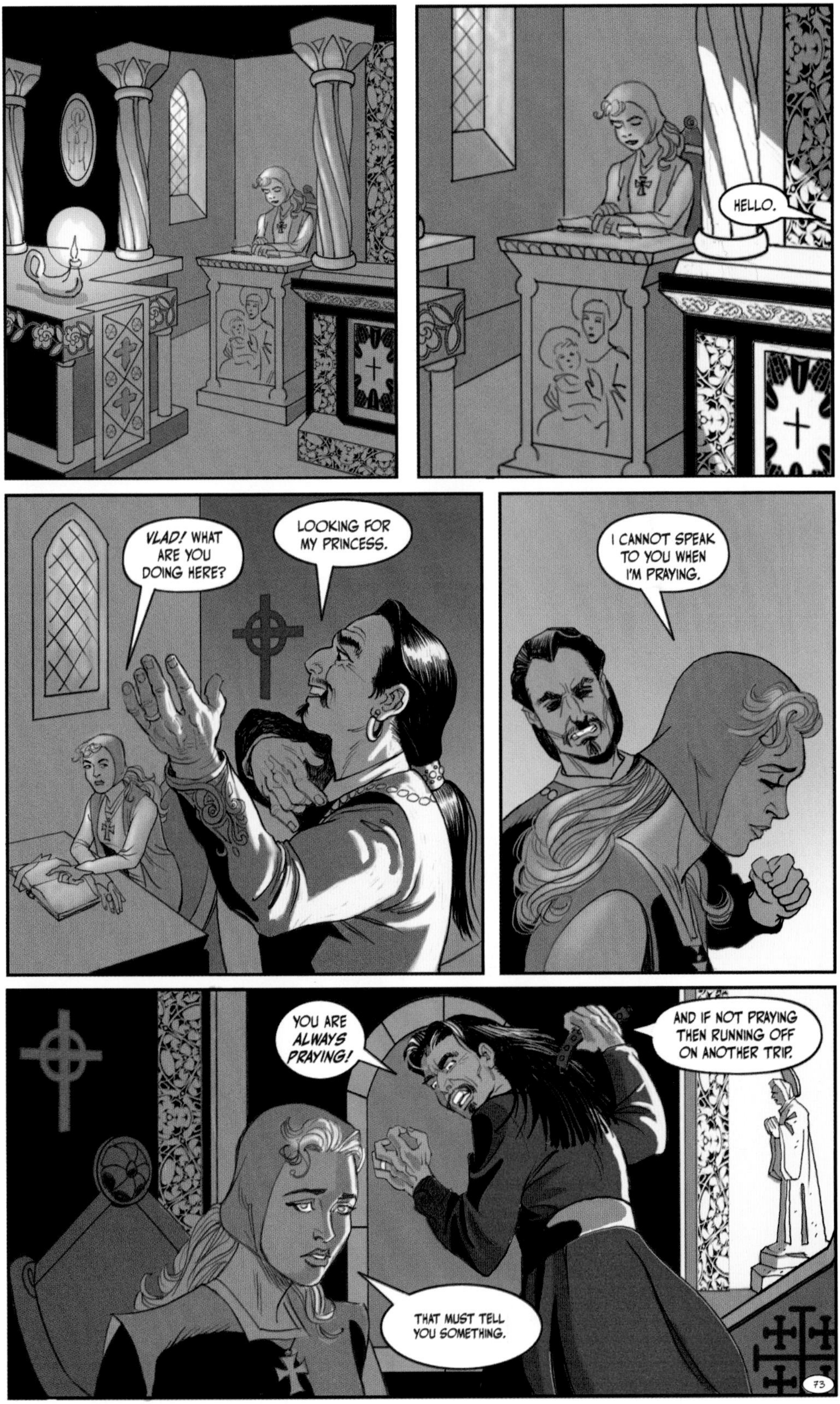
HELLO.
VLAD! WHAT ARE YOU DOING HERE?
LOOKING FOR MY PRINCESS.
I CANNOT SPEAK TO YOU WHEN I'M PRAYING.
YOU ARE ALWAYS PRAYING!
AND IF NOT PRAYING THEN RUNNING OFF ON ANOTHER TRIP.
THAT MUST TELL YOU SOMETHING.

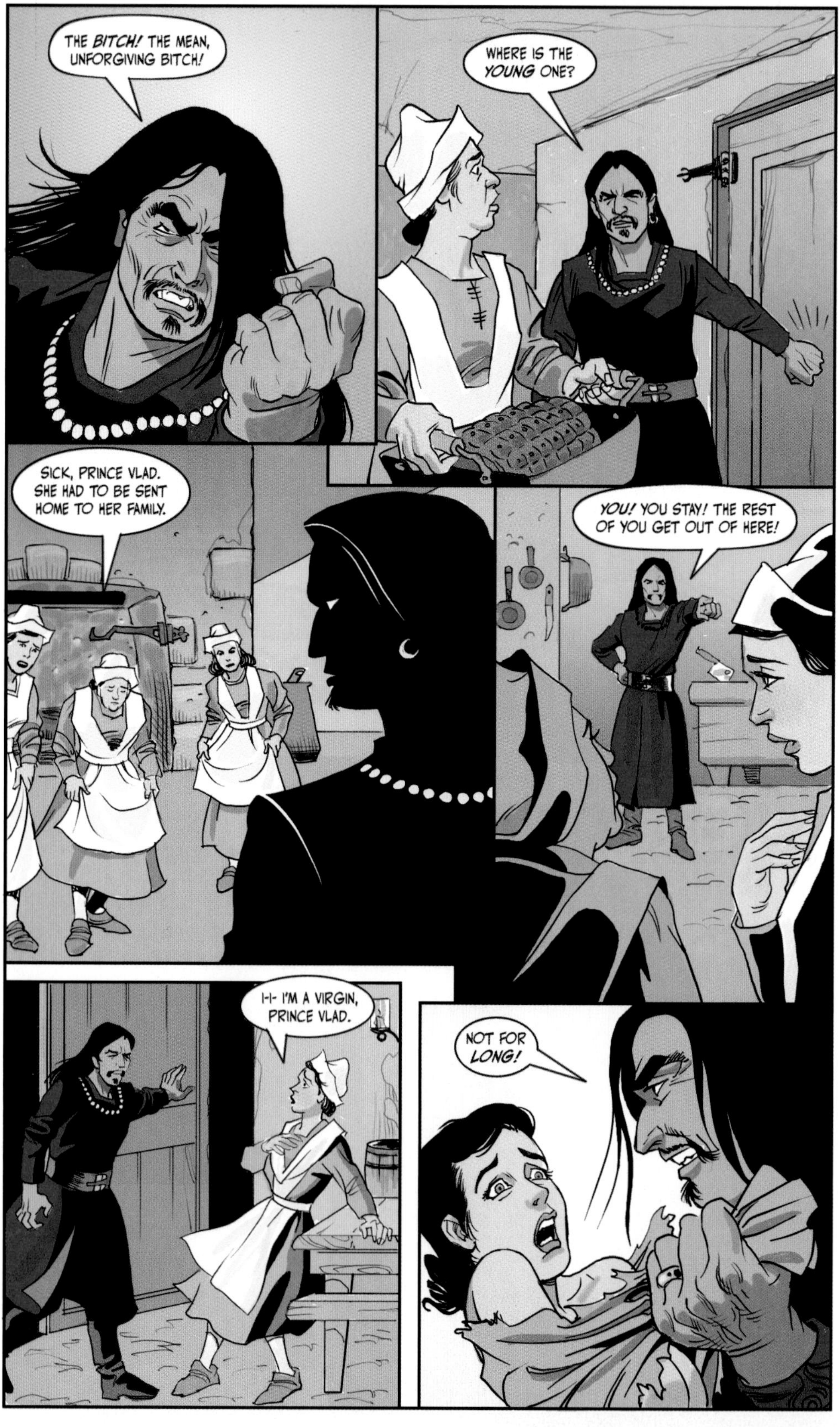
THE BITCH! THE MEAN, UNFORGIVING BITCH!
WHERE IS THE YOUNG ONE?
SICK, PRINCE VLAD. SHE HAD TO BE SENT HOME TO HER FAMILY.
YOU! YOU STAY! THE REST OF YOU GET OUT OF HERE!
I-I- I'M A VIRGIN, PRINCE VLAD.
NOT FOR LONG!

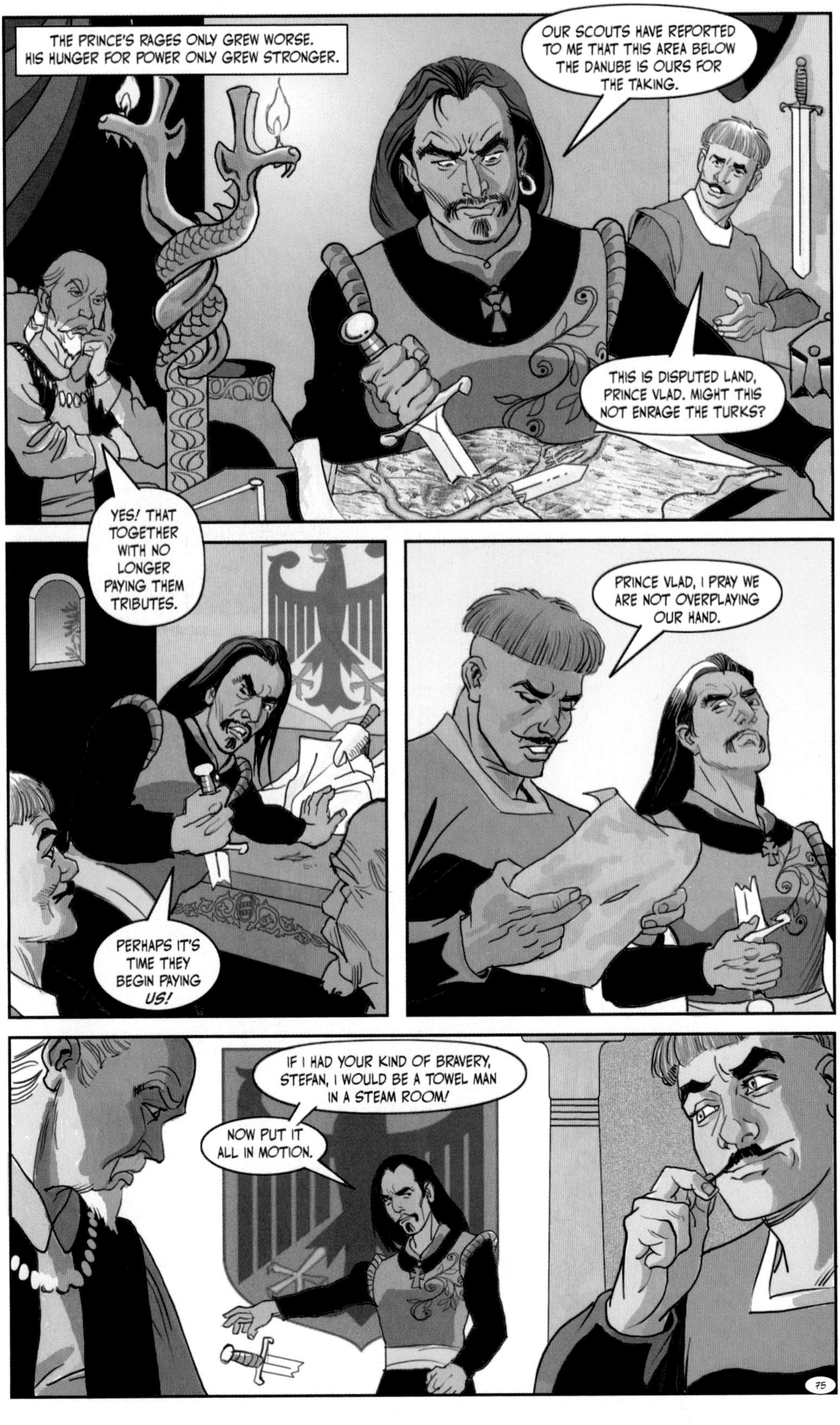
THE PRINCE'S RAGES ONLY GREW WORSE. HIS HUNGER FOR POWER ONLY GREW STRONGER.
OUR SCOUTS HAVE REPORTED TO ME THAT THIS AREA BELOW THE DANUBE IS OURS FOR THE TAKING.
THIS IS DISPUTED LAND, PRINCE VLAD. MIGHT THIS NOT ENRAGE THE TURKS?
YES! THAT TOGETHER WITH NO LONGER PAYING THEM TRIBUTES.
PERHAPS IT'S TIME THEY BEGIN PAYING *US!*
PRINCE VLAD, I PRAY WE ARE NOT OVERPLAYING OUR HAND.
IF I HAD YOUR KIND OF BRAVERY, STEFAN, I WOULD BE A TOWEL MAN IN A STEAM ROOM!
NOW PUT IT ALL IN MOTION.

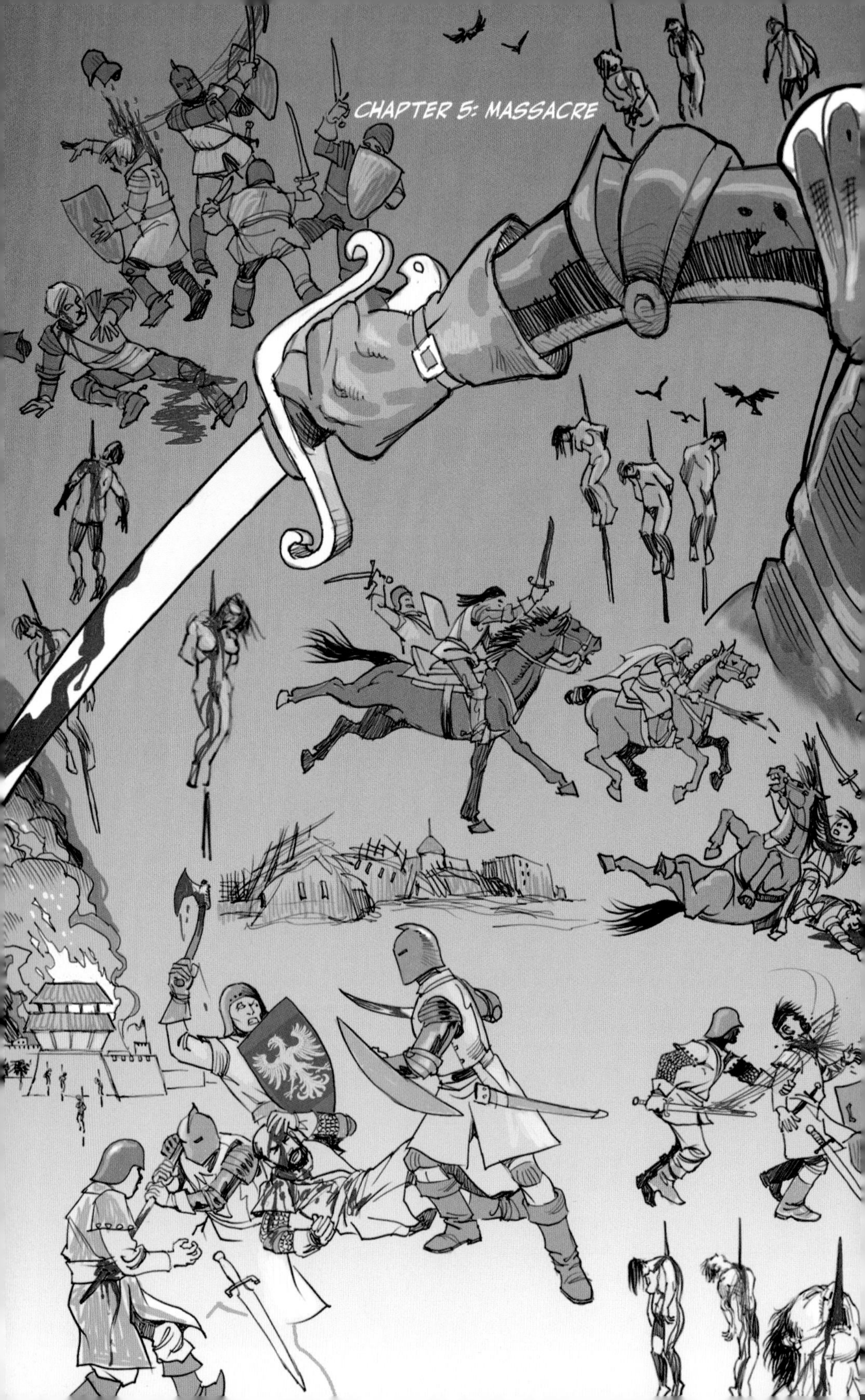
CHAPTER 5: MASSACRE

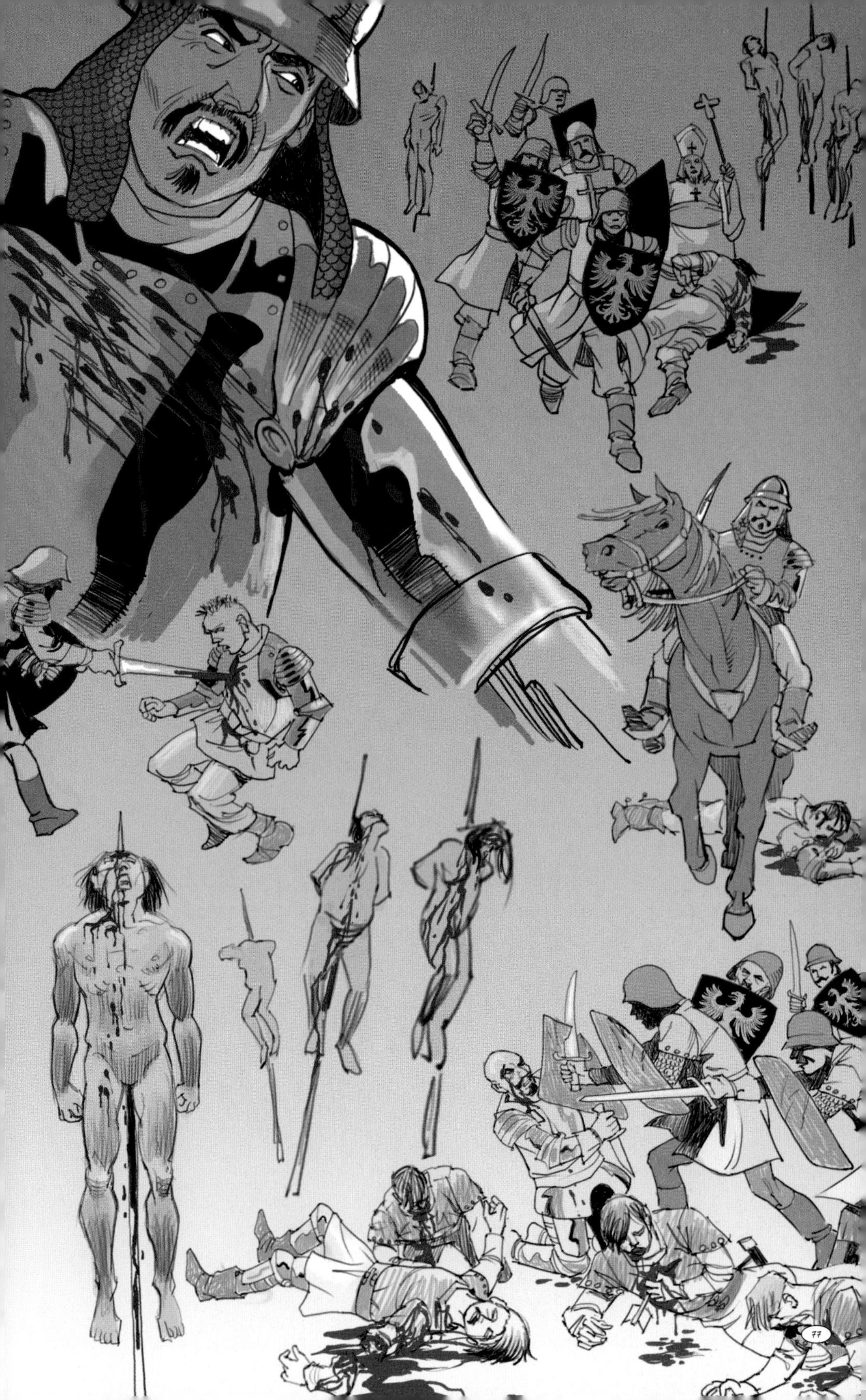

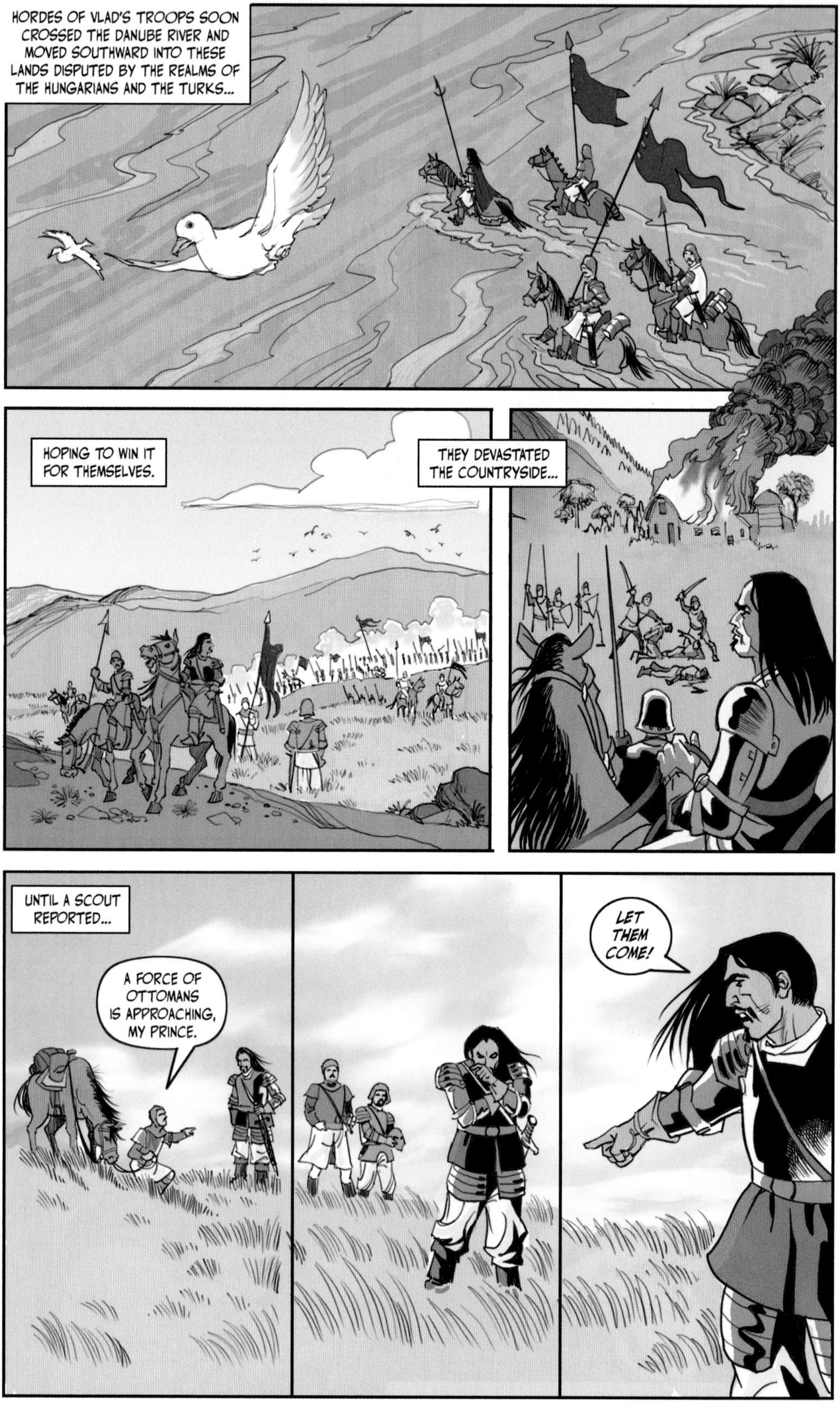
HORDES OF VLAD'S TROOPS SOON CROSSED THE DANUBE RIVER AND MOVED SOUTHWARD INTO THESE LANDS DISPUTED BY THE REALMS OF THE HUNGARIANS AND THE TURKS...
HOPING TO WIN IT FOR THEMSELVES.
THEY DEVASTATED THE COUNTRYSIDE...
UNTIL A SCOUT REPORTED...
A FORCE OF OTTOMANS IS APPROACHING, MY PRINCE.
LET THEM COME!

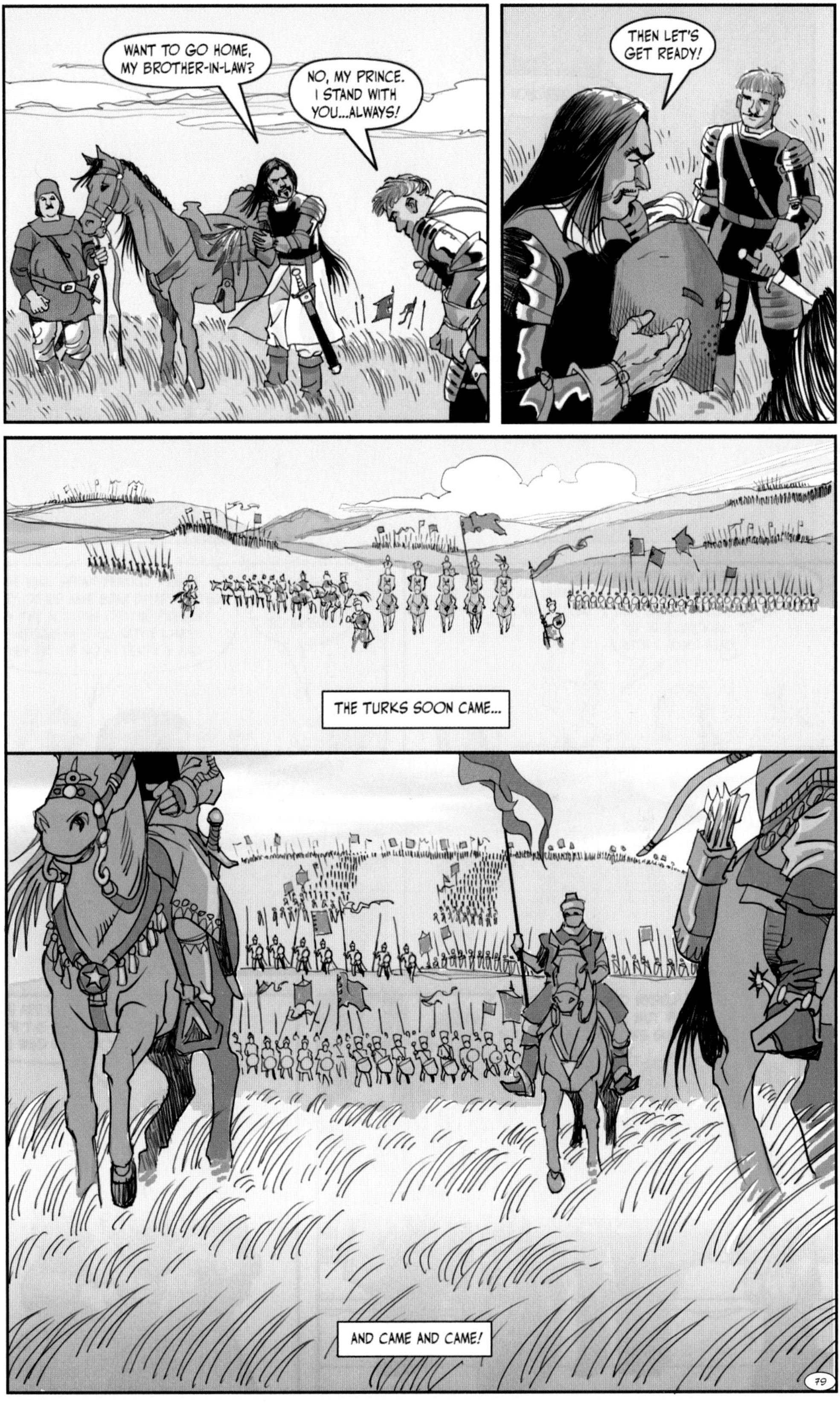
WANT TO GO HOME, MY BROTHER-IN-LAW?
NO, MY PRINCE. I STAND WITH YOU...ALWAYS!
THEN LET'S GET READY!
THE TURKS SOON CAME...
AND CAME AND CAME!

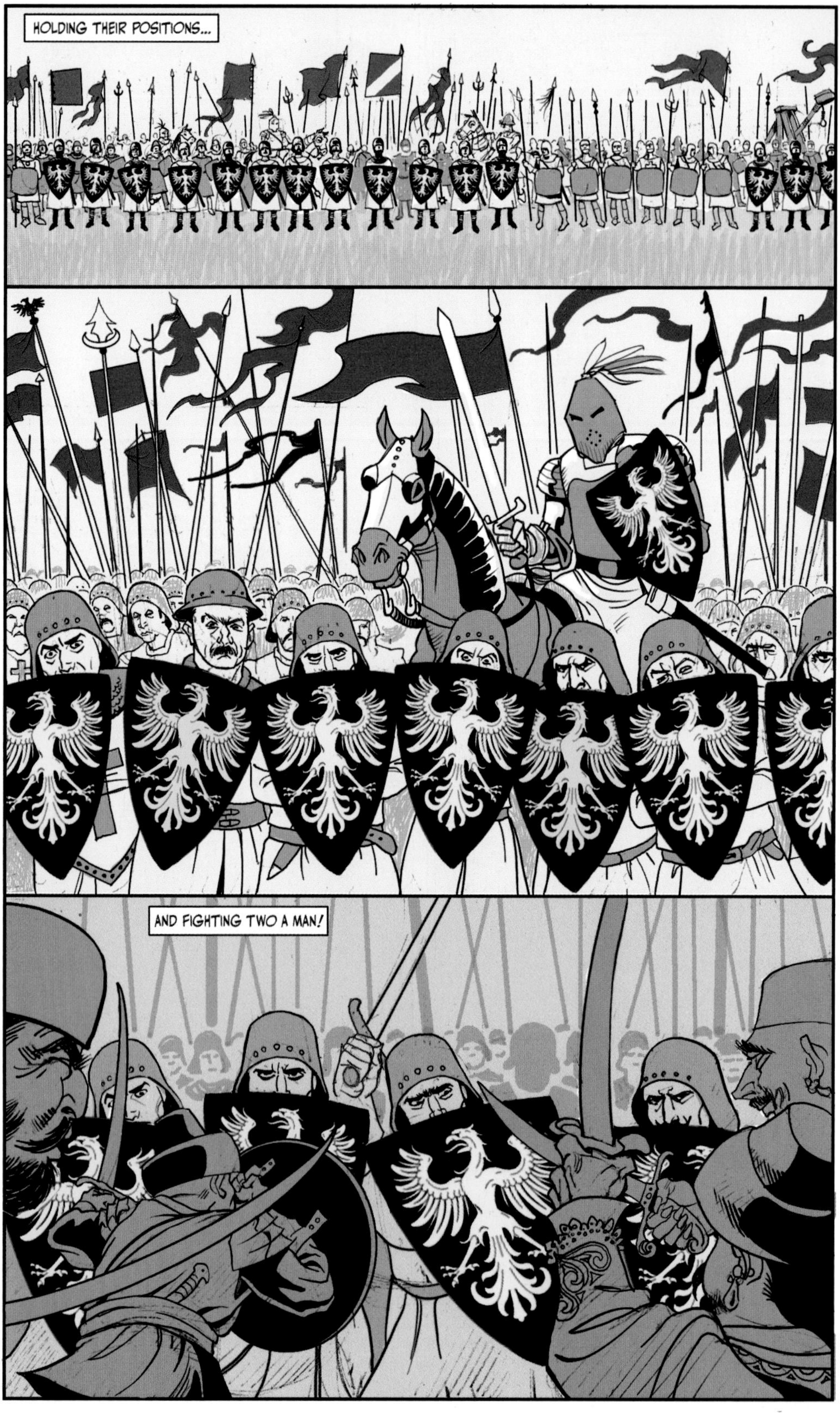
HOLDING THEIR POSITIONS...
AND FIGHTING TWO A MAN!

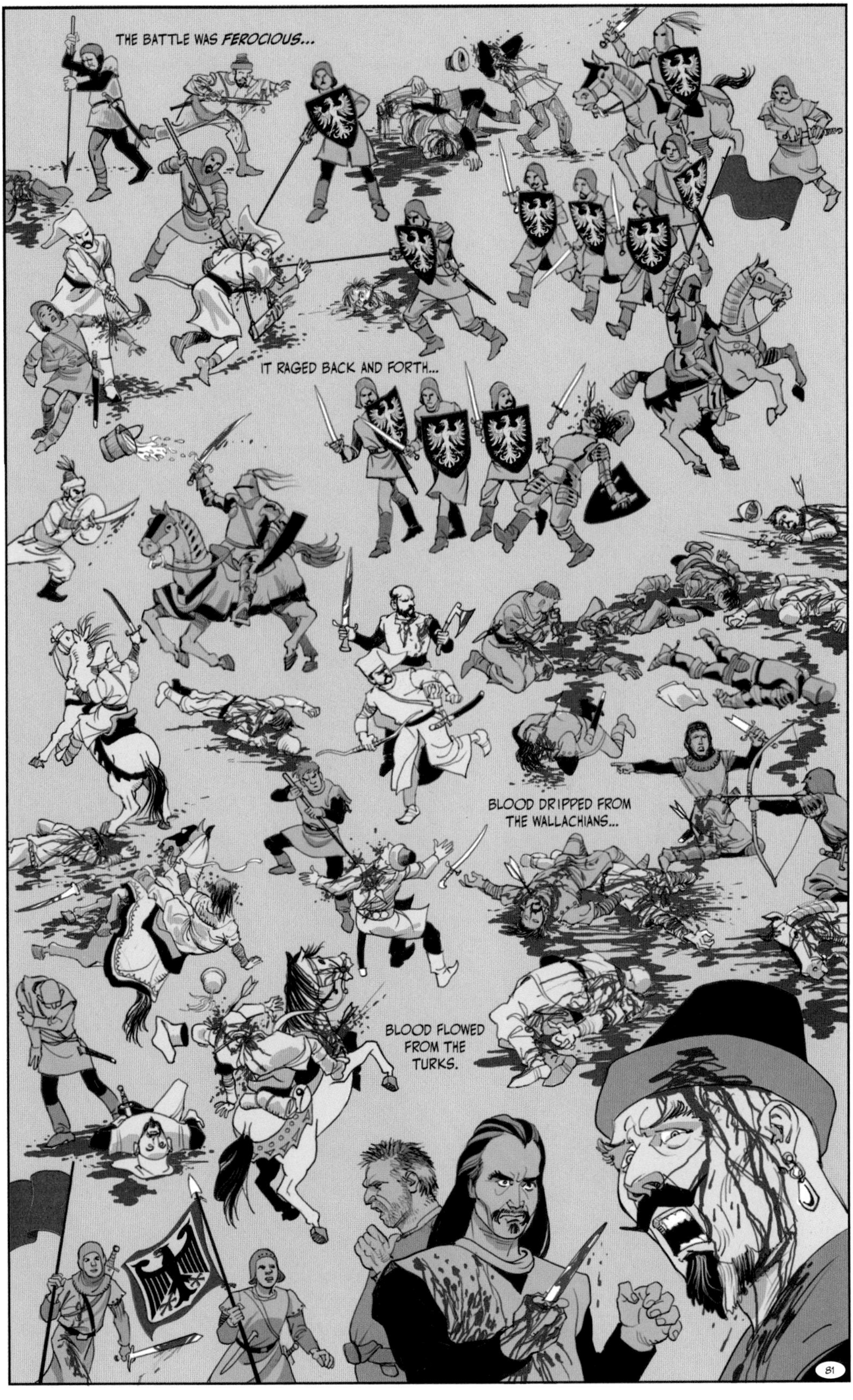
THE BATTLE WAS *FEROCIOUS...*
IT RAGED BACK AND FORTH...
BLOOD DRIPPED FROM THE WALLACHIANS...
BLOOD FLOWED FROM THE TURKS.

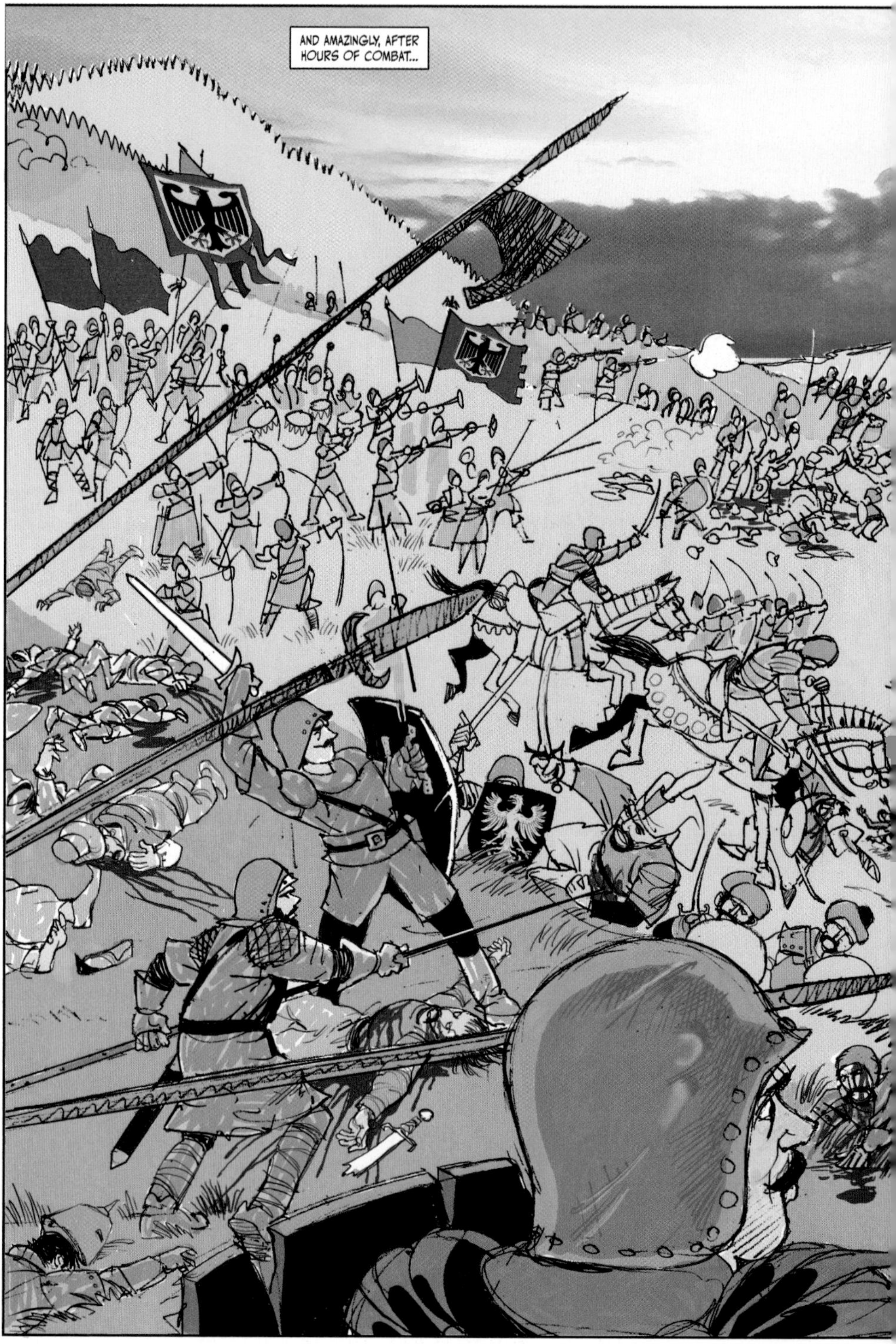
AND AMAZINGLY, AFTER HOURS OF COMBAT...

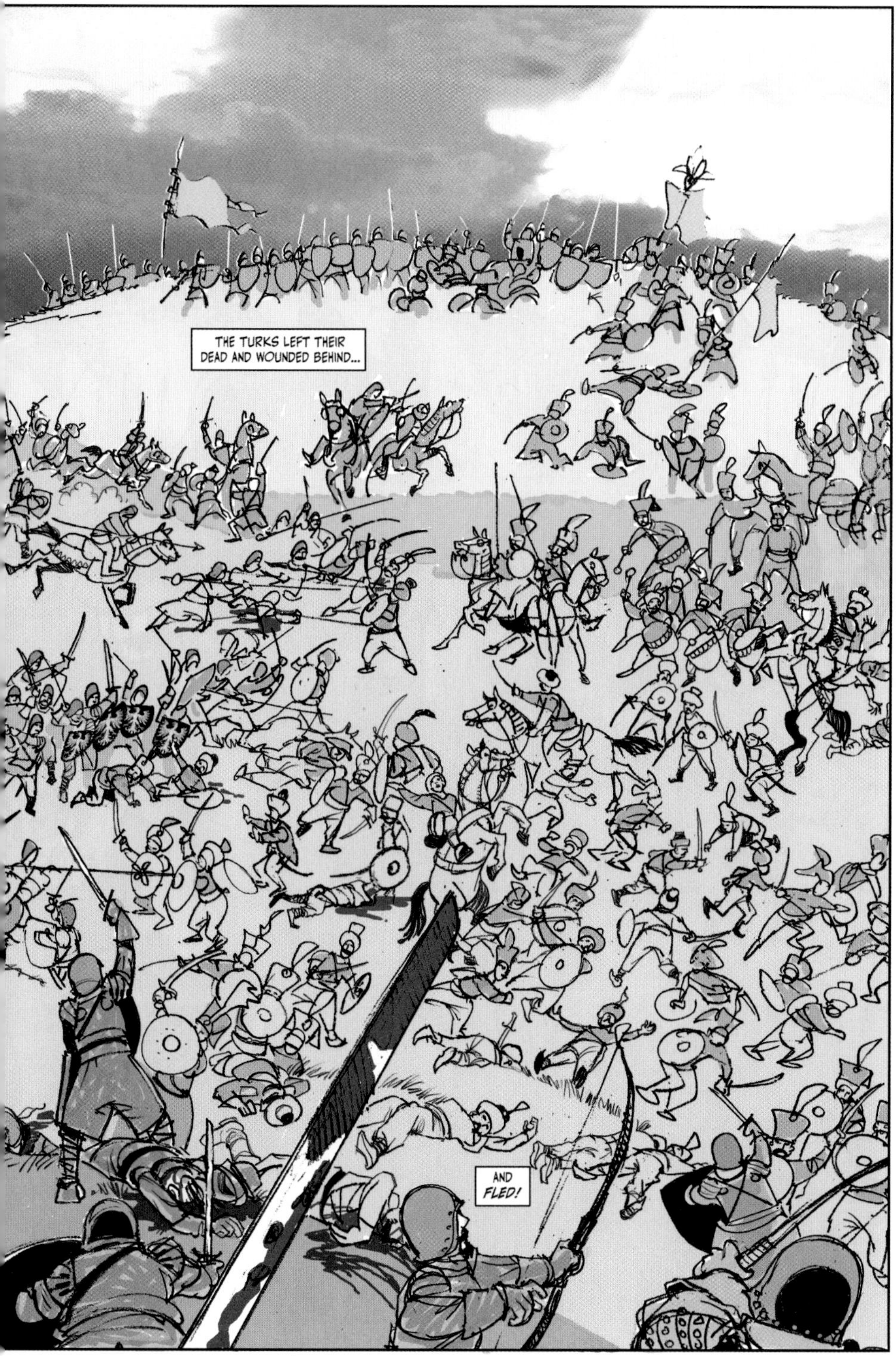
THE TURKS LEFT THEIR DEAD AND WOUNDED BEHIND...
AND *FLED!*

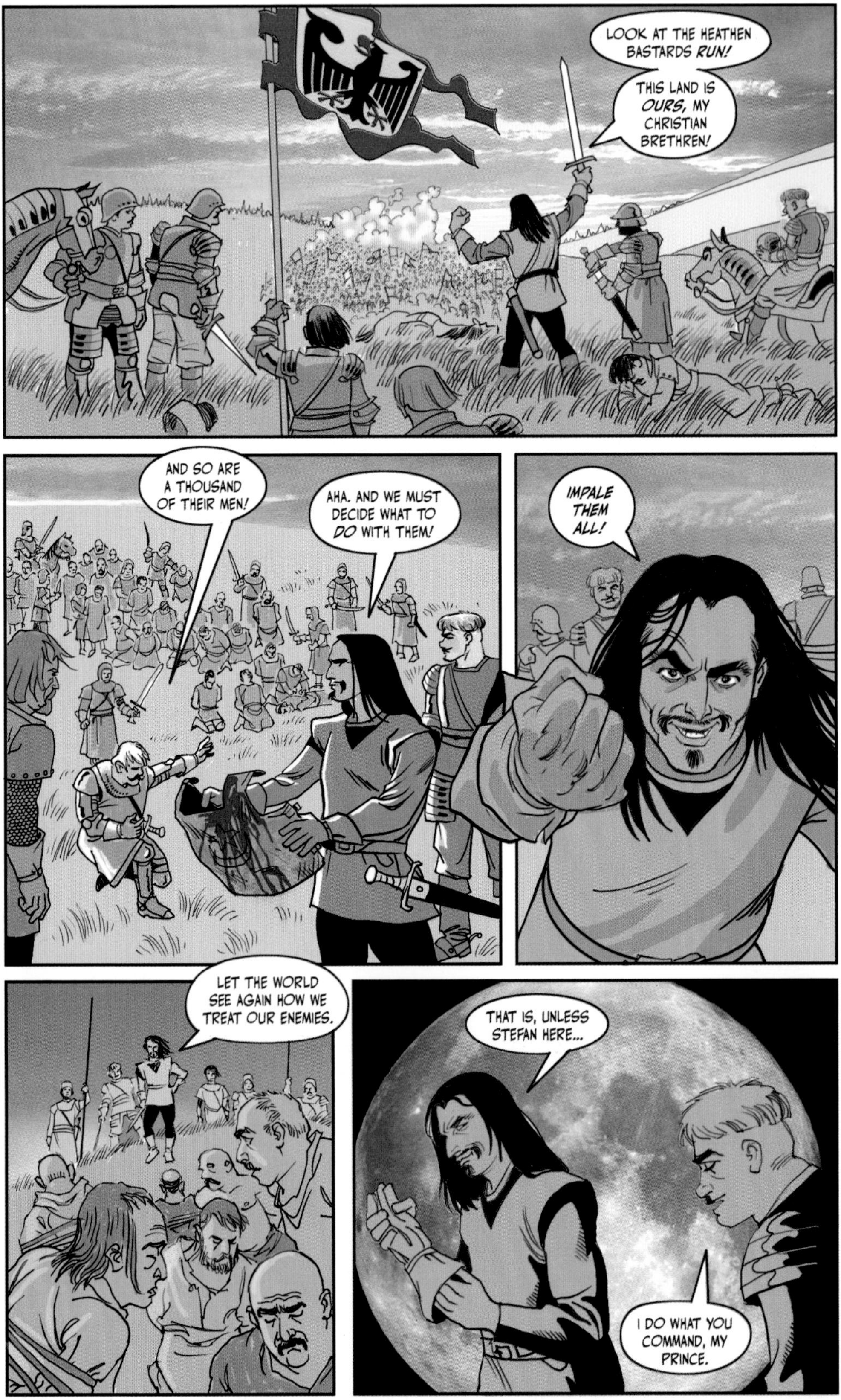
LOOK AT THE HEATHEN BASTARDS *RUN!*
THIS LAND IS *OURS,* MY CHRISTIAN BRETHREN!
AND SO ARE A THOUSAND OF THEIR MEN!
AHA. AND WE MUST DECIDE WHAT TO *DO* WITH THEM!
IMPALE THEM ALL!
LET THE WORLD SEE AGAIN HOW WE TREAT OUR ENEMIES.
THAT IS, UNLESS STEFAN HERE...
I DO WHAT YOU COMMAND, MY PRINCE.

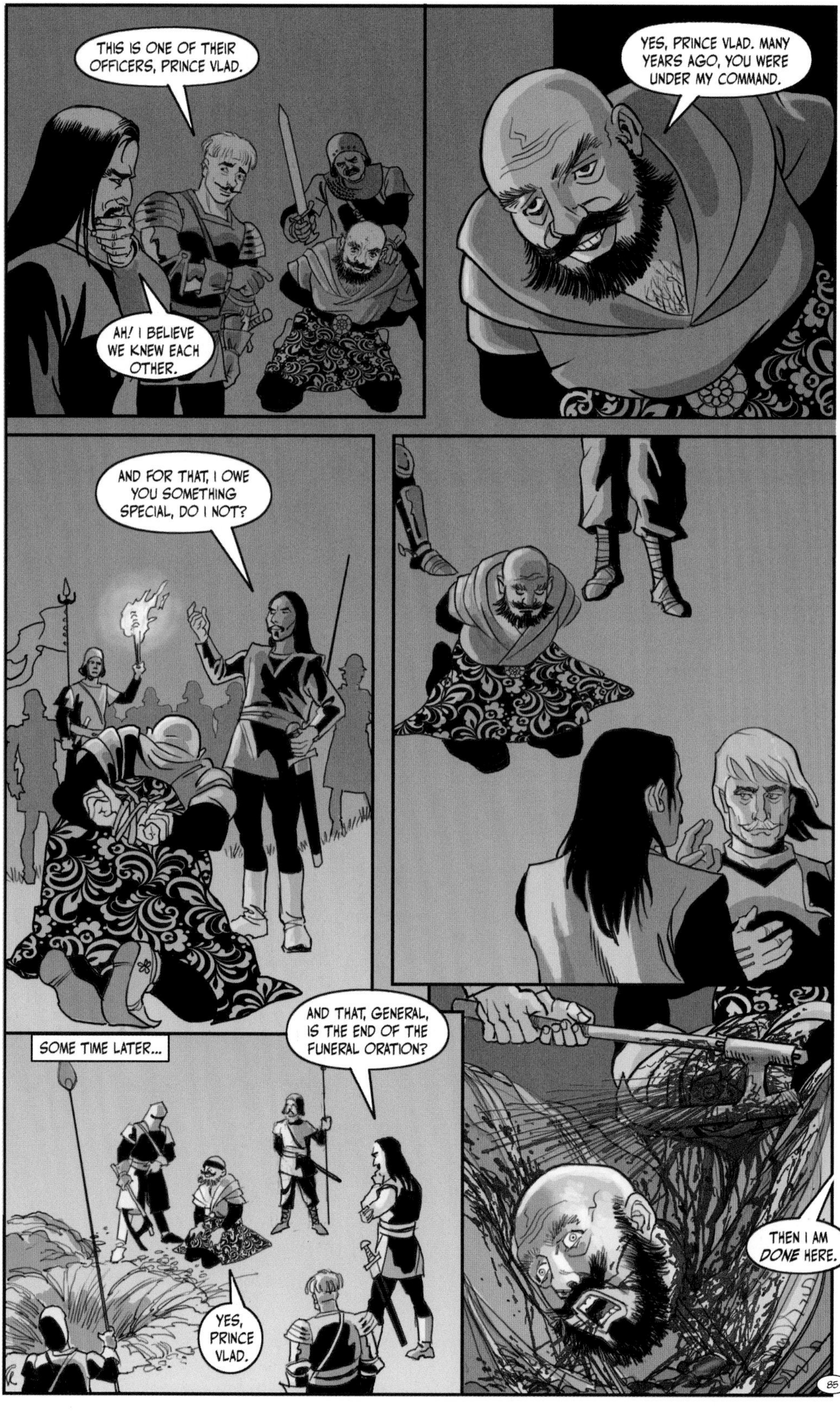
THIS IS ONE OF THEIR OFFICERS, PRINCE VLAD.
AH! I BELIEVE WE KNEW EACH OTHER.
YES, PRINCE VLAD. MANY YEARS AGO, YOU WERE UNDER MY COMMAND.
AND FOR THAT, I OWE YOU SOMETHING SPECIAL, DO I NOT?
SOME TIME LATER...
AND THAT, GENERAL, IS THE END OF THE FUNERAL ORATION?
YES, PRINCE VLAD.
THEN I AM DONE HERE.

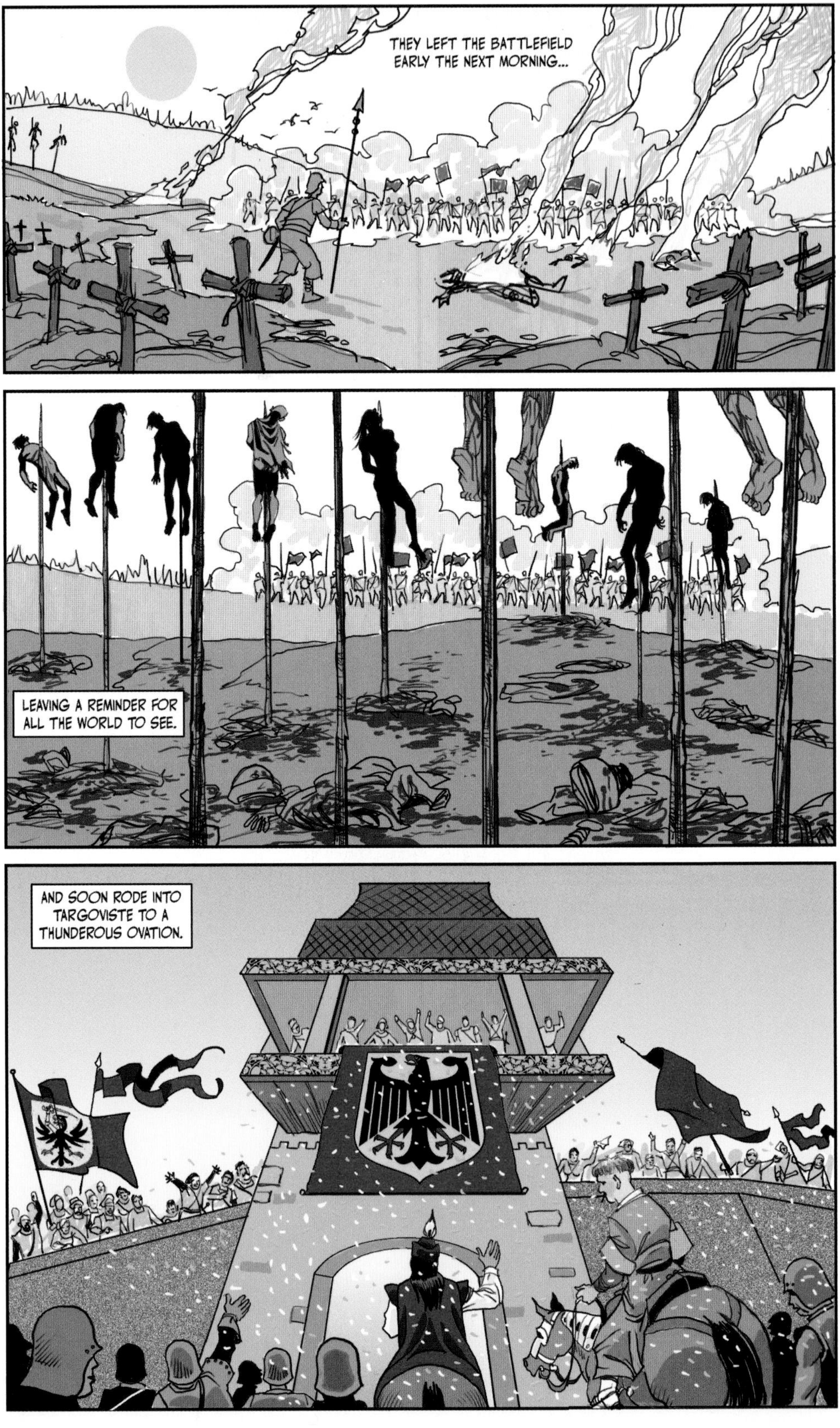

THEY LEFT THE BATTLEFIELD EARLY THE NEXT MORNING...
LEAVING A REMINDER FOR ALL THE WORLD TO SEE.
AND SOON RODE INTO TARGOVISTE TO A THUNDEROUS OVATION.

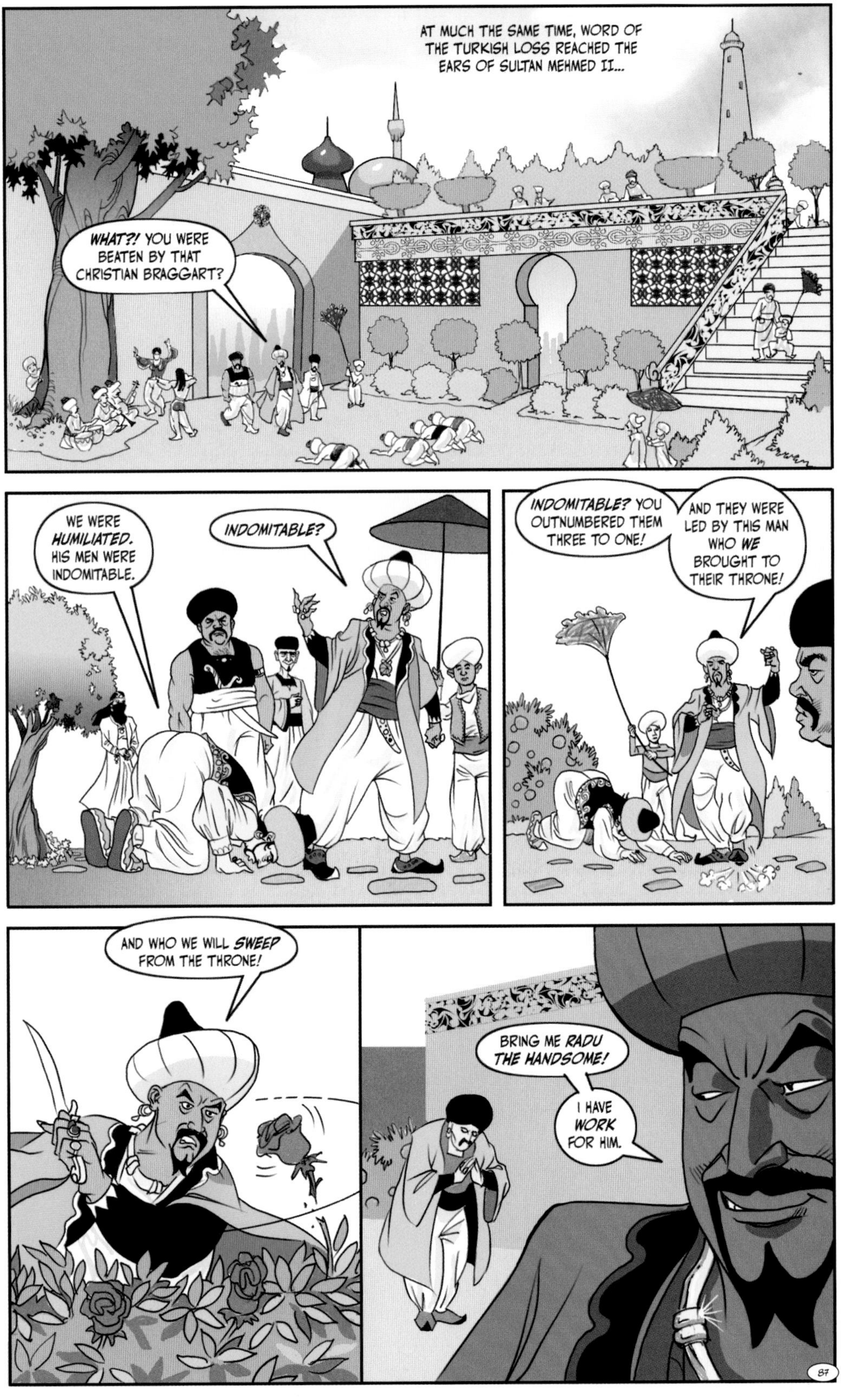
AT MUCH THE SAME TIME, WORD OF THE TURKISH LOSS REACHED THE EARS OF SULTAN MEHMED II...
WHAT?! YOU WERE BEATEN BY THAT CHRISTIAN BRAGGART?
WE WERE HUMILIATED. HIS MEN WERE INDOMITABLE.
INDOMITABLE?
INDOMITABLE? YOU OUTNUMBERED THEM THREE TO ONE!
AND THEY WERE LED BY THIS MAN WHO WE BROUGHT TO THEIR THRONE!
AND WHO WE WILL SWEEP FROM THE THRONE!
BRING ME RADU THE HANDSOME!
I HAVE WORK FOR HIM.

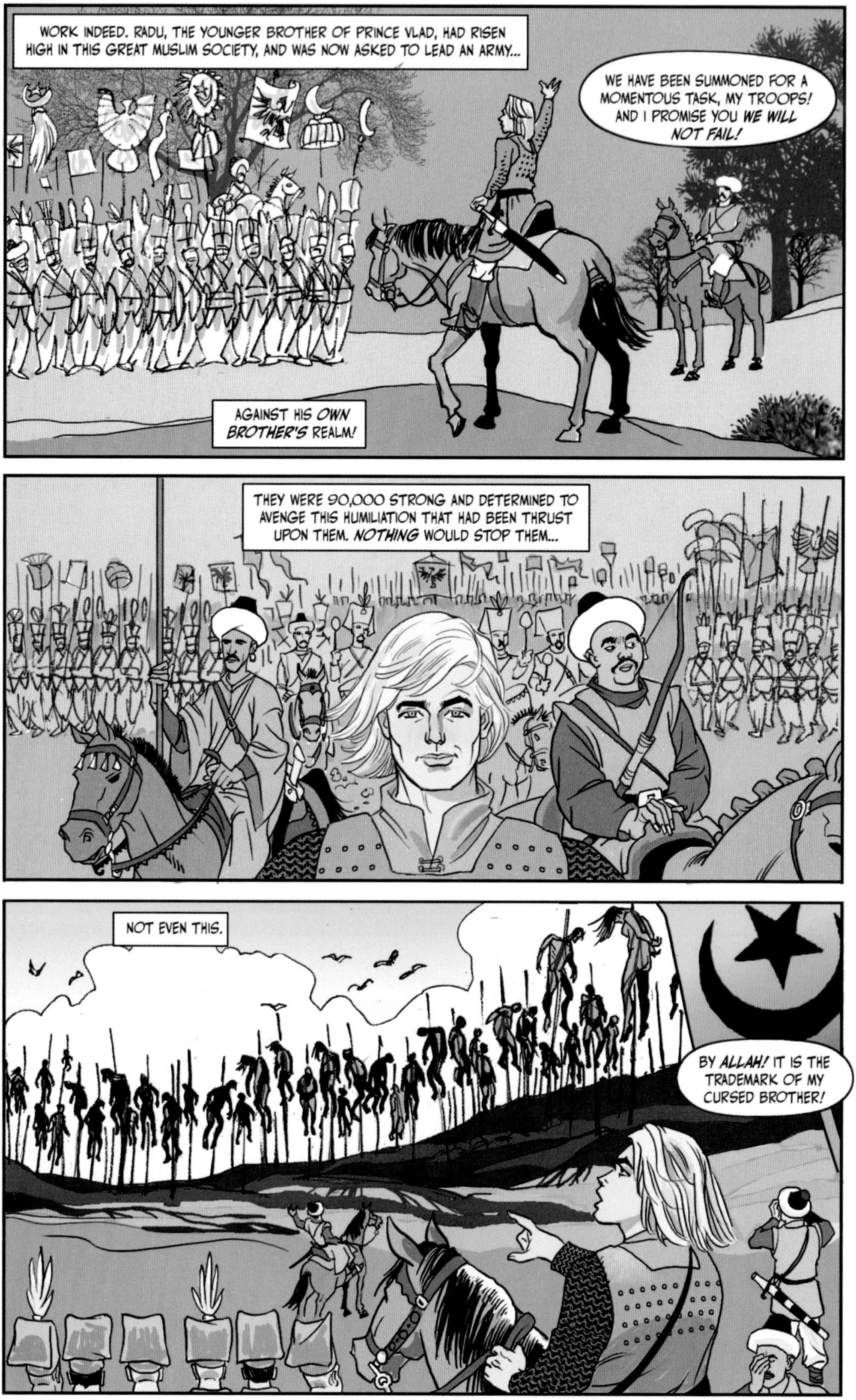
WORK INDEED. RADU, THE YOUNGER BROTHER OF PRINCE VLAD, HAD RISEN HIGH IN THIS GREAT MUSLIM SOCIETY, AND WAS NOW ASKED TO LEAD AN ARMY...
WE HAVE BEEN SUMMONED FOR A MOMENTOUS TASK, MY TROOPS! AND I PROMISE YOU *WE WILL NOT FAIL!*
AGAINST HIS *OWN BROTHER'S* REALM!
THEY WERE 90,000 STRONG AND DETERMINED TO AVENGE THIS HUMILIATION THAT HAD BEEN THRUST UPON THEM. *NOTHING* WOULD STOP THEM...
NOT EVEN THIS.
BY *ALLAH!* IT IS THE TRADEMARK OF MY CURSED BROTHER!

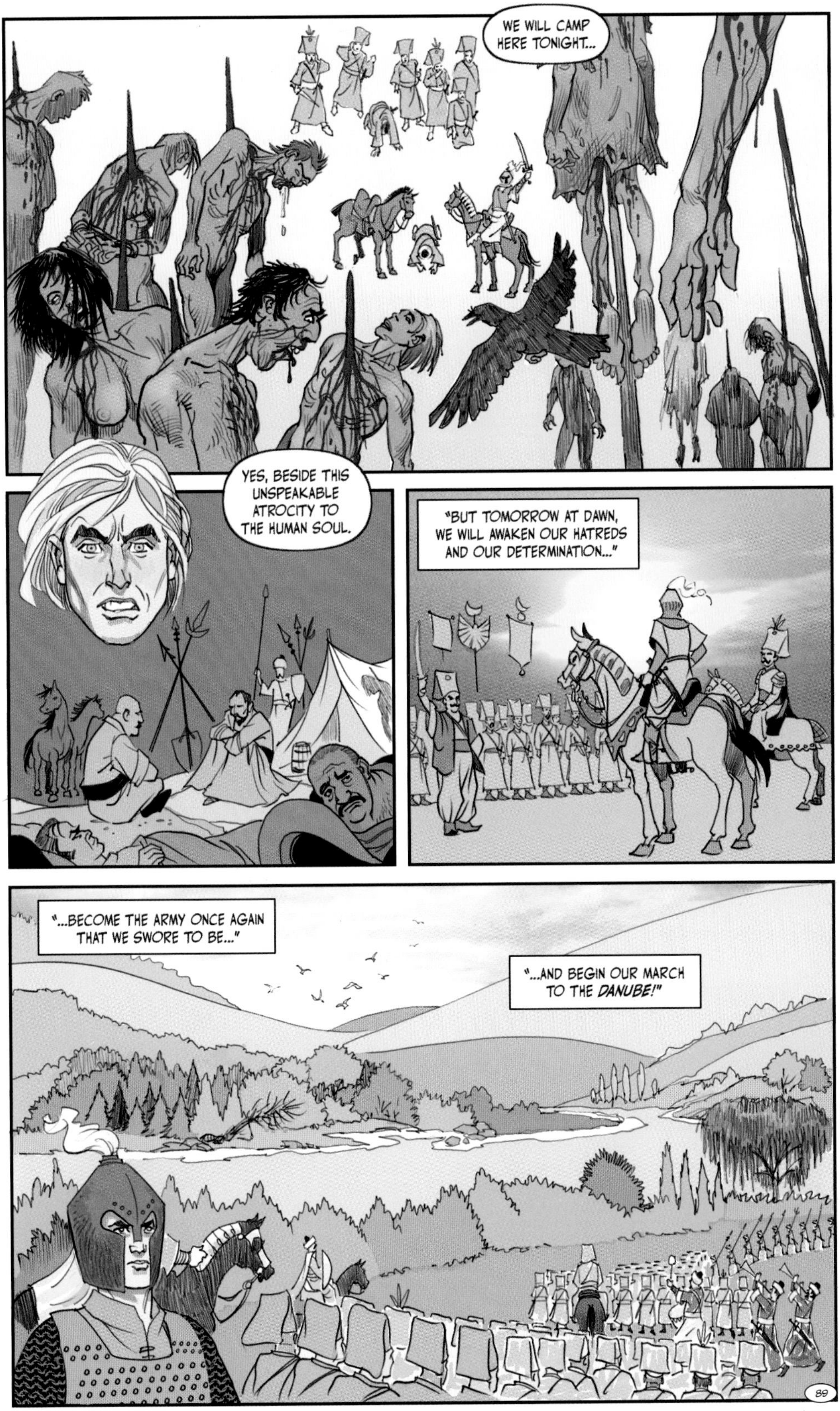

WE WILL CAMP HERE TONIGHT...
YES, BESIDE THIS UNSPEAKABLE ATROCITY TO THE HUMAN SOUL.
"BUT TOMORROW AT DAWN, WE WILL AWAKEN OUR HATREDS AND OUR DETERMINATION..."
"...BECOME THE ARMY ONCE AGAIN THAT WE SWORE TO BE..."
"...AND BEGIN OUR MARCH TO THE *DANUBE!*"

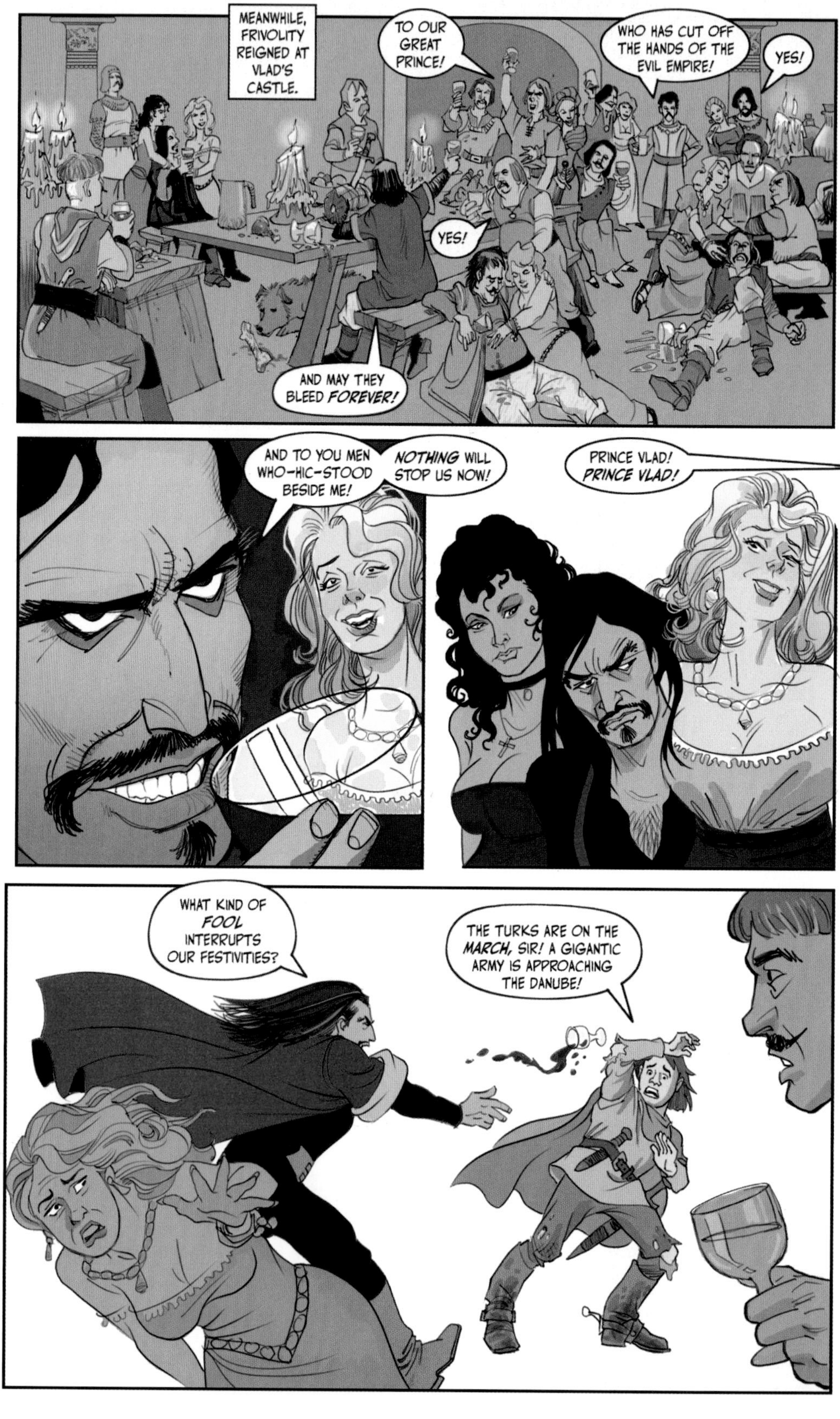

MEANWHILE, FRIVOLITY REIGNED AT VLAD'S CASTLE.
TO OUR GREAT PRINCE!
WHO HAS CUT OFF THE HANDS OF THE EVIL EMPIRE!
YES!
YES!
AND MAY THEY BLEED *FOREVER!*
AND TO YOU MEN WHO–HIC–STOOD BESIDE ME!
NOTHING WILL STOP US NOW!
PRINCE VLAD! *PRINCE VLAD!*
WHAT KIND OF *FOOL* INTERRUPTS OUR FESTIVITIES?
THE TURKS ARE ON THE *MARCH,* SIR! A GIGANTIC ARMY IS APPROACHING THE DANUBE!

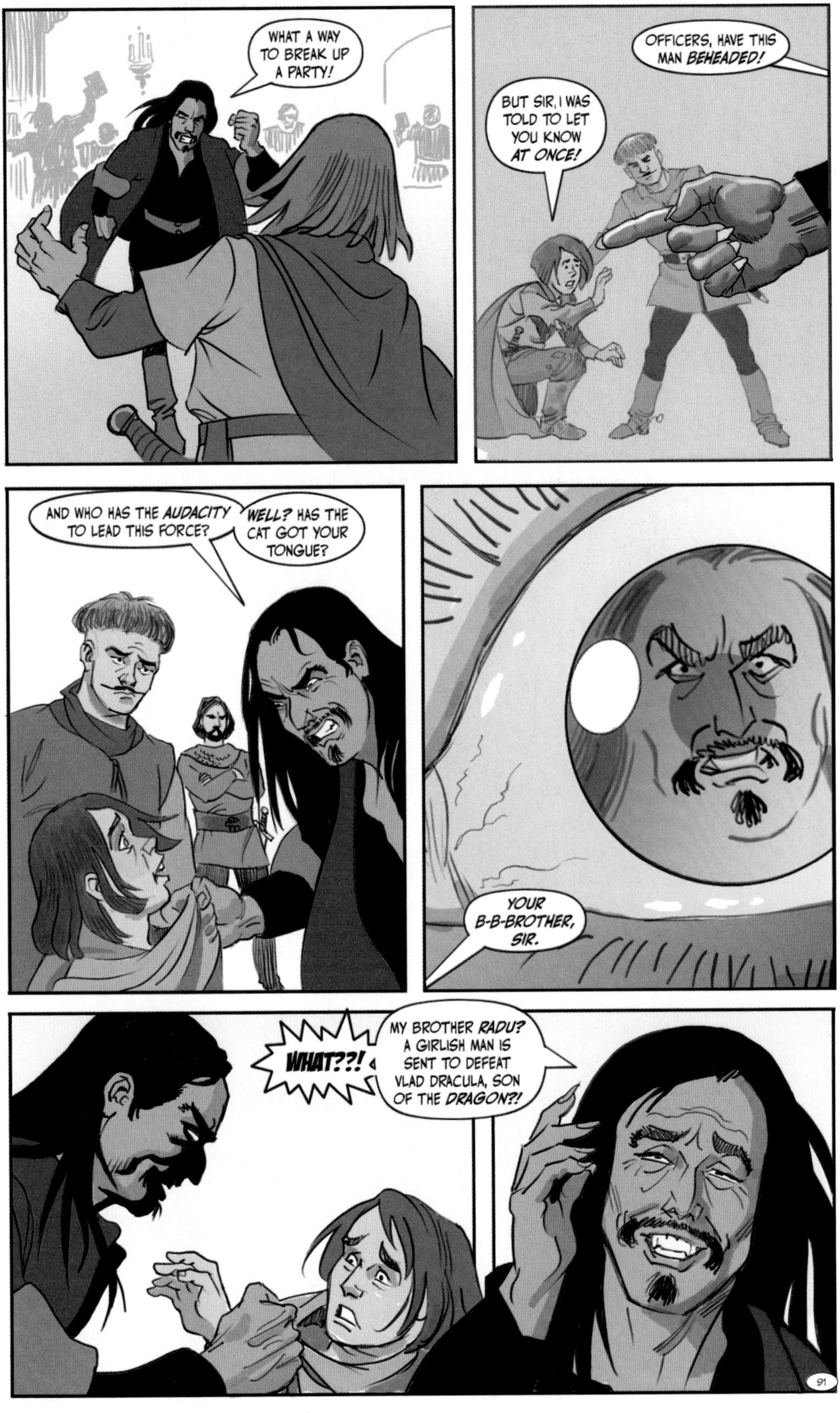
WHAT A WAY TO BREAK UP A PARTY!
OFFICERS, HAVE THIS MAN BEHEADED!
BUT SIR, I WAS TOLD TO LET YOU KNOW AT ONCE!
AND WHO HAS THE AUDACITY TO LEAD THIS FORCE?
WELL? HAS THE CAT GOT YOUR TONGUE?
YOUR B-B-BROTHER, SIR.
WHAT??!
MY BROTHER RADU? A GIRLISH MAN IS SENT TO DEFEAT VLAD DRACULA, SON OF THE DRAGON?!

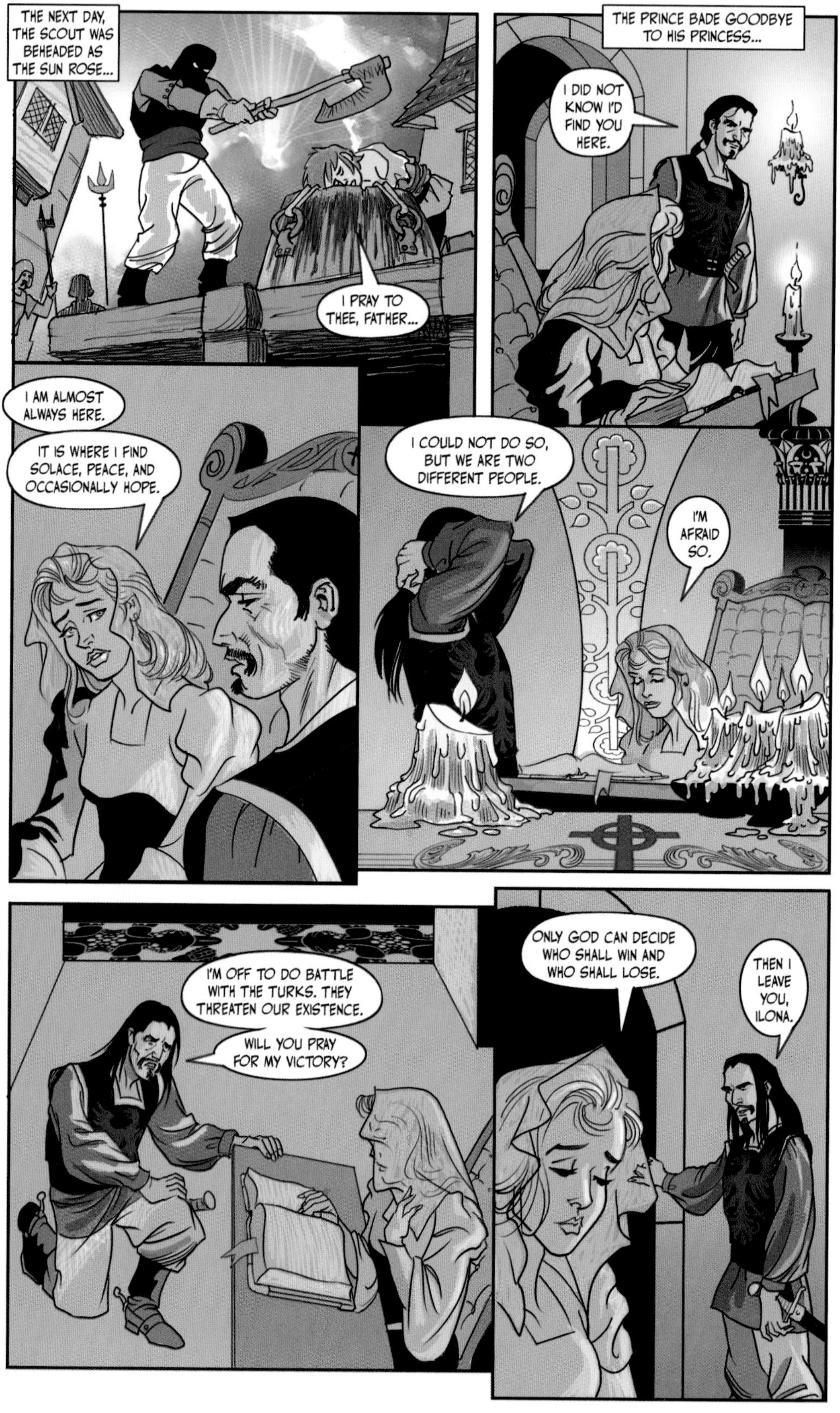
THE NEXT DAY, THE SCOUT WAS BEHEADED AS THE SUN ROSE...
I PRAY TO THEE, FATHER...
THE PRINCE BADE GOODBYE TO HIS PRINCESS...
I DID NOT KNOW I'D FIND YOU HERE.
I AM ALMOST ALWAYS HERE.
IT IS WHERE I FIND SOLACE, PEACE, AND OCCASIONALLY HOPE.
I COULD NOT DO SO, BUT WE ARE TWO DIFFERENT PEOPLE.
I'M AFRAID SO.
I'M OFF TO DO BATTLE WITH THE TURKS. THEY THREATEN OUR EXISTENCE.
WILL YOU PRAY FOR MY VICTORY?
ONLY GOD CAN DECIDE WHO SHALL WIN AND WHO SHALL LOSE.
THEN I LEAVE YOU, ILONA.

CHAPTER 6: BROTHERS

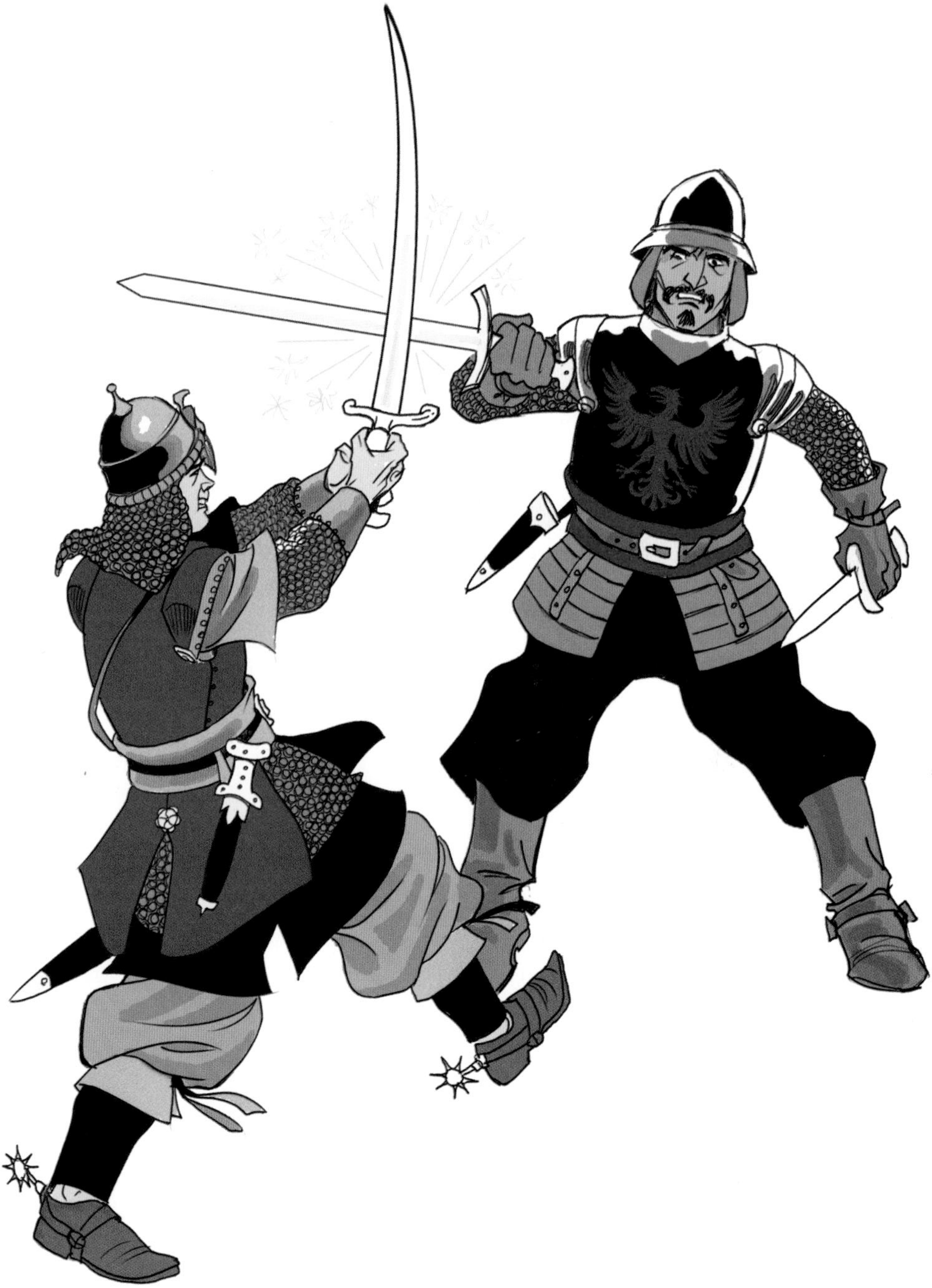

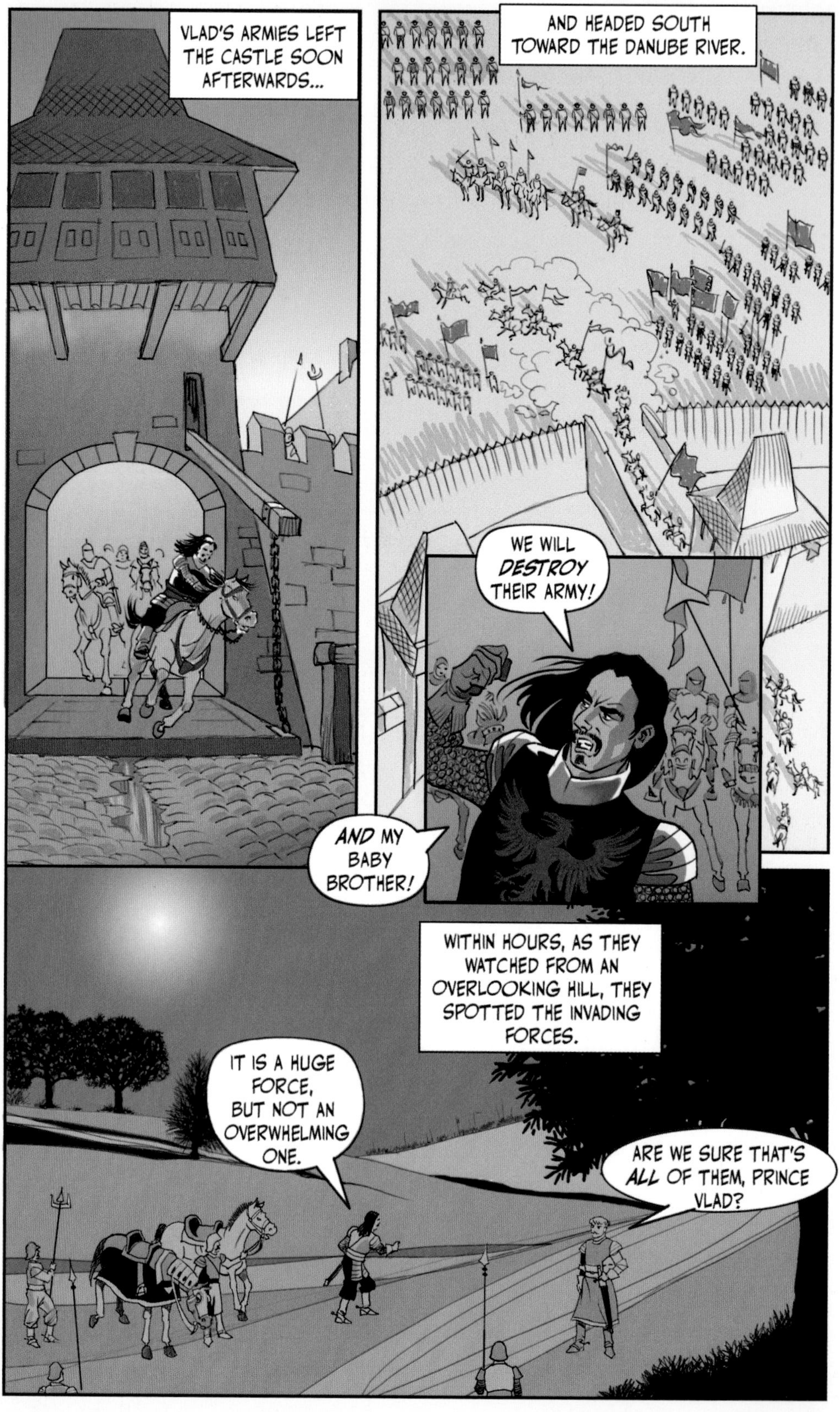
VLAD'S ARMIES LEFT THE CASTLE SOON AFTERWARDS...
AND HEADED SOUTH TOWARD THE DANUBE RIVER.
WE WILL *DESTROY* THEIR ARMY!
AND MY BABY BROTHER!
WITHIN HOURS, AS THEY WATCHED FROM AN OVERLOOKING HILL, THEY SPOTTED THE INVADING FORCES.
IT IS A HUGE FORCE, BUT NOT AN OVERWHELMING ONE.
ARE WE SURE THAT'S *ALL* OF THEM, PRINCE VLAD?

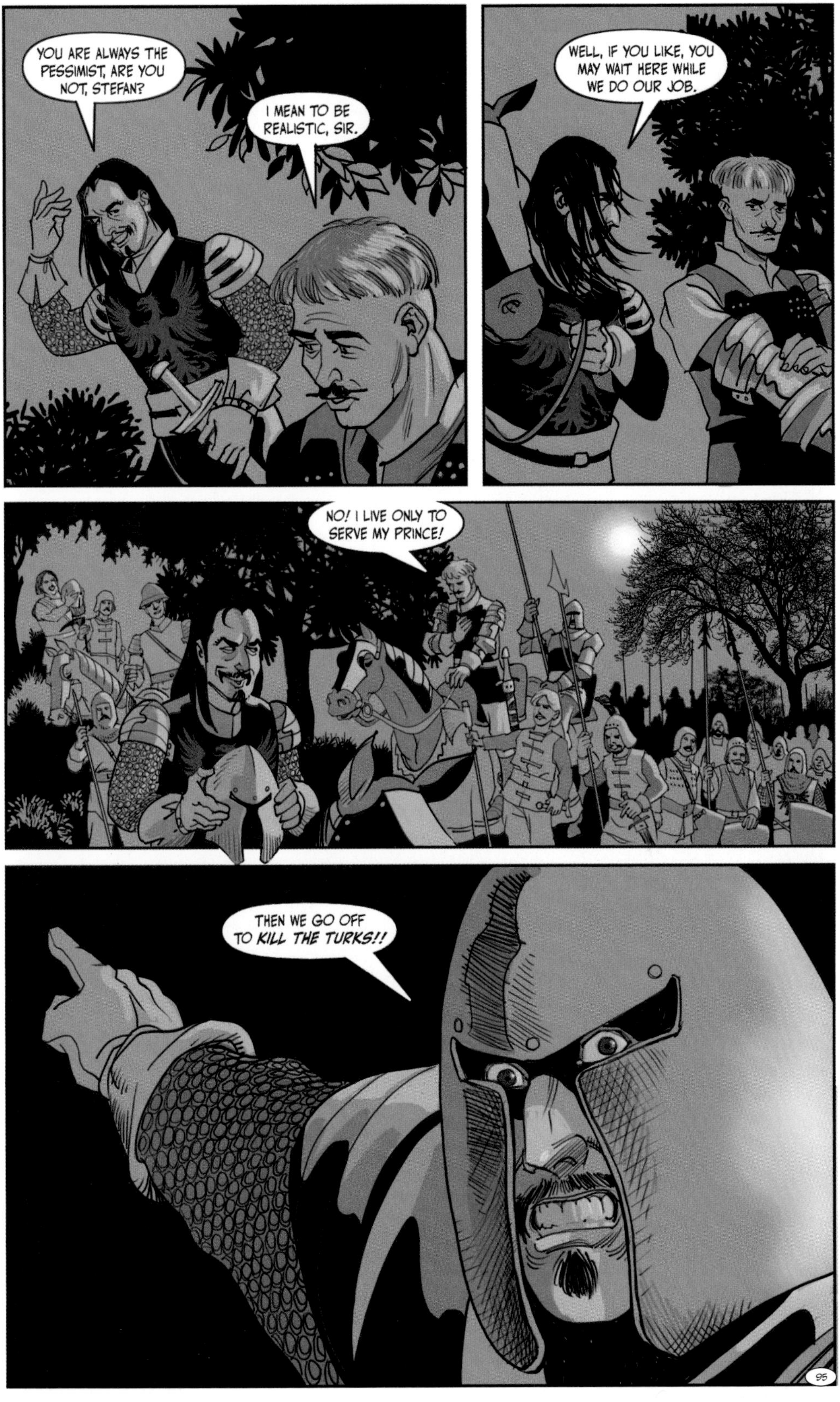
YOU ARE ALWAYS THE PESSIMIST, ARE YOU NOT, STEFAN?
I MEAN TO BE REALISTIC, SIR.
WELL, IF YOU LIKE, YOU MAY WAIT HERE WHILE WE DO OUR JOB.
NO! I LIVE ONLY TO SERVE MY PRINCE!
THEN WE GO OFF TO KILL THE TURKS!!

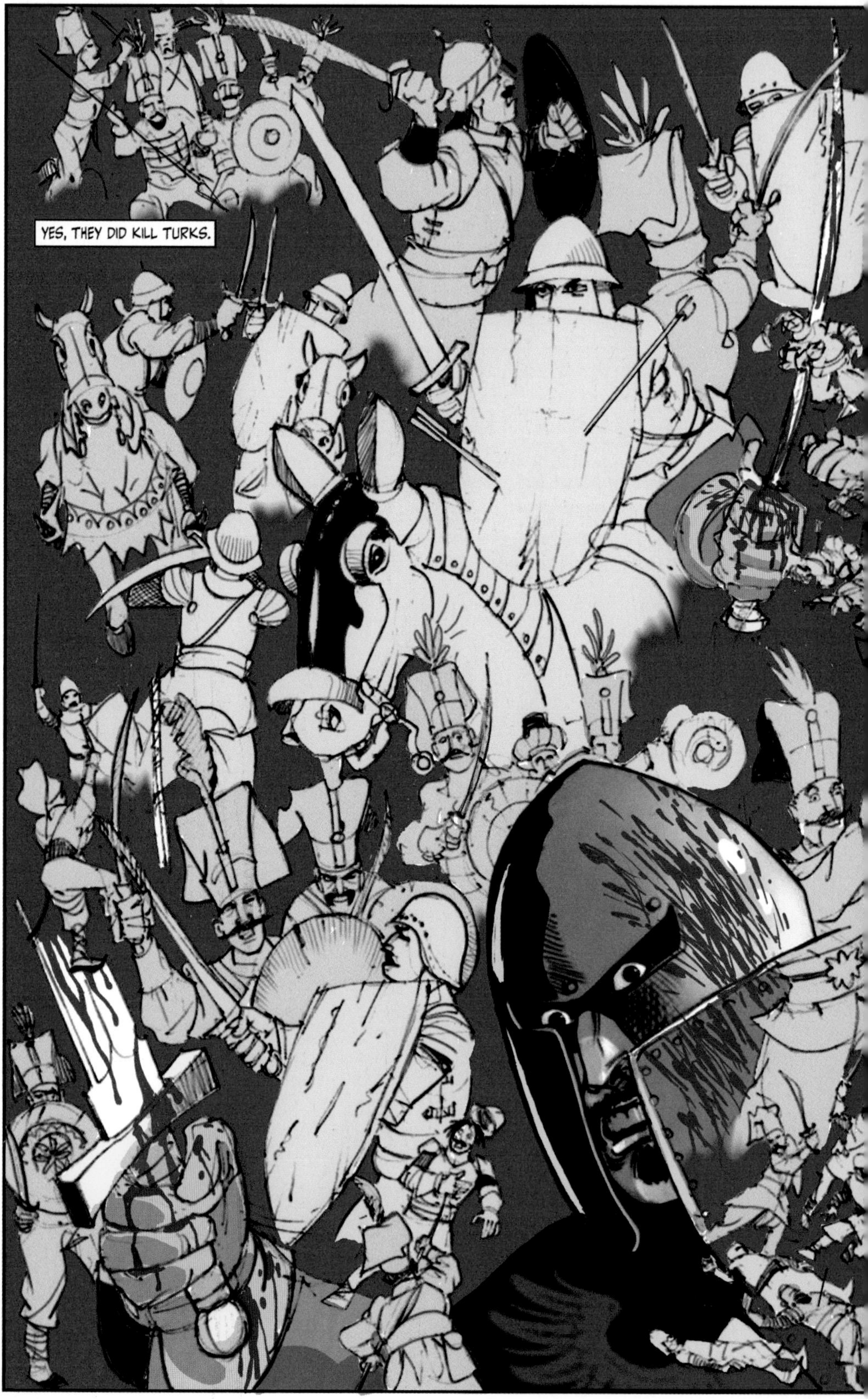
YES, THEY DID KILL TURKS.

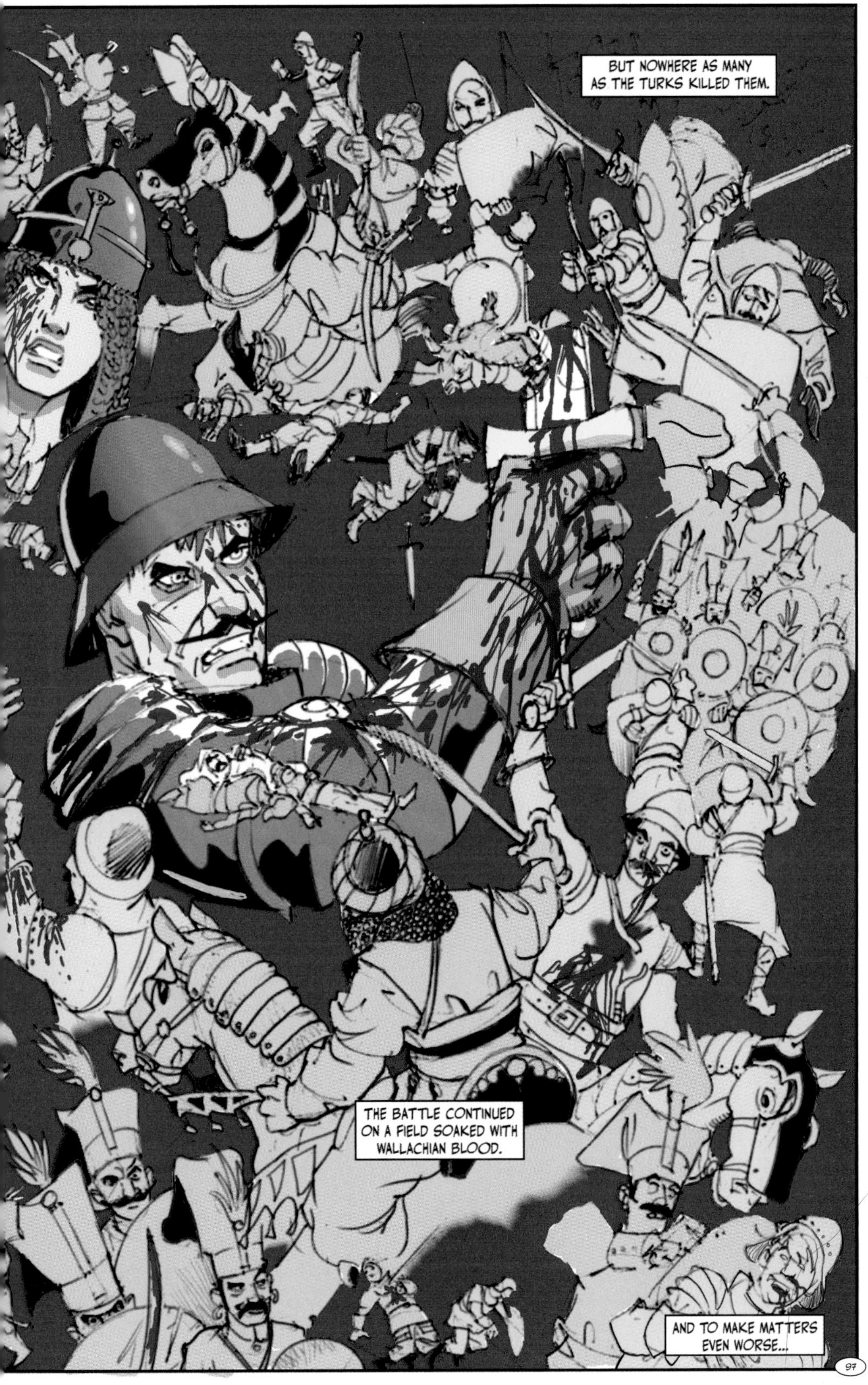
BUT NOWHERE AS MANY AS THE TURKS KILLED THEM.
THE BATTLE CONTINUED ON A FIELD SOAKED WITH WALLACHIAN BLOOD.
AND TO MAKE MATTERS EVEN WORSE...

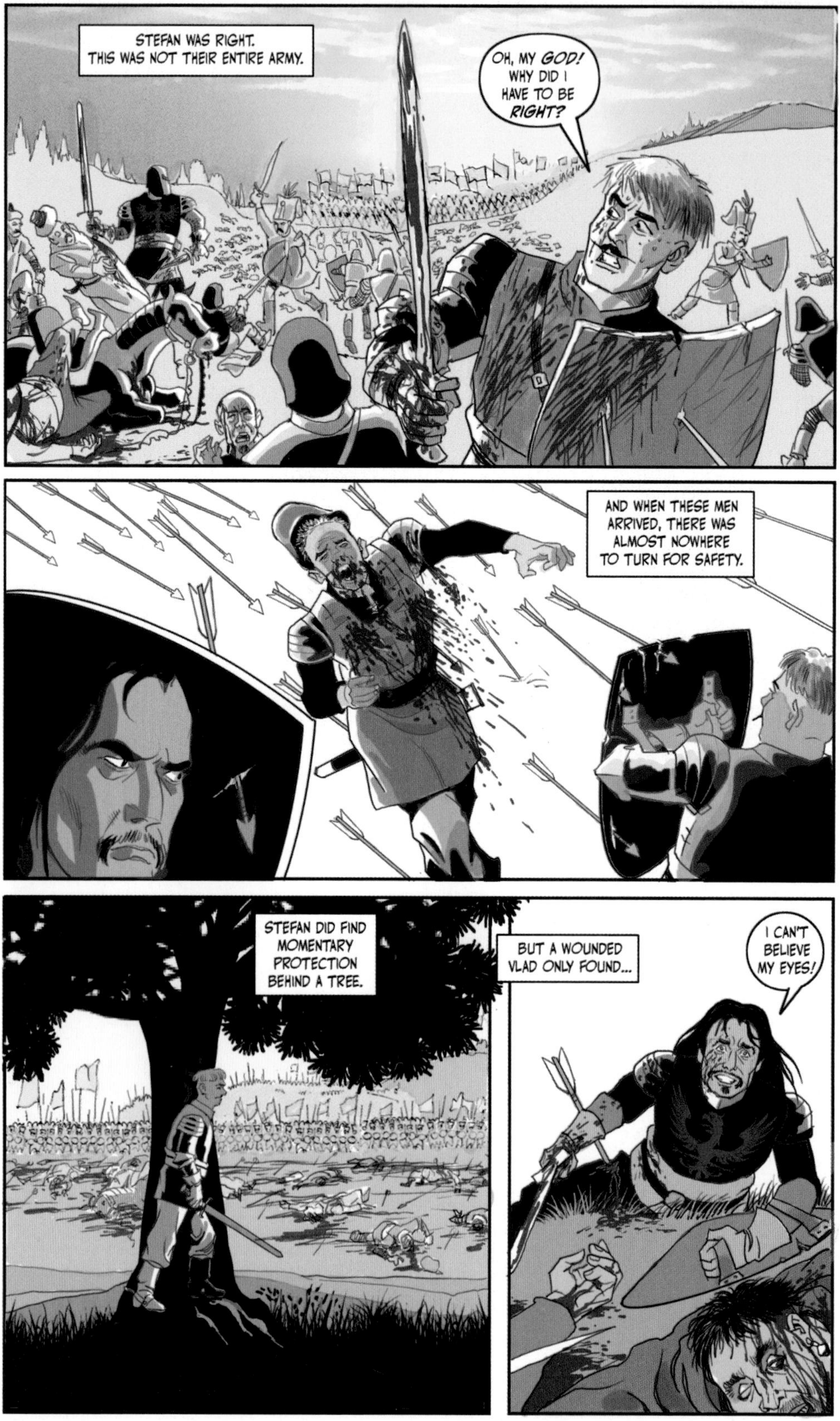
STEFAN WAS RIGHT. THIS WAS NOT THEIR ENTIRE ARMY.
OH, MY GOD! WHY DID I HAVE TO BE RIGHT?
AND WHEN THESE MEN ARRIVED, THERE WAS ALMOST NOWHERE TO TURN FOR SAFETY.
STEFAN DID FIND MOMENTARY PROTECTION BEHIND A TREE.
BUT A WOUNDED VLAD ONLY FOUND...
I CAN'T BELIEVE MY EYES!

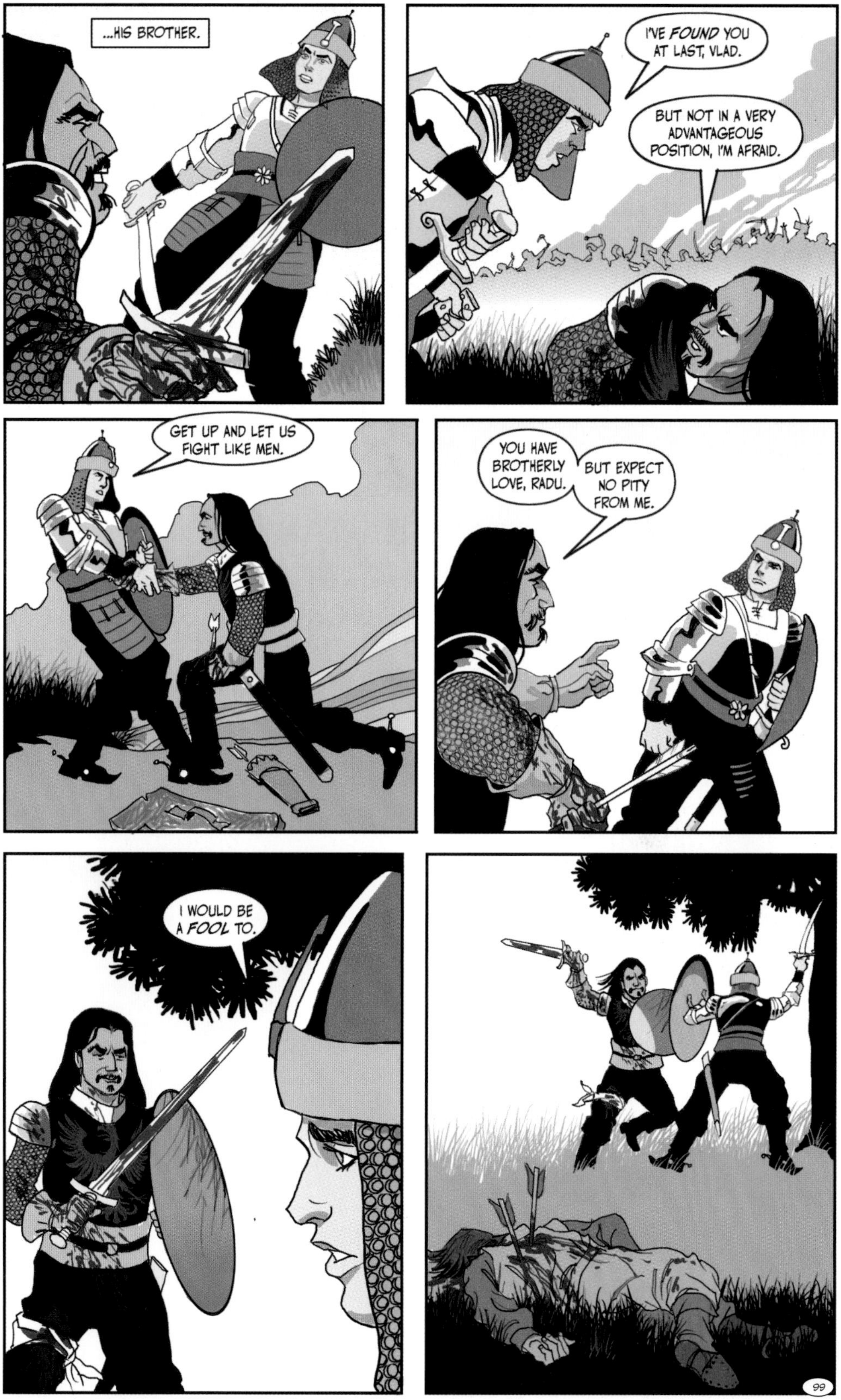
...HIS BROTHER.
I'VE FOUND YOU AT LAST, VLAD.
BUT NOT IN A VERY ADVANTAGEOUS POSITION, I'M AFRAID.
GET UP AND LET US FIGHT LIKE MEN.
YOU HAVE BROTHERLY LOVE, RADU.
BUT EXPECT NO PITY FROM ME.
I WOULD BE A FOOL TO.

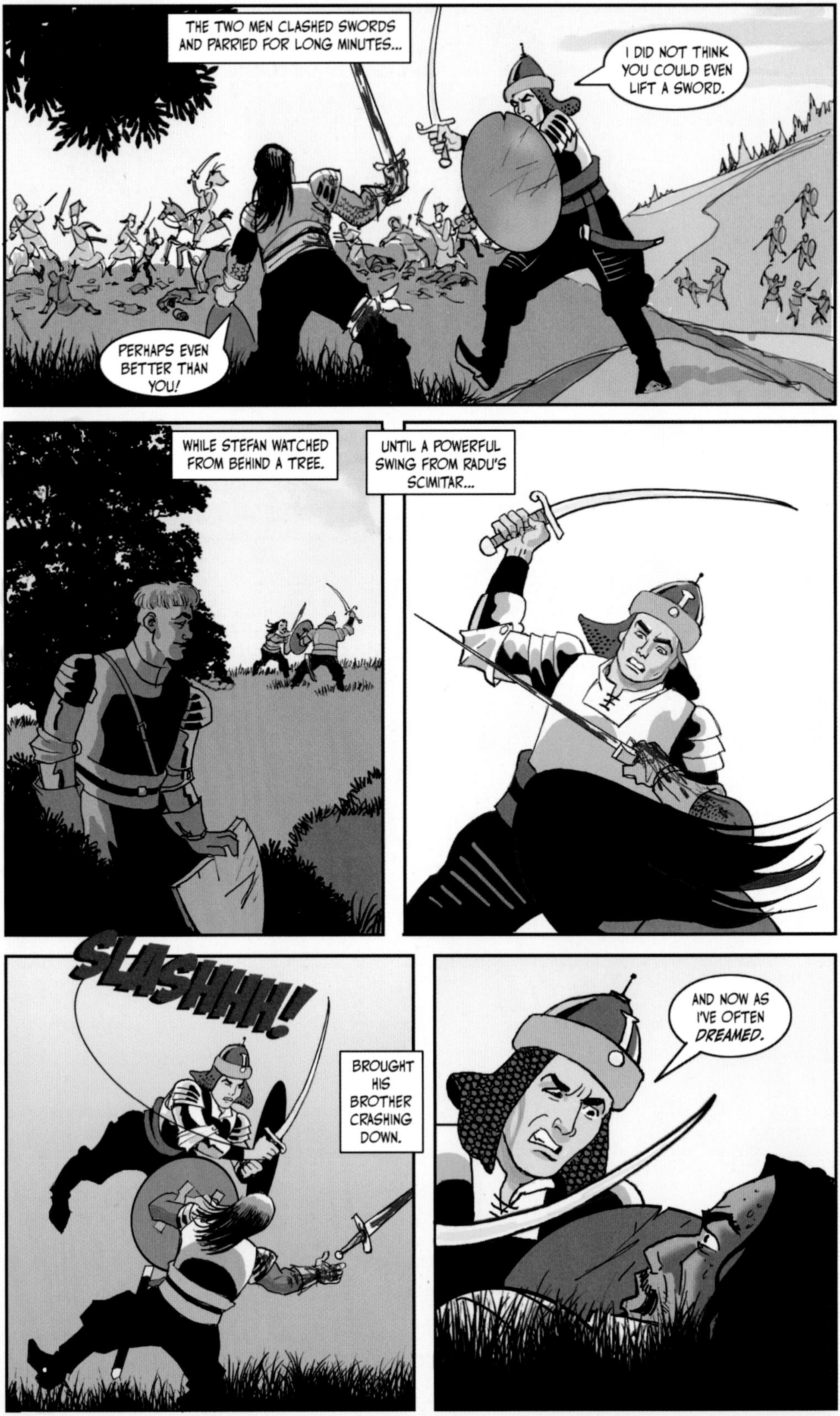
THE TWO MEN CLASHED SWORDS AND PARRIED FOR LONG MINUTES...
I DID NOT THINK YOU COULD EVEN LIFT A SWORD.
PERHAPS EVEN BETTER THAN YOU!
WHILE STEFAN WATCHED FROM BEHIND A TREE.
UNTIL A POWERFUL SWING FROM RADU'S SCIMITAR...
SLASHHH!
BROUGHT HIS BROTHER CRASHING DOWN.
AND NOW AS I'VE OFTEN *DREAMED.*

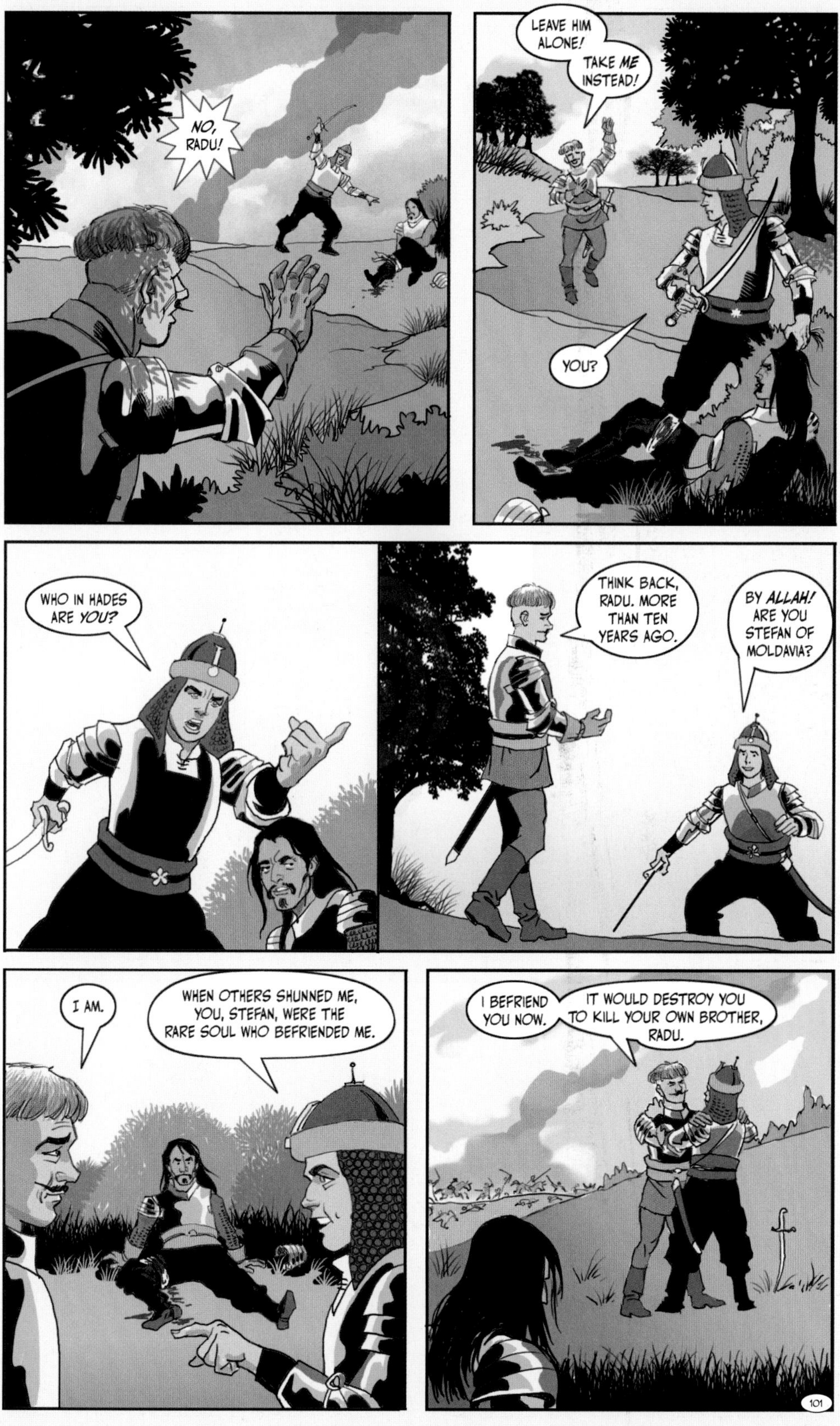
NO, RADU!
LEAVE HIM ALONE!
TAKE *ME* INSTEAD!
YOU?
WHO IN HADES ARE *YOU?*
THINK BACK, RADU. MORE THAN TEN YEARS AGO.
BY *ALLAH!* ARE YOU STEFAN OF MOLDAVIA?
I AM.
WHEN OTHERS SHUNNED ME, YOU, STEFAN, WERE THE RARE SOUL WHO BEFRIENDED ME.
I BEFRIEND YOU NOW.
IT WOULD DESTROY YOU TO KILL YOUR OWN BROTHER, RADU.

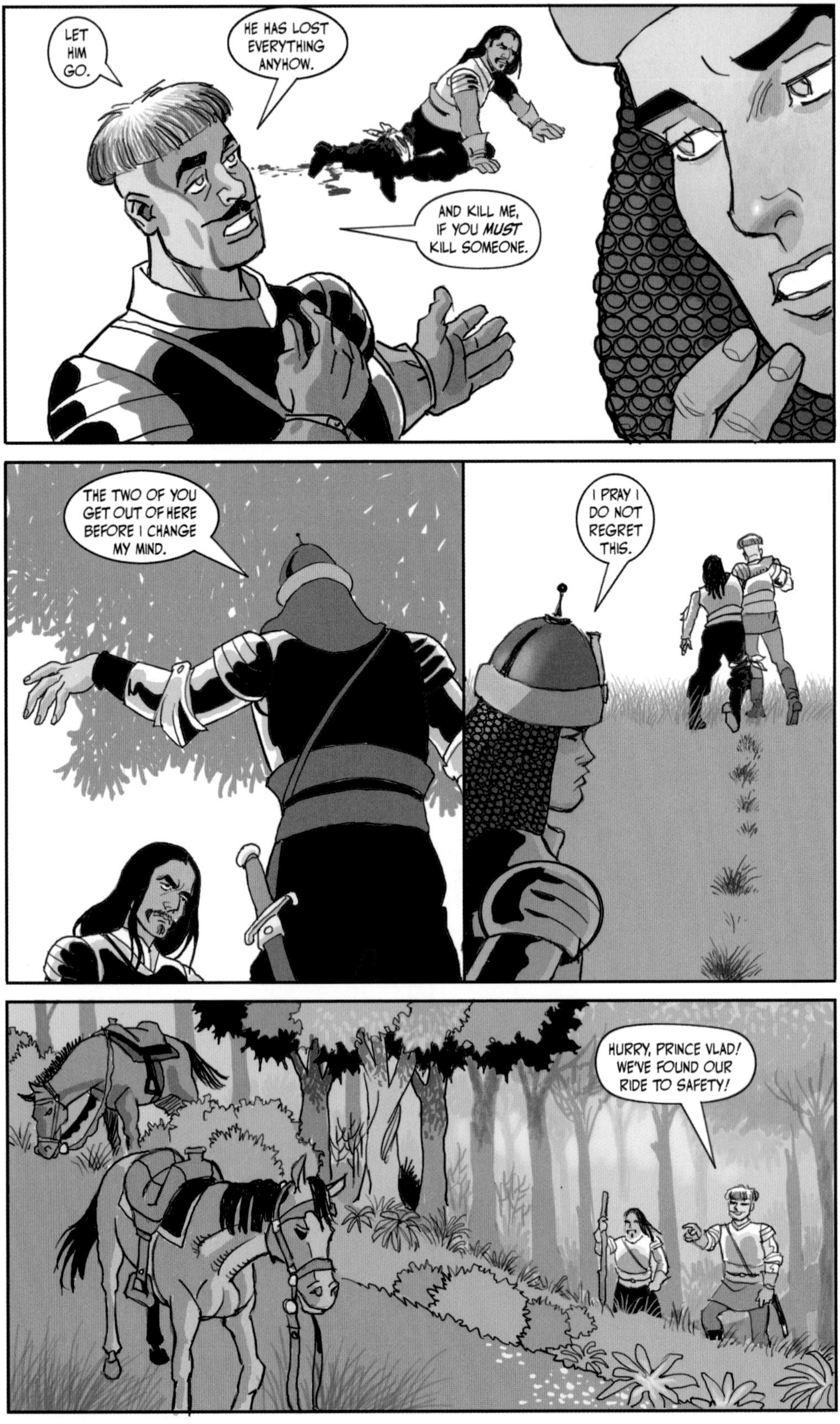
LET HIM GO.
HE HAS LOST EVERYTHING ANYHOW.
AND KILL ME, IF YOU *MUST* KILL SOMEONE.
THE TWO OF YOU GET OUT OF HERE BEFORE I CHANGE MY MIND.
I PRAY I DO NOT REGRET THIS.
HURRY, PRINCE VLAD! WE'VE FOUND OUR RIDE TO SAFETY!

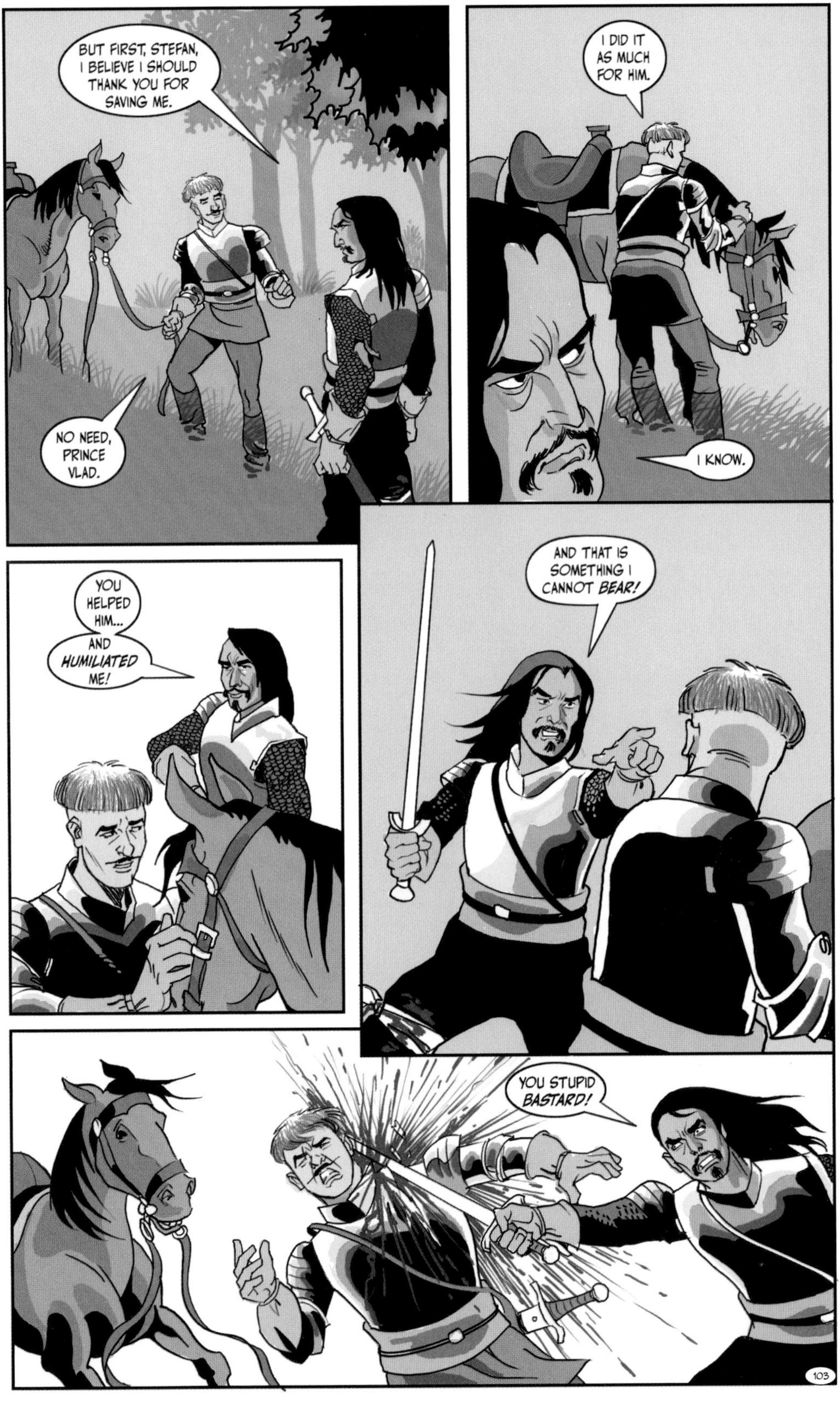
BUT FIRST, STEFAN, I BELIEVE I SHOULD THANK YOU FOR SAVING ME.
NO NEED, PRINCE VLAD.
I DID IT AS MUCH FOR HIM.
I KNOW.
YOU HELPED HIM...
AND *HUMILIATED* ME!
AND THAT IS SOMETHING I CANNOT *BEAR!*
YOU STUPID *BASTARD!*

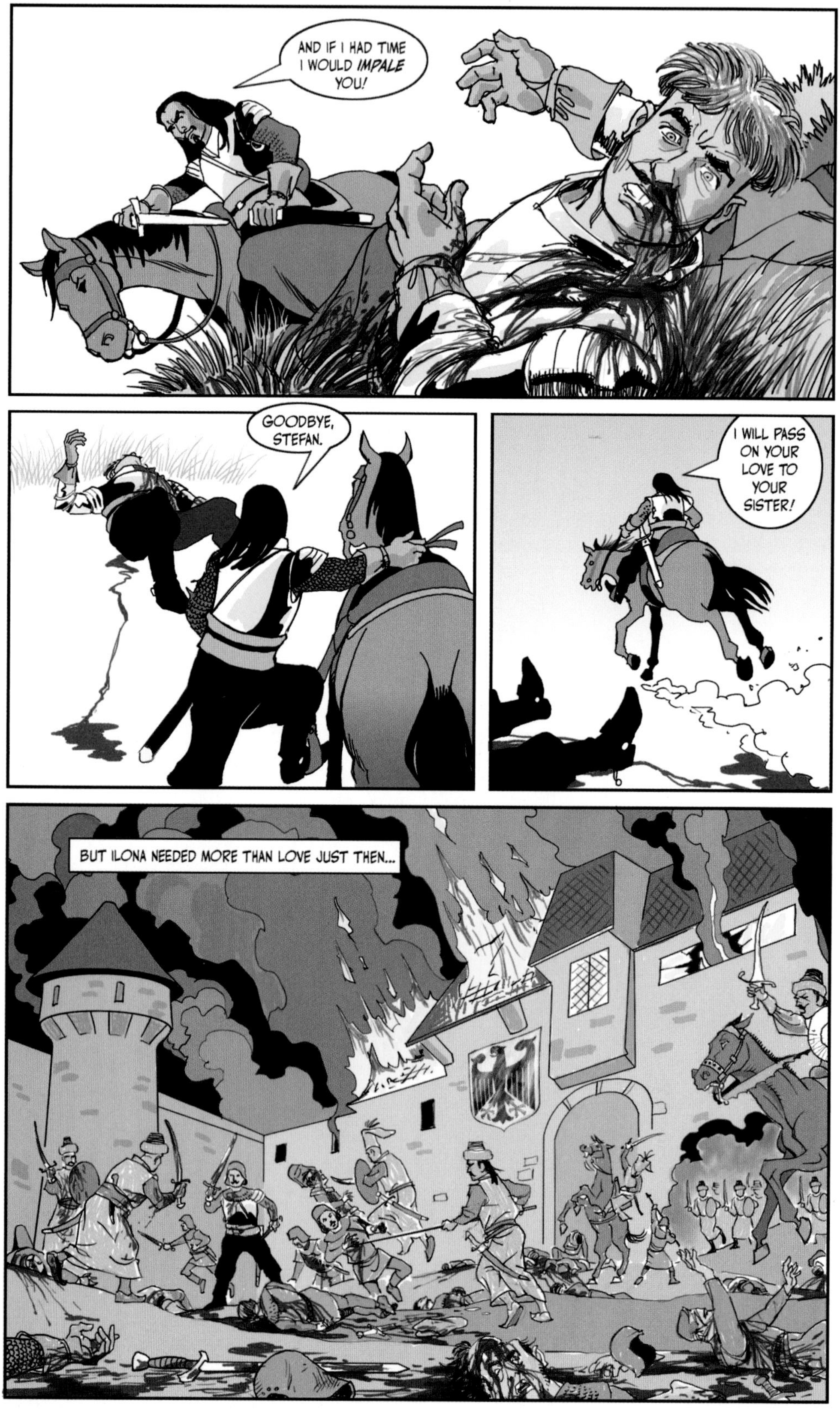
AND IF I HAD TIME I WOULD *IMPALE* YOU!
GOODBYE, STEFAN.
I WILL PASS ON YOUR LOVE TO YOUR SISTER!
BUT ILONA NEEDED MORE THAN LOVE JUST THEN...

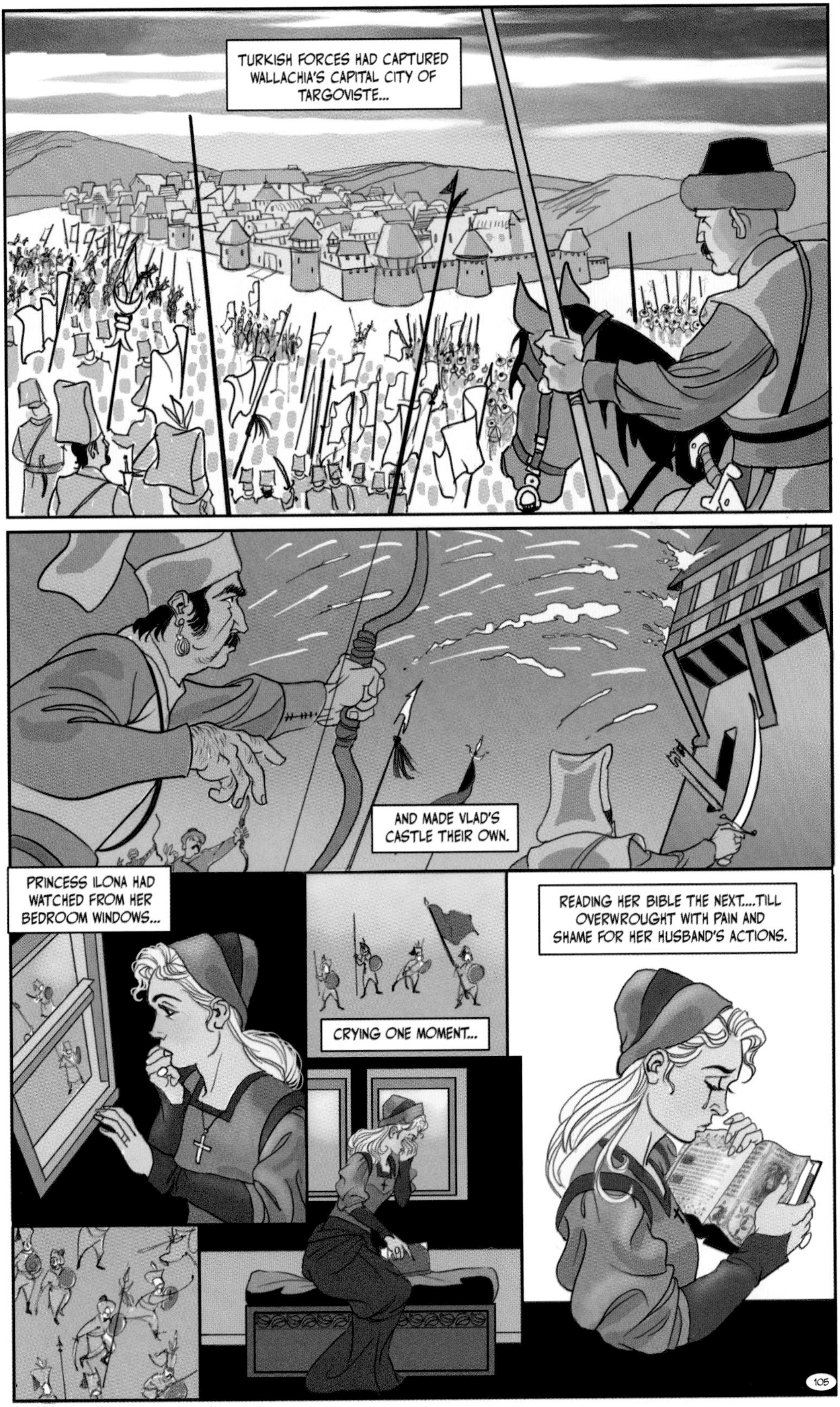
TURKISH FORCES HAD CAPTURED WALLACHIA'S CAPITAL CITY OF TARGOVISTE...
AND MADE VLAD'S CASTLE THEIR OWN.
PRINCESS ILONA HAD WATCHED FROM HER BEDROOM WINDOWS...
CRYING ONE MOMENT...
READING HER BIBLE THE NEXT....TILL OVERWROUGHT WITH PAIN AND SHAME FOR HER HUSBAND'S ACTIONS.

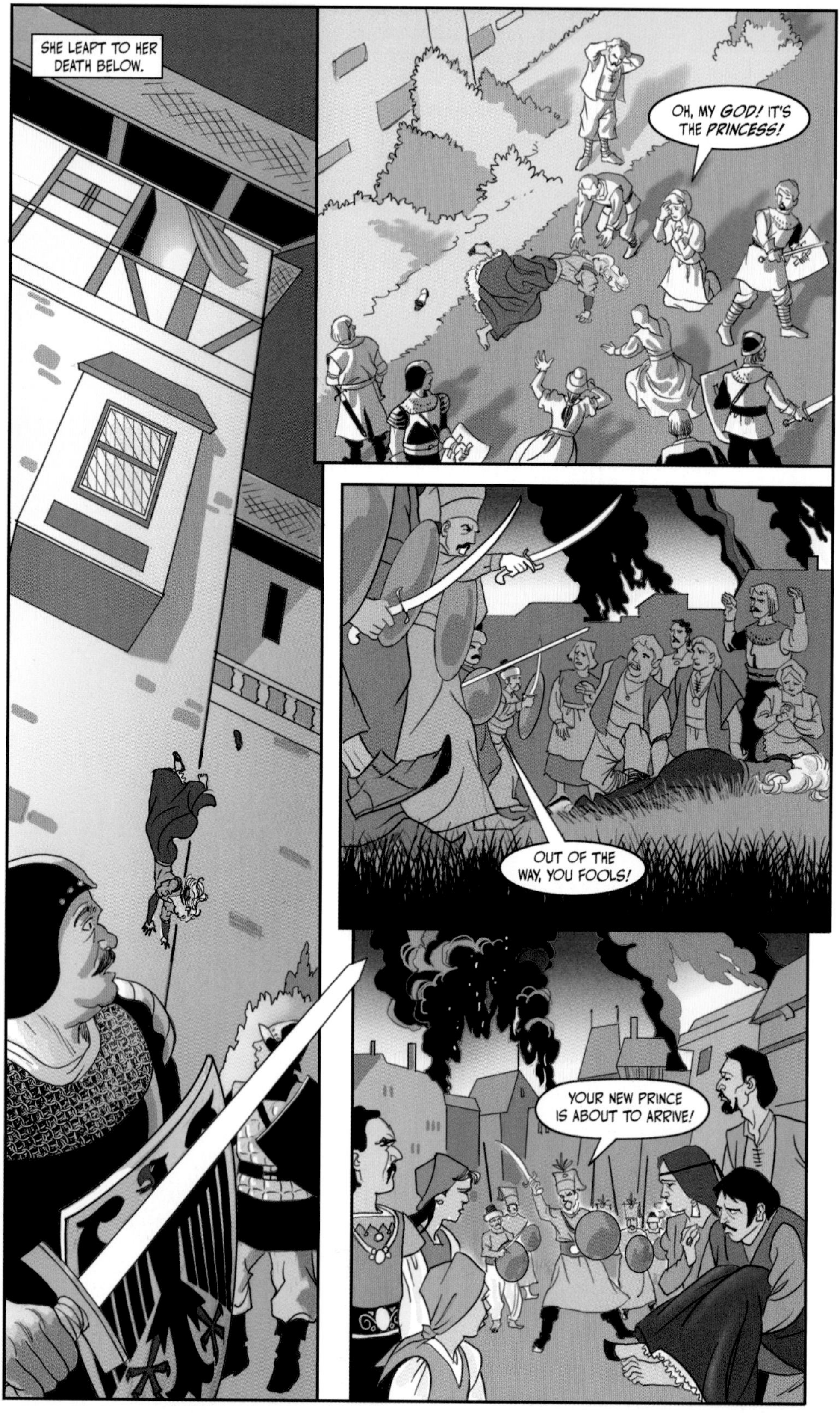
SHE LEAPT TO HER DEATH BELOW.
OH, MY GOD! IT'S THE PRINCESS!
OUT OF THE WAY, YOU FOOLS!
YOUR NEW PRINCE IS ABOUT TO ARRIVE!

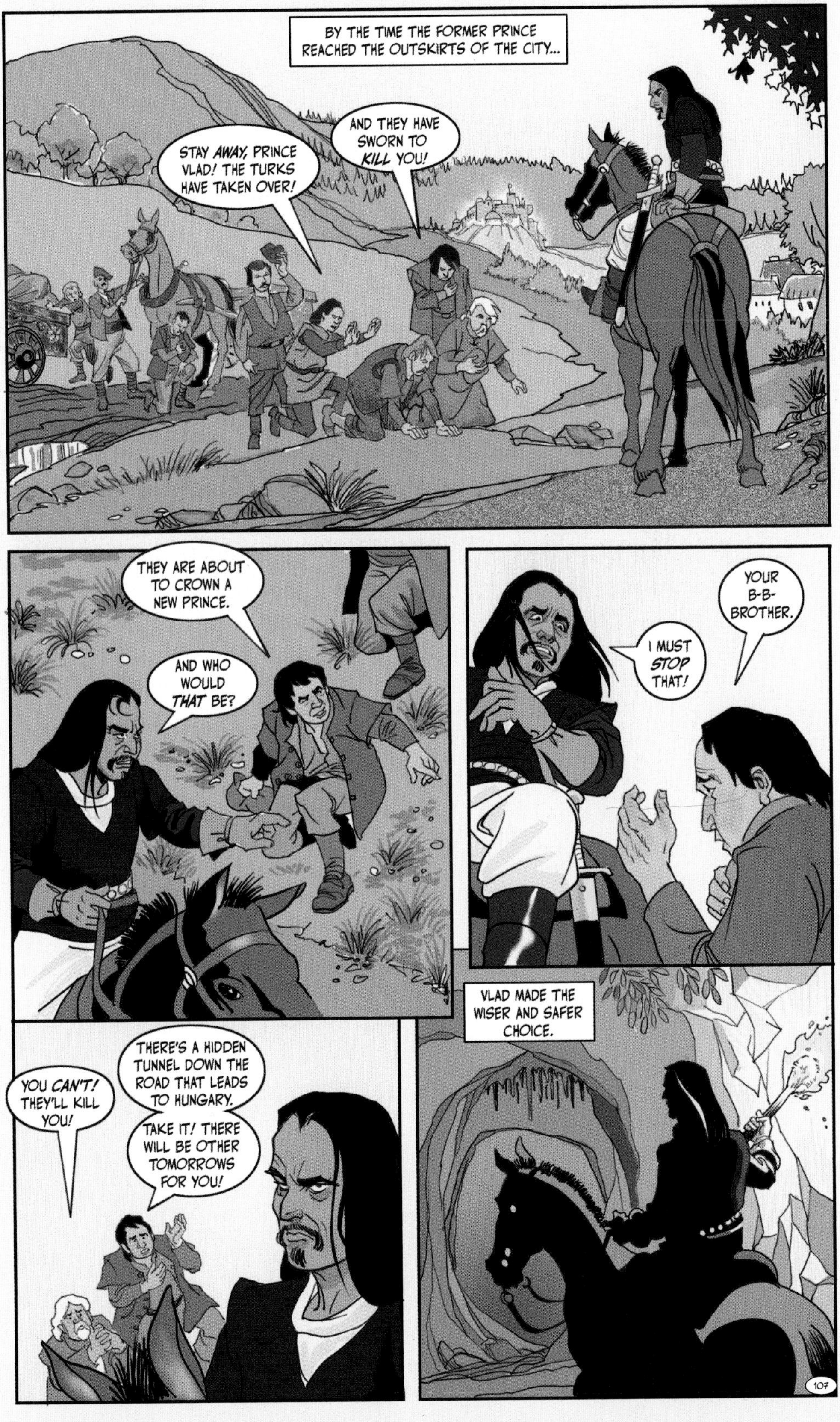
BY THE TIME THE FORMER PRINCE REACHED THE OUTSKIRTS OF THE CITY...
STAY *AWAY,* PRINCE VLAD! THE TURKS HAVE TAKEN OVER!
AND THEY HAVE SWORN TO *KILL* YOU!
THEY ARE ABOUT TO CROWN A NEW PRINCE.
AND WHO WOULD *THAT* BE?
YOUR B-B-BROTHER.
I MUST *STOP* THAT!
YOU *CAN'T!* THEY'LL KILL YOU!
THERE'S A HIDDEN TUNNEL DOWN THE ROAD THAT LEADS TO HUNGARY.
TAKE IT! THERE WILL BE OTHER TOMORROWS FOR YOU!
VLAD MADE THE WISER AND SAFER CHOICE.

CHAPTER 7: *REVELATION*

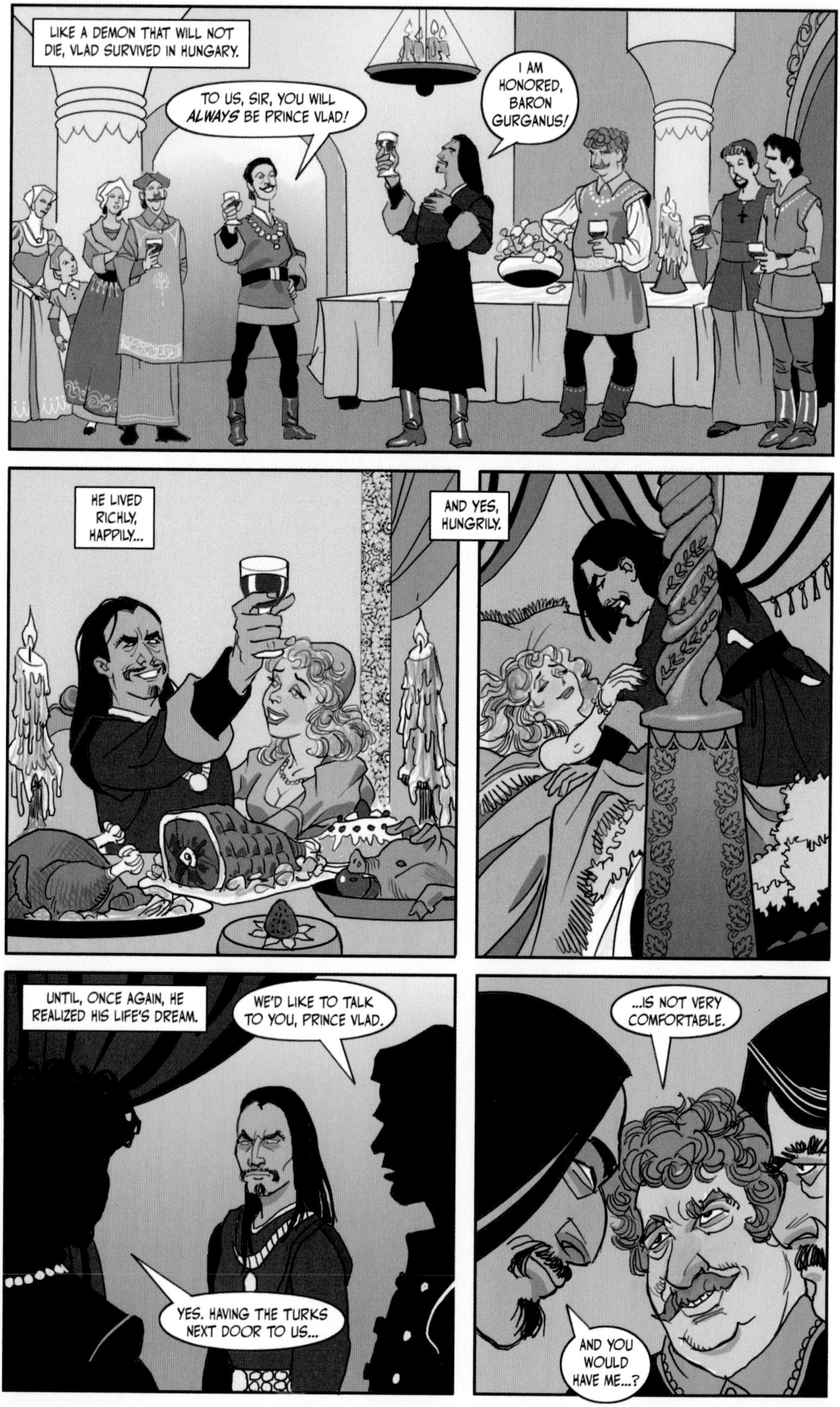
LIKE A DEMON THAT WILL NOT DIE, VLAD SURVIVED IN HUNGARY.
TO US, SIR, YOU WILL *ALWAYS* BE PRINCE VLAD!
I AM HONORED, BARON GURGANUS!
HE LIVED RICHLY, HAPPILY...
AND YES, HUNGRILY.
UNTIL, ONCE AGAIN, HE REALIZED HIS LIFE'S DREAM.
WE'D LIKE TO TALK TO YOU, PRINCE VLAD.
YES. HAVING THE TURKS NEXT DOOR TO US...
...IS NOT VERY COMFORTABLE.
AND YOU WOULD HAVE ME...?

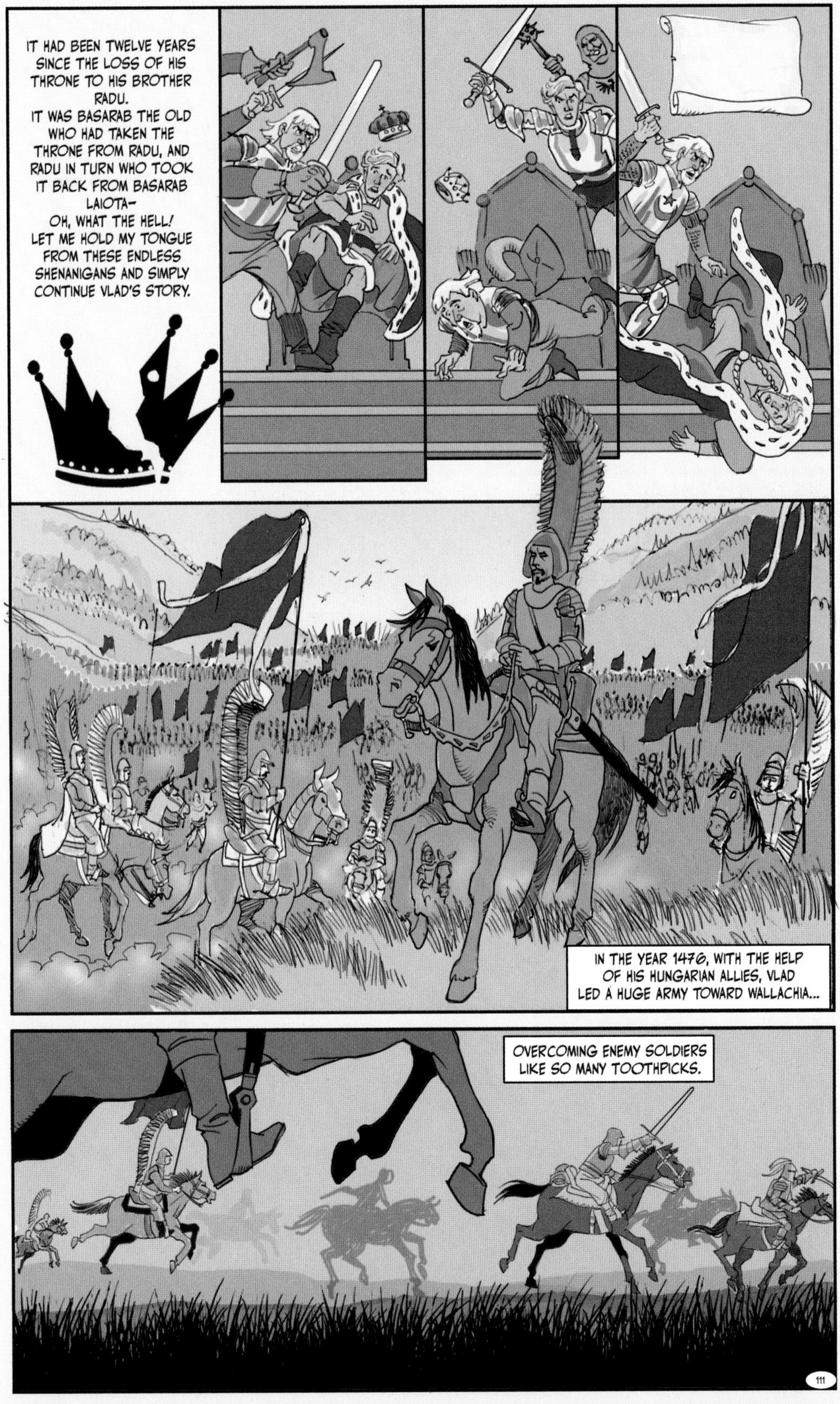
IT HAD BEEN TWELVE YEARS SINCE THE LOSS OF HIS THRONE TO HIS BROTHER RADU.
IT WAS BASARAB THE OLD WHO HAD TAKEN THE THRONE FROM RADU, AND RADU IN TURN WHO TOOK IT BACK FROM BASARAB LAIOTA–
OH, WHAT THE HELL! LET ME HOLD MY TONGUE FROM THESE ENDLESS SHENANIGANS AND SIMPLY CONTINUE VLAD'S STORY.
IN THE YEAR 1476, WITH THE HELP OF HIS HUNGARIAN ALLIES, VLAD LED A HUGE ARMY TOWARD WALLACHIA...
OVERCOMING ENEMY SOLDIERS LIKE SO MANY TOOTHPICKS.

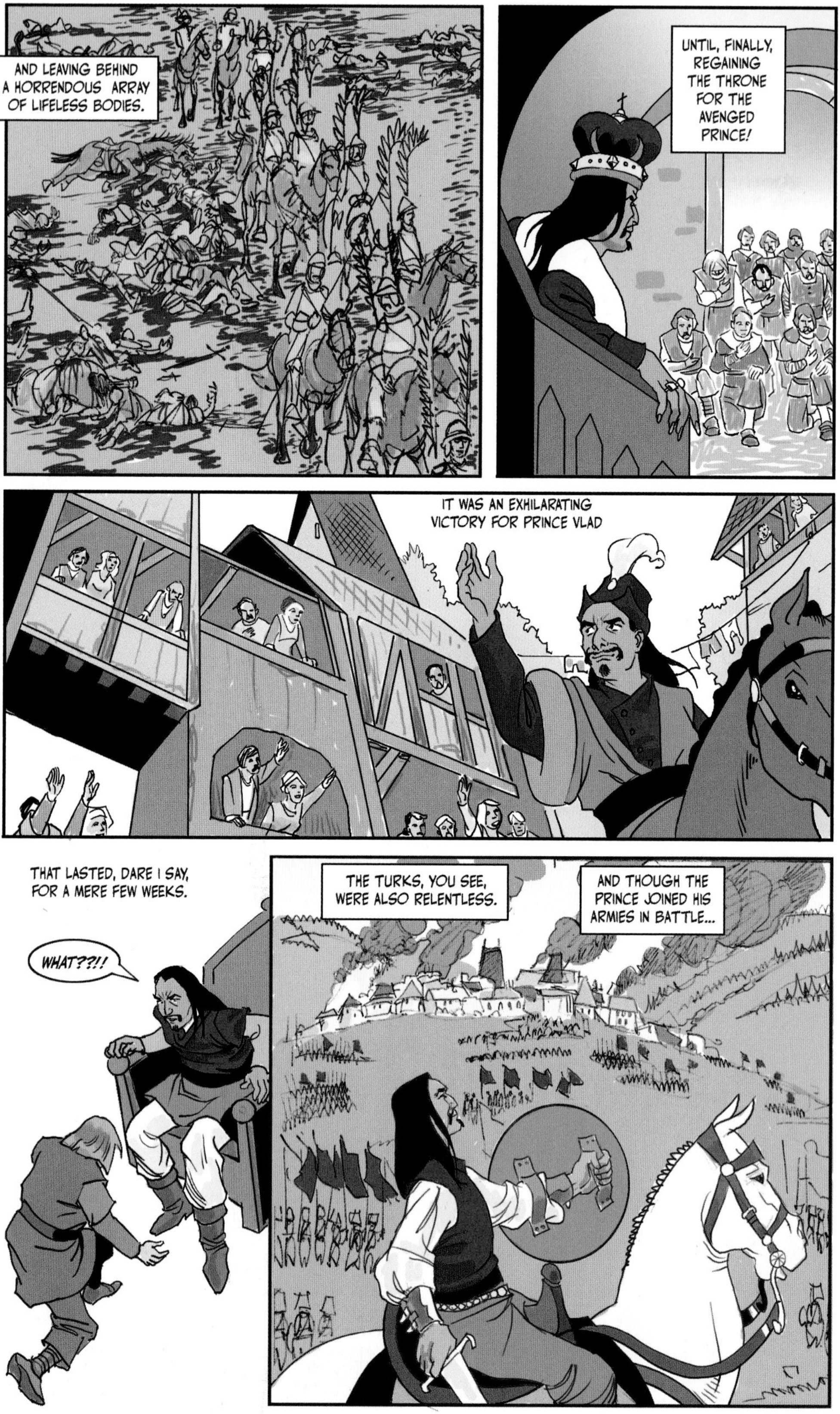
AND LEAVING BEHIND A HORRENDOUS ARRAY OF LIFELESS BODIES.
UNTIL, FINALLY, REGAINING THE THRONE FOR THE AVENGED PRINCE!
IT WAS AN EXHILARATING VICTORY FOR PRINCE VLAD
THAT LASTED, DARE I SAY, FOR A MERE FEW WEEKS.
WHAT??!!
THE TURKS, YOU SEE, WERE ALSO RELENTLESS.
AND THOUGH THE PRINCE JOINED HIS ARMIES IN BATTLE...

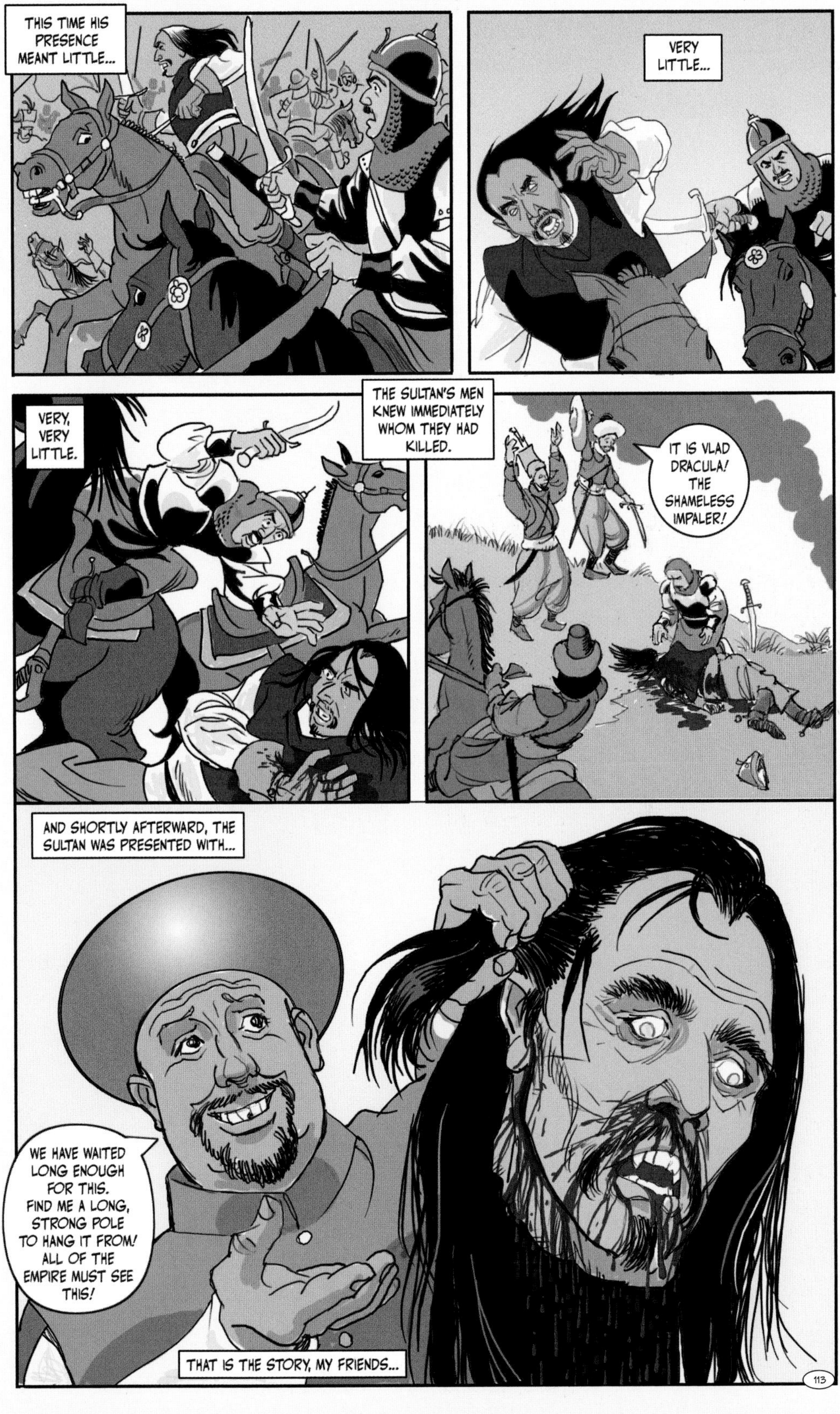

THIS TIME HIS PRESENCE MEANT LITTLE...
VERY LITTLE...
VERY, VERY LITTLE.
THE SULTAN'S MEN KNEW IMMEDIATELY WHOM THEY HAD KILLED.
IT IS VLAD DRACULA! THE SHAMELESS IMPALER!
AND SHORTLY AFTERWARD, THE SULTAN WAS PRESENTED WITH...
WE HAVE WAITED LONG ENOUGH FOR THIS. FIND ME A LONG, STRONG POLE TO HANG IT FROM! ALL OF THE EMPIRE MUST SEE THIS!
THAT IS THE STORY, MY FRIENDS...

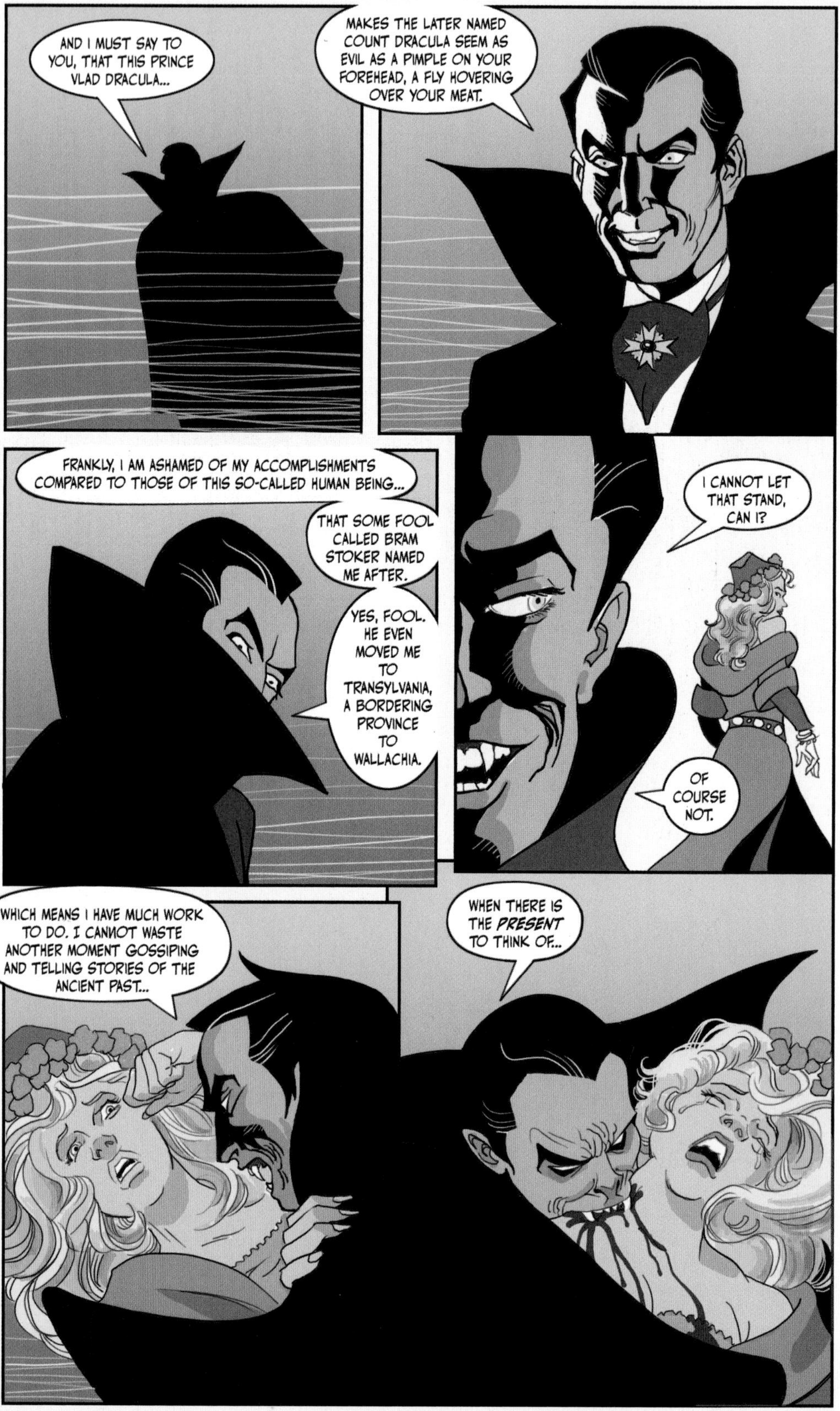
AND I MUST SAY TO YOU, THAT THIS PRINCE VLAD DRACULA...
MAKES THE LATER NAMED COUNT DRACULA SEEM AS EVIL AS A PIMPLE ON YOUR FOREHEAD, A FLY HOVERING OVER YOUR MEAT.
FRANKLY, I AM ASHAMED OF MY ACCOMPLISHMENTS COMPARED TO THOSE OF THIS SO-CALLED HUMAN BEING...
THAT SOME FOOL CALLED BRAM STOKER NAMED ME AFTER.
YES, FOOL. HE EVEN MOVED ME TO TRANSYLVANIA, A BORDERING PROVINCE TO WALLACHIA.
I CANNOT LET THAT STAND, CAN I?
OF COURSE NOT.
WHICH MEANS I HAVE MUCH WORK TO DO. I CANNOT WASTE ANOTHER MOMENT GOSSIPING AND TELLING STORIES OF THE ANCIENT PAST...
WHEN THERE IS THE *PRESENT* TO THINK OF...

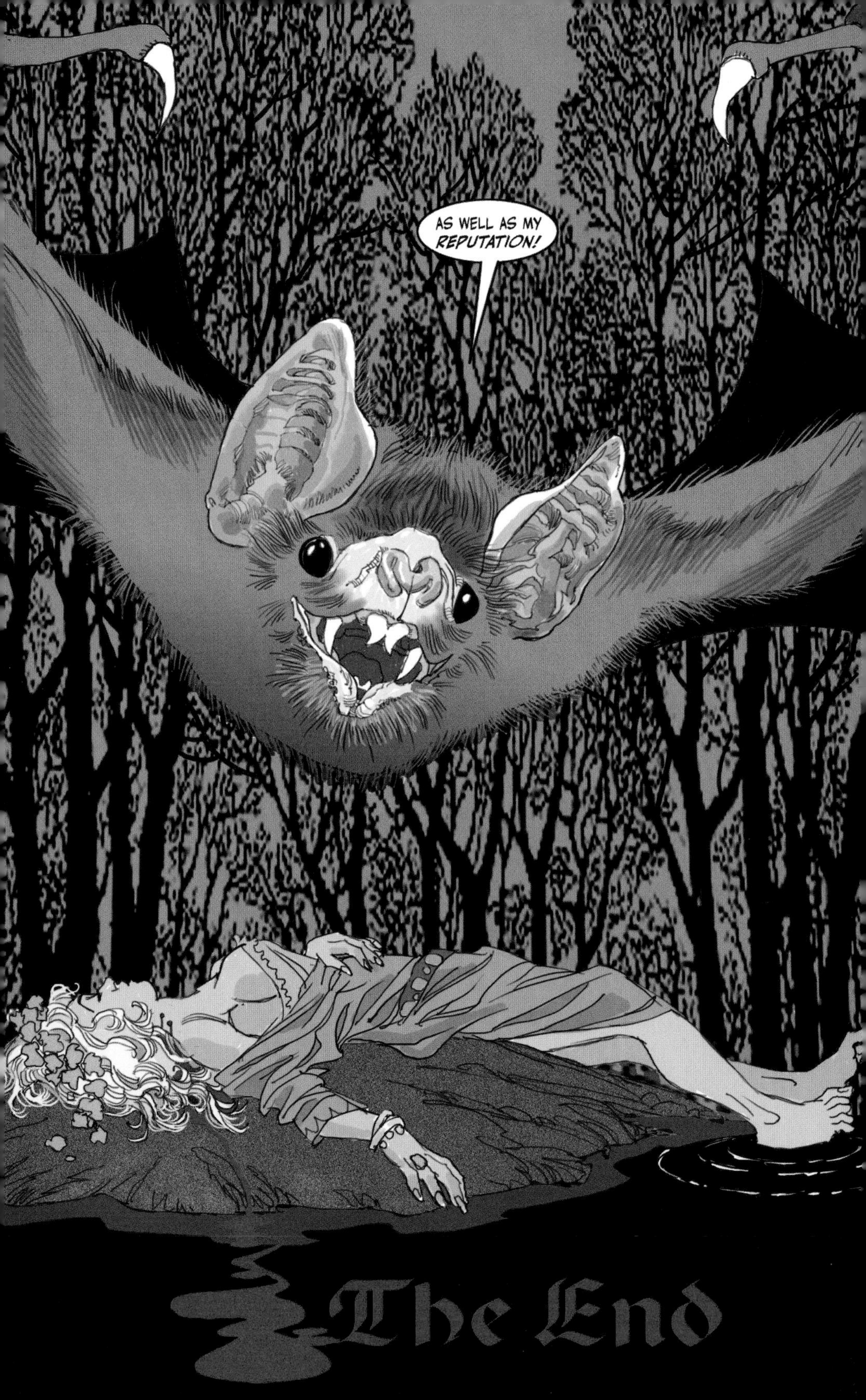
AS WELL AS MY *REPUTATION!*
The End